STATUTORY APPENDIX

Criminal Law

CASES AND READINGS

Fourth Edition

JEROME HALL
Professor of Law
University of California
Hastings College of the Law

ROBERT FORCE
Professor of Law
Tulane University School of Law

B. J. GEORGE, JR.
Professor of Law
New York Law School

THE MICHIE COMPANY
Law Publishers
CHARLOTTESVILLE, VIRGINIA

ISBN 0-87215-671-0

Copyright © 1983
by The Michie Company
Printed in the United States of America
All Rights Reserved

The publisher thanks the American Bar Association for permission to reprint from the ABA Standards for Criminal Justice (2d edition 1980). Reprinted by permission of Little, Brown and Company.

Table of Contents

APPENDIX A

MODEL PENAL CODE

PART I. GENERAL PROVISIONS
ARTICLE 1. PRELIMINARY

ARTICLE 7. AUTHORITY OF COURT IN SENTENCING

PART II. DEFINITION OF SPECIFIC CRIMES

OFFENSES AGAINST EXISTENCE OR STABILITY OF THE STATE

OFFENSES INVOLVING DANGER TO THE PERSON

ARTICLE 210. CRIMINAL HOMICIDE

ARTICLE 211. ASSAULT; RECKLESS ENDANGERING; THREATS

ARTICLE 212. KIDNAPPING AND RELATED OFFENSES; COERCION

ARTICLE 213. SEXUAL OFFENSES

OFFENSES AGAINST PROPERTY

ARTICLE 220. ARSON, CRIMINAL MISCHIEF, AND OTHER PROPERTY DESTRUCTION

ARTICLE 221. BURGLARY AND OTHER CRIMINAL INTRUSION

ARTICLE 222. ROBBERY

ARTICLE 223. THEFT AND RELATED OFFENSES

ARTICLE 224. FORGERY AND FRAUDULENT PRACTICE

OFFENSES AGAINST THE FAMILY

ARTICLE 230. OFFENSES AGAINST THE FAMILY

OFFENSES AGAINST PUBLIC ADMINISTRATION

ARTICLE 240. BRIBERY AND CORRUPT INFLUENCE

ARTICLE 241. PERJURY AND OTHER FALSIFICATION IN OFFICIAL MATTERS

ARTICLE 242. OBSTRUCTING GOVERNMENTAL OPERATIONS; ESCAPES

ARTICLE 243. ABUSE OF OFFICE

OFFENSES AGAINST PUBLIC ORDER AND DECENCY

ARTICLE 250. RIOT, DISORDERLY CONDUCT, AND RELATED OFFENSES

ARTICLE 251. PUBLIC INDECENCY

PART I. GENERAL PROVISIONS

ARTICLE 1. PRELIMINARY

Section 1.01. Title and Effective Date.

(1) This Act is called the Penal and Correctional Code and may be cited as P.C.C. It shall become effective on _____.

(2) Except as provided in Subsections (3) and (4) of this Section, the Code does not apply to offenses committed prior to its effective date and prosecutions for such offenses shall be governed by the prior law, which is continued in effect for that purpose, as if this Code were not in force. For the purposes of this Section, an offense was committed prior to the effective date of the Code if any of the elements of the offense occurred prior thereto.

(3) In any case pending on or after the effective date of the Code, involving an offense committed prior to such date:

(a) procedural provisions of the Code shall govern, insofar as they are justly applicable and their application does not introduce confusion or delay;

(b) provisions of the Code according a defense or mitigation shall apply, with the consent of the defendant;

(c) the Court, with the consent of the defendant, may impose sentence under the provisions of the Code applicable to the offense and the offender.

(4) Provisions of the Code governing the treatment and the release or discharge of prisoners, probationers and parolees shall apply to persons under sentence for offenses committed prior to the effective date of the Code, except that the minimum or maximum period of their detention or supervision shall in no case be increased.

Section 1.02. Purposes; Principles of Construction.

(1) The general purposes of the provisions governing the definition of offenses are:

(a) to forbid and prevent conduct that unjustifiably and inexcusably inflicts or threatens substantial harm to individual or public interests;

(b) to subject to public control persons whose conduct indicates that they are disposed to commit crimes;

(c) to safeguard conduct that is without fault from condemnation as criminal;

(d) to give fair warning of the nature of the conduct declared to constitute an offense;

(e) to differentiate on reasonable grounds between serious and minor offenses.

(2) The general purposes of the provisions governing the sentencing and treatment of offenders are:

(a) to prevent the commission of offenses;

(b) to promote the correction and rehabilitation of offenders;

(c) to safeguard offenders against excessive, disproportionate or arbitrary punishment;

(d) to give fair warning of the nature of the sentences that may be imposed on conviction of an offense;

(e) to differentiate among offenders with a view to a just individualization in their treatment;

(f) to define, coordinate and harmonize the powers, duties and functions of the courts and of administrative officers and agencies responsible for dealing with offenders;

(g) to advance the use of generally accepted scientific methods and knowledge in the sentencing and treatment of offenders;

(h) to integrate responsibility for the administration of the correctional system in a State Department of Correction [or other single department or agency].

(3) The provisions of the Code shall be construed according to the fair import of their terms but when the language is susceptible of differing constructions it shall be interpreted to further the general purposes stated in this Section and the special purposes of the particular provision involved. The discretionary powers conferred by the Code shall be exercised in accordance with the criteria stated in the Code and, insofar as such criteria are not decisive, to further the general purposes stated in this Section.

Section 1.03. Territorial Applicability.

(1) Except as otherwise provided in this Section, a person may be convicted under the law of this State of an offense committed by his own conduct or the conduct of another for which he is legally accountable if:

(a) either the conduct which is an element of the offense or the result which is such an element occurs within this State; or

(b) conduct occurring outside the State is sufficient under the law of this State to constitute an attempt to commit an offense within the State; or

(c) conduct occurring outside the State is sufficient under the law of this State to constitute a conspiracy to commit an offense within the State and an overt act in furtherance of such conspiracy occurs within the State; or

(d) conduct occurring within the State establishes complicity in the commission of, or an attempt, solicitation or conspiracy to commit, an offense in another jurisdiction which also is an offense under the law of this State; or

(e) the offense consists of the omission to perform a legal duty imposed by the law of this State with respect to domicile, residence or a relationship to a person, thing or transaction in the State; or

(f) the offense is based on a statute of this State which expressly prohibits conduct outside the State, when the conduct bears a reasonable relation to a legitimate interest of this State and the actor knows or should know that his conduct is likely to affect that interest.

(2) Subsection (1)(a) does not apply when either causing a specified result or a purpose to cause or danger of causing such a result is an element of an offense and the result occurs or is designed or likely to occur only in another jurisdiction where the conduct charged would not constitute an offense, unless a legislative purpose plainly appears to declare the conduct criminal regardless of the place of the result.

(3) Subsection (1)(a) does not apply when causing a particular result is an element of an offense and the result is caused by conduct occurring outside the State which would not constitute an offense if the result had occurred there, unless the actor purposely or knowingly caused the result within the State.

(4) When the offense is homicide, either the death of the victim or the bodily impact causing death constitutes a "result," within the meaning of Subsection (1)(a) and if the body of a homicide victim is found within the State, it is presumed that such result occurred within the State.

(5) This State includes the land and water and the air space above such land and water with respect to which the State has legislative jurisdiction.

Section 1.04. Classes of Crimes; Violations.

(1) An offense defined by this Code or by any other statute of this State, for which a sentence of [death or of] imprisonment is authorized, constitutes a crime. Crimes are classified as felonies, misdemeanors or petty misdemeanors.

(2) A crime is a felony if it is so designated in this Code or if persons convicted thereof may be sentenced [to death or] to imprisonment for a term which, apart from an extended term, is in excess of one year.

(3) A crime is a misdemeanor if it is so designated in this Code or in a statute other than this Code enacted subsequent thereto.

(4) A crime is a petty misdemeanor if it is so designated in this Code or in a statute other than this Code enacted subsequent thereto or if it is defined by a statute other than this Code which now provides that persons convicted thereof may be sentenced to imprisonment for a term of which the maximum is less than one year.

(5) An offense defined by this Code or by any other statute of this State constitutes a violation if it is so designated in this Code or in the law defining the offense or if no other sentence than a fine, or fine and forfeiture or other civil penalty is authorized upon conviction or if it is defined by a statute other than this Code which now provides that the offense shall not constitute a crime. A violation does not constitute a crime and conviction of a violation shall not give rise to any disability or legal disadvantage based on conviction of a criminal offense.

(6) Any offense declared by law to constitute a crime, without specification of the grade thereof or of the sentence authorized upon conviction, is a misdemeanor.

(7) An offense defined by any statute of this State other than this Code shall be classified as provided in this Section and the sentence that may be imposed upon conviction thereof shall hereafter be governed by this Code.

Section 1.05. All Offenses Defined by Statute; Application of General Provisions of the Code.

(1) No conduct constitutes an offense unless it is a crime or violation under this Code or another statute of this State.

(2) The provisions of Part I of the Code are applicable to offenses defined by other statutes, unless the Code otherwise provides.

(3) This Section does not affect the power of a court to punish for contempt or to employ any sanction authorized by law for the enforcement of an order or a civil judgment or decree.

Section 1.06. Time Limitations.

(1) A prosecution for murder may be commenced at any time.

(2) Except as otherwise provided in this Section, prosecutions for other offenses are subject to the following periods of limitation:

(a) a prosecution for a felony of the first degree must be commenced within six years after it is committed;

(b) a prosecution for any other felony must be commenced within three years after it is committed;

(c) a prosecution for a misdemeanor must be commenced within two years after it is committed;

(d) a prosecution for a petty misdemeanor or a violation must be commenced within six months after it is committed.

(3) If the period prescribed in Subsection (2) has expired, a prosecution may nevertheless be commenced for:

(a) any offense a material element of which is either fraud or a breach of fiduciary obligation within one year after discovery of the offense by an aggrieved party or by a person who has legal duty to represent an aggrieved party and who is himself not a party to the offense, but in no case shall this provision extend the period of limitation otherwise applicable by more than three years; and

(b) any offense based upon misconduct in office by a public officer or employee at any time when the defendant is in public office or employment or within two years thereafter, but in no case shall this provision extend the period of limitation otherwise applicable by more than three years.

(4) An offense is committed either when every element occurs, or, if a legislative purpose to prohibit a continuing course of conduct plainly appears, at the time when the course of conduct or the defendant's complicity therein is terminated. Time starts to run on the day after the offense is committed.

(5) A prosecution is commenced either when an indictment is found [or an information filed] or when a warrant or other process is issued, provided that such warrant or process is executed without unreasonable delay.

(6) The period of limitation does not run:

(a) during any time when the accused is continuously absent from the State or has no reasonably ascertainable place of abode or work within the State, but in no case shall this provision extend the period of limitation otherwise applicable by more than three years; or

(b) during any time when a prosecution against the accused for the same conduct is pending in this State.

Section 1.07. Method of Prosecution When Conduct Constitutes More Than One Offense.

(1) *Prosecution for Multiple Offenses; Limitation on Convictions.* When the same conduct of a defendant may establish the commission of more than one offense, the defendant may be prosecuted for each such offense. He may not, however, be convicted of more than one offense if:

(a) one offense is included in the other, as defined in Subsection (4) of this Section; or

(b) one offense consists only of a conspiracy or other form of preparation to commit the other; or

(c) inconsistent findings of fact are required to establish the commission of the offenses; or

(d) the offenses differ only in that one is defined to prohibit a designated kind of conduct generally and the other to prohibit a specific instance of such conduct; or

(e) the offense is defined as a continuing course of conduct and the defendant's course of conduct was uninterrupted, unless the law provides that specific periods of such conduct constitute separate offenses.

(2) *Limitation on Separate Trials for Multiple Offenses.* Except as provided in Subsection (3) of this Section, a defendant shall not be subject to separate trials for multiple offenses based on the same conduct or arising from the same criminal episode, if such offenses are known to the appropriate prosecuting officer at the time of the commencement of the first trial and are within the jurisdiction of a single court.

(3) *Authority of Court to Order Separate Trials.* When a defendant is charged with two or more offenses based on the same conduct or arising from the same criminal episode, the Court, on application of the prosecuting attorney or of the defendant, may order any such charge to be tried separately, if it is satisfied that justice so requires.

(4) *Conviction of Included Offense Permitted.* A defendant may be convicted of an offense included in an offense charged in the indictment [or the information]. An offense is so included when:

(a) it is established by proof of the same or less than all the facts required to establish the commission of the offense charged; or

(b) it consists of an attempt or solicitation to commit the offense charged or to commit an offense otherwise included therein; or

(c) it differs from the offense charged only in the respect that a less serious injury or risk of injury to the same person, property or public interest or a lesser kind of culpability suffices to establish its commission.

(5) *Submission of Included Offense to Jury.* The Court shall not be obligated to charge the jury with respect to an included offense unless there is a rational

basis for a verdict acquitting the defendant of the offense charged and convicting him of the included offense.

Section 1.08. When Prosecution Barred by Former Prosecution for the Same Offense.

When a prosecution is for a violation of the same provision of the statutes and is based upon the same facts as a former prosecution, it is barred by such former prosecution under the following circumstances:

(1) The former prosecution resulted in an acquittal. There is an acquittal if the prosecution resulted in a finding of not guilty by the trier of fact or in a determination that there was insufficient evidence to warrant a conviction. A finding of guilty of a lesser included offense is an acquittal of the greater inclusive offense, although the conviction is subsequently set aside.

(2) The former prosecution was terminated, after the information had been filed or the indictment found, by a final order or judgment for the defendant, which has not been set aside, reversed, or vacated and which necessarily required a determination inconsistent with a fact or a legal proposition that must be established for conviction of the offense.

(3) The former prosecution resulted in a conviction. There is a conviction if the prosecution resulted in a judgment of conviction which has not been reversed or vacated, a verdict of guilty which has not been set aside and which is capable of supporting a judgment, or a plea of guilty accepted by the Court. In the latter two cases failure to enter judgment must be for a reason other than a motion of the defendant.

(4) The former prosecution was improperly terminated. Except as provided in this Subsection, there is an improper termination of a prosecution if the termination is for reasons not amounting to an acquittal, and it takes place after the first witness is sworn but before verdict. Termination under any of the following circumstances is not improper:

(a) The defendant consents to the termination or waives, by motion to dismiss or otherwise, his right to object to the termination.

(b) The trial court finds that the termination is necessary because:

(1) it is physically impossible to proceed with the trial in conformity with law; or

(2) there is a legal defect in the proceedings which would make any judgment entered upon a verdict reversible as a matter of law; or

(3) prejudicial conduct, in or outside the courtroom, makes it impossible to proceed with the trial without injustice to either the defendant or the State; or

(4) the jury is unable to agree upon a verdict; or

(5) false statements of a juror on voir dire prevent a fair trial.

Section 1.09. When Prosecution Barred by Former Prosecution for Different Offense.

Although a prosecution is for a violation of a different provision of the statutes than a former prosecution or is based on different facts, it is barred by such former prosecution under the following circumstances:

(1) The former prosecution resulted in an acquittal or in a conviction as defined in Section 1.08 and the subsequent prosecution is for:

(a) any offense of which the defendant could have been convicted on the first prosecution; or

(b) any offense for which the defendant should have been tried on the first prosecution under Section 1.07, unless the Court ordered a separate trial of the charge of such offense; or

(c) the same conduct, unless (i) the offense of which the defendant was formerly convicted or acquitted and the offense for which he is subsequently prosecuted each requires proof of a fact not required by the other and the law defining each of such offenses is intended to prevent a substantially different harm or evil, or (ii) the second offense was not consummated when the former trial began.

(2) The former prosecution was terminated, after the information was filed or the indictment found, by an acquittal or by a final order or judgment for the defendant which has not been set aside, reversed or vacated and which acquittal, final order or judgment necessarily required a determination inconsistent with a fact which must be established for conviction of the second offense.

(3) The former prosecution was improperly terminated, as improper termination is defined in Section 1.08, and the subsequent prosecution is for an offense of which the defendant could have been convicted had the former prosecution not been improperly terminated.

Section 1.10. Former Prosecution in Another Jurisdiction: When a Bar.

When conduct constitutes an offense within the concurrent jurisdiction of this State and of the United States or another State, a prosecution in any such other jurisdiction is a bar to a subsequent prosecution in this State under the following circumstances:

(1) The first prosecution resulted in an acquittal or in a conviction as defined in Section 1.08 and the subsequent prosecution is based on the same conduct, unless (a) the offense of which the defendant was formerly convicted or acquitted and the offense for which he is subsequently prosecuted each requires proof of a fact not required by the other and the law defining each of such offenses is intended to prevent a substantially different harm or evil or (b) the second offense was not consummated when the former trial began; or

(2) The former prosecution was terminated, after the information was filed or the indictment found, by an acquittal or by a final order or judgment for the defendant which has not been set aside, reversed or vacated and which acquittal, final order or judgment necessarily required a determination inconsistent with a fact which must be established for conviction of the offense of which the defendant is subsequently prosecuted.

Section 1.11. Former Prosecution Before Court Lacking Jurisdiction or When Fraudulently Procured by the Defendant.

A prosecution is not a bar within the meaning of Sections 1.08, 1.09 and 1.10 under any of the following circumstances:

(1) The former prosecution was before a court which lacked jurisdiction over the defendant or the offense; or

(2) The former prosecution was procured by the defendant without the knowledge of the appropriate prosecuting officer and with the purpose of avoiding the sentence which might otherwise be imposed; or

(3) The former prosecution resulted in a judgment of conviction which was held invalid in a subsequent proceeding on a writ of habeas corpus, coram nobis or similar process.

Section 1.12. Proof Beyond a Reasonable Doubt; Affirmative Defenses; Burden of Proving Fact When Not an Element of an Offense; Presumptions.

(1) No person may be convicted of an offense unless each element of such offense is proved beyond a reasonable doubt. In the absence of such proof, the innocence of the defendant is assumed.

(2) Subsection (1) of this Section does not:

(a) require the disproof of an affirmative defense unless and until there is evidence supporting such defense; or

(b) apply to any defense which the Code or another statute plainly requires the defendant to prove by a preponderance of evidence.

(3) A ground of defense is affirmative, within the meaning of Subsection (2)(a) of this Section, when:

(a) it arises under a section of the Code which so provides; or

(b) it relates to an offense defined by a statute other than the Code and such statute so provides; or

(c) it involves a matter of excuse or justification peculiarly within the knowledge of the defendant on which he can fairly be required to adduce supporting evidence.

(4) When the application of the Code depends upon the finding of a fact which is not an element of an offense, unless the Code otherwise provides:

(a) the burden of proving the fact is on the prosecution or defendant, depending on whose interest or contention will be furthered if the finding should be made; and

(b) the fact must be proved to the satisfaction of the Court or jury, as the case may be.

(5) When the Code establishes a presumption with respect to any fact which is an element of an offense, it has the following consequences:

(a) when there is evidence of the facts which give rise to the presumption, the issue of the existence of the presumed fact must be submitted to the jury, unless the Court is satisfied that the evidence as a whole clearly negatives the presumed fact; and

(b) when the issue of the existence of the presumed fact is submitted to the jury, the Court shall charge that while the presumed fact must, on all the evidence, be proved beyond a reasonable doubt, the law declares that the jury may regard the facts giving rise to the presumption as sufficient evidence of the presumed fact.

(6) A presumption not established by the Code or inconsistent with it has the consequences otherwise accorded it by law.

Section 1.13. General Definitions.

In this Code, unless a different meaning plainly is required:

(1) "statute" includes the Constitution and a local law or ordinance of a political subdivision of the State;

(2) "act" or "action" means a bodily movement whether voluntary or involuntary;

(3) "voluntary" has the meaning specified in Section 2.01;

(4) "omission" means a failure to act;

(5) "conduct" means an action or omission and its accompanying state of mind, or, where relevant, a series of acts and omissions;

(6) "actor" includes, where relevant, a person guilty of an omission;

(7) "acted" includes, where relevant, "omitted to act";

(8) "person," "he" and "actor" include any natural person and, where relevant, a corporation or an unincorporated association;

(9) "element of an offense" means (i) such conduct or (ii) such attendant circumstances or (iii) such a result of conduct as

(a) is included in the description of the forbidden conduct in the definition of the offense; or

(b) establishes the required kind of culpability; or

(c) negatives an excuse or jusitification for such conduct; or

(d) negatives a defense under the statute of limitations; or

(e) establishes jurisdiction or venue;

(10) "material element of an offense" means an element that does not relate exclusively to the statute of limitations, jurisdiction, venue or to any other matter similarly unconnected with (i) the harm or evil, incident to conduct, sought to be prevented by the law defining the offense, or (ii) the existence of a justification or excuse for such conduct;

(11) "purposely" has the meaning specified in Section 2.02 and equivalent terms such as "with purpose," "designed" or "with design" have the same meaning;

(12) "intentionally" or "with intent" means purposely;

(13) "knowingly" has the meaning specified in Section 2.02 and equivalent terms such as "knowing" or "with knowledge" have the same meaning;

(14) "recklessly" has the meaning specified in Section 2.02 and equivalent terms such as "recklessness" or "with recklessness" have the same meaning;

(15) "negligently" has the meaning specified in Section 2.02 and equivalent terms such as "negligence" or "with negligence" have the same meaning;

(16) "reasonably believes" or "reasonable belief" designates a belief which the actor is not reckless or negligent in holding.

ARTICLE 2. GENERAL PRINCIPLES OF LIABILITY

Section 2.01. Requirement of Voluntary Act; Omission as Basis of Liability; Possession as an Act.

(1) A person is not guilty of an offense unless his liability is based on conduct which includes a voluntary act or the omission to perform an act of which he is physically capable.

(2) The following are not voluntary acts within the meaning of this Section:

(a) a reflex or convulsion;

(b) a bodily movement during unconsciousness or sleep;

(c) conduct during hypnosis or resulting from hypnotic suggestion;

(d) a bodily movement that otherwise is not a product of the effort or determination of the actor, either conscious or habitual.

(3) Liability for the commission of an offense may not be based on an omission unaccompanied by action unless:

(a) the omission is expressly made sufficient by the law defining the offense; or

(b) a duty to perform the omitted act is otherwise imposed by law.

(4) Possession is an act, within the meaning of this Section, if the possessor knowingly procured or received the thing possessed or was aware of his control thereof for a sufficient period to have been able to terminate his possession.

Section 2.02. General Requirements of Culpability.

(1) *Minimum Requirements of Culpability.* Except as provided in Section 2.05, a person is not guilty of an offense unless he acted purposely, knowingly, recklessly or negligently, as the law may require, with respect to each material element of the offense.

(2) *Kinds of Culpability Defined.*

(a) *Purposely.*

A person acts purposely with respect to a material element of an offense when:

(i) if the element involves the nature of his conduct or a result thereof, it is his conscious object to engage in conduct of that nature or to cause such a result; and

(ii) if the element involves the attendant circumstances, he is aware of the existence of such circumstances or he believes or hopes that they exist.

(b) *Knowingly.*

A person acts knowingly with respect to a material element of an offense when:

(i) if the element involves the nature of his conduct or the attendant circumstances, he is aware that his conduct is of that nature or that such circumstances exist; and

(ii) if the element involves a result of his conduct, he is aware that it is practically certain that his conduct will cause such a result.

(c) *Recklessly.*

A person acts recklessly with respect to a material element of an offense when he consciously disregards a substantial and unjustifiable risk that the material element exists or will result from his conduct. The risk must be of such a nature and degree that, considering the nature and purpose of the actor's conduct and the circumstances known to him, its disregard involves a gross deviation from the standard of conduct that a law-abiding person would observe in the actor's situation.

(d) *Negligently.*

A person acts negligently with respect to a material element of an offense when he should be aware of a substantial and unjustifiable risk that the material element exists or will result from his conduct. The risk must be of such a nature and degree that the actor's failure to perceive it, considering the nature and purpose of his conduct and the circumstances known to him, involves a gross deviation from the standard of care that a reasonable person would observe in the actor's situation.

(3) *Culpability Required Unless Otherwise Provided.* When the culpability sufficient to establish a material element of an offense is not prescribed by law, such element is established if a person acts purposely, knowingly or recklessly with respect thereto.

(4) *Prescribed Culpability Requirement Applies to All Material Elements.* When the law defining an offense prescribes the kind of culpability that is sufficient for the commission of an offense, without distinguishing among the material elements thereof, such provision shall apply to all the material elements of the offense, unless a contrary purpose plainly appears.

(5) *Substitutes for Negligence, Recklessness and Knowledge.* When the law provides that negligence suffices to establish an element of an offense, such element also is established if a person acts purposely, knowingly or recklessly. When recklessness suffices to establish an element, such element also is established if a person acts purposely or knowingly. When acting knowingly suffices to establish an element, such element also is established if a person acts purposely.

(6) *Requirement of Purpose Satisfied if Purpose Is Conditional.* When a particular purpose is an element of an offense, the element is established although such purpose is conditional, unless the condition negatives the harm or evil sought to be prevented by the law defining the offense.

(7) *Requirement of Knowledge Satisfied by Knowledge of High Probability.* When knowledge of the existence of a particular fact is an element of an offense, such knowledge is established if a person is aware of a high probability of its existence, unless he actually believes that it does not exist.

(8) *Requirement of Wilfulness Satisfied by Acting Knowingly.* A requirement that an offense be committed wilfully is satisfied if a person acts knowingly with respect to the material elements of the offense, unless a purpose to impose further requirements appears.

(9) *Culpability as to Illegality of Conduct.* Neither knowledge nor recklessness or negligence as to whether conduct constitutes an offense or as to the existence, meaning or application of the law determining the elements of an offense is an element of such offense, unless the definition of the offense or the Code so provides.

(10) *Culpability as Determinant of Grade of Offense.* When the grade or degree of an offense depends on whether the offense is committed purposely, knowingly, recklessly or negligently, its grade or degree shall be the lowest for which the determinative kind of culpability is established with respect to any material element of the offense.

Section 2.03. Causal Relationship Between Conduct and Result; Divergence Between Result Designed or Contemplated and Actual Result or Between Probable and Actual Result.

(1) Conduct is the cause of a result when:

(a) it is an antecedent but for which the result in question would not have occurred; and

(b) the relationship between the conduct and result satisfies any additional causal requirements imposed by the Code or by the law defining the offense.

(2) When purposely or knowingly causing a particular result is an element of an offense, the element is not established if the actual result is not within the purpose or the contemplation of the actor unless:

(a) the actual result differs from that designed or contemplated, as the case may be, only in the respect that a different person or different property is injured or affected or that the injury or harm designed or contemplated would have been more serious or more extensive than that caused; or

(b) the actual result involves the same kind of injury or harm as that designed or contemplated and is not too remote or accidental in its occurrence to have a [just] bearing on the actor's liability or on the gravity of his offense.

(3) When recklessly or negligently causing a particular result is an element of an offense, the element is not established if the actual result is not within the risk of which the actor is aware or, in the case of negligence, of which he should be aware unless:

(a) the actual result differs from the probable result only in the respect that a different person or different property is injured or affected or that the probable injury or harm would have been more serious or more extensive than that caused; or

(b) the actual result involves the same kind of injury or harm as the probable result and is not too remote or accidental in its occurrence to have a [just] bearing on the actor's liability or on the gravity of his offense.

(4) When causing a particular result is a material element of an offense for which absolute liability is imposed by law, the element is not established unless the actual result is a probable consequence of the actor's conduct.

Section 2.04. Ignorance or Mistake.

(1) Ignorance or mistake as to a matter of fact or law is a defense if:

(a) the ignorance or mistake negatives the purpose, knowledge, belief, recklessness or negligence required to establish a material element of the offense; or

(b) the law provides that the state of mind established by such ignorance or mistake constitutes a defense.

(2) Although ignorance or mistake would otherwise afford a defense to the offense charged, the defense is not available if the defendant would be guilty of another offense had the situation been as he supposed. In such case, however, the ignorance or mistake of the defendant shall reduce the grade and degree of the offense of which he may be convicted to those of the offense of which he would be guilty had the situation been as he supposed.

(3) A belief that conduct does not legally constitute an offense is a defense to a prosecution for that offense based upon such conduct when:

(a) the statute or other enactment defining the offense is not known to the actor and has not been published or otherwise reasonably made available prior to the conduct alleged; or

(b) he acts in reasonable reliance upon an official statement of the law, afterward determined to be invalid or erroneous, contained in (i) a statute or other enactment; (ii) a judicial decision, opinion or judgment; (iii) an administrative order or grant of permission; or (iv) an official interpretation of the public officer or body charged by law with responsibility for the interpretation, administration or enforcement of the law defining the offense.

(4) The defendant must prove a defense arising under Subsection (3) of this Section by a preponderance of evidence.

Section 2.05. When Culpability Requirements Are Inapplicable to Violations and to Offenses Defined by Other Statutes; Effect of Absolute Liability in Reducing Grade of Offense to Violation.

(1) The requirements of culpability prescribed by Sections 2.01 and 2.02 do not apply to:

(a) offenses which constitute violations, unless the requirement involved is included in the definition of the offense or the Court determines that its application is consistent with effective enforcement of the law defining the offense; or

(b) offenses defined by statutes other than the Code, insofar as a legislative purpose to impose absolute liability for such offenses or with respect to any material element thereof plainly appears.

(2) Notwithstanding any other provision of existing law and unless a subsequent statute otherwise provides:

(a) when absolute liability is imposed with respect to any material element of an offense defined by a statute other than the Code and a conviction is based upon such liability, the offense constitutes a violation; and

(b) although absolute liability is imposed by law with respect to one or more of the material elements of an offense defined by a statute other than the Code, the culpable commission of the offense may be charged and proved, in which event negligence with respect to such elements constitutes sufficient culpability and the classification of the offense and the sentence that may be imposed therefor upon conviction are determined by Section 1.04 and Article 6 of the Code.

Section 2.06. Liability for Conduct of Another; Complicity.

(1) A person is guilty of an offense if it is committed by his own conduct or by the conduct of another person for which he is legally accountable, or both.

(2) A person is legally accountable for the conduct of another person when:

(a) acting with the kind of culpability that is sufficient for the commission of the offense, he causes an innocent or irresponsible person to engage in such conduct; or

(b) he is made accountable for the conduct of such other person by the Code or by the law defining the offense; or

(c) he is an accomplice of such other person in the commission of the offense.

(3) A person is an accomplice of another person in the commission of an offense if:

(a) with the purpose of promoting or facilitating the commission of the offense, he

(i) solicits such other person to commit it; or

(ii) aids or agrees or attempts to aid such other person in planning or committing it; or

(iii) having a legal duty to prevent the commission of the offense, fails to make proper effort so to do; or

(b) his conduct is expressly declared by law to establish his complicity.

(4) When causing a particular result is an element of an offense, an accomplice in the conduct causing such result is an accomplice in the commission of that offense, if he acts with the kind of culpability, if any, with respect to that result that is sufficient for the commission of the offense.

(5) A person who is legally incapable of committing a particular offense himself may be guilty thereof if it is committed by the conduct of another person for which he is legally accountable, unless such liability is inconsistent with the purpose of the provision establishing his incapacity.

(6) Unless otherwise provided by the Code or by the law defining the offense, a person is not an accomplice in an offense committed by another person if:

(a) he is a victim of that offense; or
(b) the offense is so defined that his conduct is inevitably incident to its commission; or
(c) he terminates his complicity prior to the commission of the offense; and
　(i) wholly deprives it of effectiveness in the commission of the offense; or
　(ii) gives timely warning to the law enforcement authorities or otherwise makes proper effort to prevent the commission of the offense.

(7) An accomplice may be convicted on proof of the commission of the offense and of his complicity therein, though the person claimed to have committed the offense has not been prosecuted or convicted or has been convicted of a different offense or degree of offense or has an immunity to prosecution or conviction or has been acquitted.

Section 2.07. Liability of Corporations, Unincorporated Associations and Persons Acting, or Under a Duty to Act, in Their Behalf.

(1) A corporation may be convicted of the commission of an offense if:

(a) the offense is a violation or the offense is defined by a statute other than the Code in which a legislative purpose to impose liability on corporations plainly appears and the conduct is performed by an agent of the corporation acting in behalf of the corporation within the scope of his office or employment, except that if the law defining the offense designates the agents for whose conduct the corporation is accountable or the circumstances under which it is accountable, such provisions shall apply; or
(b) the offense consists of an omission to discharge a specific duty of affirmative performance imposed on corporations by law; or
(c) the commission of the offense was authorized, requested, commanded, performed or recklessly tolerated by the board of directors or by a high managerial agent acting in behalf of the corporation within the scope of his office or employment.

(2) When absolute liability is imposed for the commission of an offense, a legislative purpose to impose liability on a corporation shall be assumed, unless the contrary plainly appears.

(3) An unincorporated association may be convicted of the commission of an offense if:

(a) the offense is defined by a statute other than the Code which expressly provides for the liability of such an association and the conduct is performed by an agent of the association acting in behalf of the association within the scope of his office or employment, except that if the law defining the offense designates the agents for whose conduct the association is accountable or the circumstances under which it is accountable, such provisions shall apply; or

(b) the offense consists of an omission to discharge a specific duty of affirmative performance imposed on associations by law.

(4) As used in this Section:

(a) "corporation" does not include an entity organized as or by a governmental agency for the execution of a governmental program;

(b) "agent" means any director, officer, servant, employee or other person authorized to act in behalf of the corporation or association and, in the case of an unincorporated association, a member of such association;

(c) "high managerial agent" means an officer of a corporation or an unincorporated association, or, in the case of a partnership, a partner, or any other agent of a corporation or association having duties of such responsibility that his conduct may fairly be assumed to represent the policy of the corporation or association.

(5) In any prosecution of a corporation or an unincorporated association for the commission of an offense included within the terms of Subsection (1)(a) or Subsection (3)(a) of this Section, other than an offense for which absolute liability has been imposed, it shall be a defense if the defendant proves by a preponderance of evidence that the high managerial agent having supervisory responsibility over the subject matter of the offense employed due diligence to prevent its commission. This paragraph shall not apply if it is plainly inconsistent with the legislative purpose in defining the particular offense.

(6) (a) A person is legally accountable for any conduct he performs or causes to be performed in the name of the corporation or an unincorporated association or in its behalf to the same extent as if it were performed in his own name or behalf.

(b) Whenever a duty to act is imposed by law upon a corporation or an unincorporated association, any agent of the corporation or association having primary responsibility for the discharge of the duty is legally accountable for a reckless omission to perform the required act to the same extent as if the duty were imposed by law directly upon himself.

(c) When a person is convicted of an offense by reason of his legal accountability for the conduct of a corporation or an unincorporated association, he is subject to the sentence authorized by law when a natural person is convicted of an offense of the grade and the degree involved.

Section 2.08. Intoxication.

(1) Except as provided in Subsection (4) of this Section, intoxication of the actor is not a defense unless it negatives an element of the offense.

(2) When recklessness establishes an element of the offense, if the actor, due to self-induced intoxication, is unaware of a risk of which he would have been aware had he been sober, such unawareness is immaterial.

(3) Intoxication does not, in itself, constitute mental disease within the meaning of Section 4.01.

(4) Intoxication which (a) is not self-induced or (b) is pathological is an affirmative defense if by reason of such intoxication the actor at the time of his conduct lacks substantial capacity either to appreciate its criminality [wrongfulness] or to conform his conduct to the requirements of law.

(5) *Definitions.* In this Section unless a different meaning plainly is required:

(a) "intoxication" means a disturbance of mental or physical capacities resulting from the introduction of substances into the body;

(b) "self-induced intoxication" means intoxication caused by substances which the actor knowingly introduces into his body, the tendency of which to cause intoxication he knows or ought to know, unless he introduces them pursuant to medical advice or under such circumstances as would afford a defense to a charge of crime;

(c) "pathological intoxication" means intoxication grossly excessive in degree, given the amount of the intoxicant, to which the actor does not know he is susceptible.

Section 2.09. Duress.

(1) It is an affirmative defense that the actor engaged in the conduct charged to constitute an offense because he was coerced to do so by the use of, or a threat to use, unlawful force against his person or the person of another, which a person of reasonable firmness in his situation would have been unable to resist.

(2) The defense provided by this Section is unavailable if the actor recklessly placed himself in a situation in which it was probable that he would be subjected to duress. The defense is also unavailable if he was negligent in placing himself in such a situation, whenever negligence suffices to establish culpability for the offense charged.

(3) It is not a defense that a woman acted on the command of her husband, unless she acted under such coercion as would establish a defense under this Section. [The presumption that a woman, acting in the presence of her husband, is coerced is abolished.]

(4) When the conduct of the actor would otherwise be justifiable under Section 3.02, this Section does not preclude such defense.

Section 2.10. Military Orders.

It is an affirmative defense that the actor, in engaging in the conduct charged to constitute an offense, does no more than execute an order of his superior in the armed services which he does not know to be unlawful.

Section 2.11. Consent.

(1) *In General.* The consent of the victim to conduct charged to constitute an offense or to the result thereof is a defense if such consent negatives an element of the offense or precludes the infliction of the harm or evil sought to be prevented by the law defining the offense.

(2) *Consent to Bodily Harm.* When conduct is charged to constitute an offense because it causes or threatens bodily harm, consent to such conduct or to the infliction of such harm is a defense if:

(a) the bodily harm consented to or threatened by the conduct consented to is not serious; or

(b) The conduct and the harm are reasonably foreseeable hazards of joint participation in a lawful athletic contest or competitive sport; or

(c) the consent establishes a justification for the conduct under Article 3 of the Code.

(3) *Ineffective Consent.* Unless otherwise provided by the Code or by the law defining the offense, assent does not constitute consent if:

(a) it is given by a person who is legally incompetent to authorize the conduct charged to constitute the offense; or

(b) it is given by a person who by reason of youth, mental disease or defect or intoxication is manifestly unable or known by the actor to be unable to make a reasonable judgment as to the nature or harmfulness of the conduct charged to constitute the offense; or

(c) it is given by a person whose improvident consent is sought to be prevented by the law defining the offense; or

(d) it is induced by force, duress or deception of a kind sought to be prevented by the law defining the offense.

Section 2.12. De Minimis Infractions.

The Court shall dismiss a prosecution if, having regard to the nature of the conduct charged to constitute an offense and the nature of the attendant circumstances, it finds that the defendant's conduct:

(1) was within a customary license or tolerance, neither expressly negatived by the person whose interest was infringed nor inconsistent with the purpose of the law defining the offense; or

(2) did not actually cause or threaten the harm or evil sought to be prevented by the law defining the offense or did so only to an extent too trivial to warrant the condemnation of conviction; or

(3) presents such other extenuations that it cannot reasonably be regarded as envisaged by the legislature in forbidding the offense.

The Court shall not dismiss a prosecution under Subsection (3) of this Section without filing a written statement of its reasons.

Section 2.13. Entrapment.

(1) A public law enforcement official or a person acting in cooperation with such an official perpetrates an entrapment if for the purpose of obtaining evidence of the commission of an offense, he induces or encourages another person to engage in conduct constituting such offense by either:

(a) making knowingly false representations designed to induce the belief that such conduct is not prohibited; or

(b) employing methods of persuasion or inducement which create a substantial risk that such an offense will be committed by persons other than those who are ready to commit it.

(2) Except as provided in Subsection (3) of this Section, a person prosecuted for an offense shall be acquitted if he proves by a preponderance of evidence that his conduct occurred in response to an entrapment. The issue of entrapment shall be tried by the Court in the absence of the jury.

(3) The defense afforded by this Section is unavailable when causing or threatening bodily injury is an element of the offense charged and the prosecution is based on conduct causing or threatening such injury to a person other than the person perpetrating the entrapment.

ARTICLE 3. GENERAL PRINCIPLES OF JUSTIFICATION

Section 3.01. Justification an Affirmative Defense; Civil Remedies Unaffected.

(1) In any prosecution based on conduct which is justifiable under this Article, justification is an affirmative defense.

(2) The fact that conduct is justifiable under this Article does not abolish or impair any remedy for such conduct which is available in any civil action.

Section 3.02. Justification Generally: Choice of Evils.

(1) Conduct which the actor believes to be necessary to avoid a harm or evil to himself or to another is justifiable, provided that:

(a) the harm or evil sought to be avoided by such conduct is greater than that sought to be prevented by the law defining the offense charged; and

(b) neither the Code nor other law defining the offense provides exceptions or defenses dealing with the specific situation involved; and

(c) a legislative purpose to exclude the justification claimed does not otherwise plainly appear.

(2) When the actor was reckless or negligent in bringing about the situation requiring a choice of harms or evils or in appraising the necessity for his conduct, the justification afforded by this Section is unavailable in a prosecution for any offense for which recklessness or negligence, as the case may be, suffices to establish culpability.

Section 3.03. Execution of Public Duty.

(1) Except as provided in Subsection (2) of this Section, conduct is justifiable when it is required or authorized by:

(a) the law defining the duties or functions of a public officer or the assistance to be rendered to such officer in the performance of his duties; or

(b) the law governing the execution of legal process; or

(c) the judgment or order of a competent court or tribunal; or

(d) the law governing the armed services or the lawful conduct of war; or

(e) any other provision of law imposing a public duty.

(2) The other sections of this Article apply to:

(a) the use of force upon or toward the person of another for any of the purposes dealt with in such sections; and

(b) the use of deadly force for any purpose, unless the use of such force is otherwise expressly authorized by law or occurs in the lawful conduct of war.

(3) The justification afforded by Subsection (1) of this Section applies:

(a) when the actor believes his conduct to be required or authorized by the judgment or direction of a competent court or tribunal or in the lawful execution of legal process, notwithstanding lack of jurisdiction of the court or defect in the legal process; and

(b) when the actor believes his conduct to be required or authorized to assist a public officer in the performance of his duties, notwithstanding that the officer exceeded his legal authority.

Section 3.04. Use of Force in Self-Protection.

(1) *Use of Force Justifiable for Protection of the Person.* Subject to the provisions of this Section and of Section 3.09, the use of force upon or toward another person is justifiable when the actor believes that such force is immediately necessary for the purpose of protecting himself against the use of unlawful force by such other person on the present occasion.

(2) *Limitations on Justifying Necessity for Use of Force.*

(a) The use of force is not justifiable under this Section:

(i) to resist an arrest which the actor knows is being made by a peace officer, although the arrest is unlawful; or

(ii) to resist force used by the occupier or possessor of property or by another person on his behalf, where the actor knows that the person using the force is doing so under a claim of right to protect the property, except that this limitation shall not apply if:

(1) the actor is a public officer acting in the performance of his duties or a person lawfully assisting him therein or a person making or assisting in a lawful arrest; or

(2) the actor has been unlawfully dispossessed of the property and is making a re-entry or recaption justified by Section 3.06; or

(3) the actor believes that such force is necessary to protect himself against death or serious bodily harm.

(b) The use of deadly force is not justifiable under this Section unless the actor believes that such force is necessary to protect himself against death, serious bodily harm, kidnapping or sexual intercourse compelled by force or threat; nor is it justifiable if:

(i) the actor, with the purpose of causing death or serious bodily harm, provoked the use of force against himself in the same encounter; or

(ii) the actor knows that he can avoid the necessity of using such force with complete safety by retreating or by surrendering possession of a thing to a person asserting a claim of right thereto or by complying with a demand that he abstain from any action which he has no duty to take, except that:

(1) the actor is not obliged to retreat from his dwelling or place of work, unless he was the initial aggressor or is assailed in his place of work by another person whose place of work the actor knows it to be; and

(2) a public officer justified in using force in the performance of his duties or a person justified in using force in his assistance or a person justified in using force in making an arrest or preventing an escape is not obliged to desist from efforts to perform such duty, effect such arrest or prevent such escape because of resistance or threatened resistance by or on behalf of the person against whom such action is directed.

(c) Except as required by paragraphs (a) and (b) of this Subsection, a person employing protective force may estimate the necessity thereof under the circumstances as he believes them to be when the force is used, without retreating, surrendering possession, doing any other act which he has no legal duty to do or abstaining from any lawful action.

(3) *Use of Confinement as Protective Force.* The justification afforded by this Section extends to the use of confinement as protective force only if the actor takes all reasonable measures to terminate the confinement as soon as he knows that he safely can, unless the person confined has been arrested on a charge of crime.

Section 3.05. Use of Force for the Protection of Other Persons.

(1) Subject to the provisions of this Section and of Section 3.09, the use of force upon or toward the person of another is justifiable to protect a third person when:

   (a) the actor would be justified under Section 3.04 in using such force to protect himself against the injury he believes to be threatened to the person whom he seeks to protect; and
   (b) under the circumstances as the actor believes them to be, the person whom he seeks to protect would be justified in using such protective force; and
   (c) the actor believes that his intervention is necessary for the protection of such other person.

(2) Notwithstanding Subsection (1) of this Section:

   (a) when the actor would be obliged under Section 3.04 to retreat, to surrender the possession of a thing or to comply with a demand before using force in self-protection, he is not obliged to do so before using force for the protection of another person, unless he knows that he can thereby secure the complete safety of such other person; and
   (b) when the person whom the actor seeks to protect would be obliged under Section 3.04 to retreat, to surrender the possession of a thing or to comply with a demand if he knew that he could obtain complete safety by so doing, the actor is obliged to try to cause him to do so before using force in his protection if the actor knows that he can obtain complete safety in that way; and
   (c) neither the action nor the person whom he seeks to protect is obliged to retreat when in the other's dwelling or place of work to any greater extent than in his own.

Section 3.06. Use of Force for the Protection of Property.

(1) *Use of Force Justifiable for Protection of Property.* Subject to the provisions of this Section and of Section 3.09, the use of force upon or toward the person of another is justifiable when the actor believes that such force is immediately necessary:

   (a) to prevent or terminate an unlawful entry or other trespass upon land or a trespass against or the unlawful carrying away of tangible, movable property, provided that such land or movable property is, or is believed by the actor to be, in his possession or in the possession of another person for whose protection he acts; or
   (b) to effect an entry or re-entry upon land or to retake tangible movable property, provided that the actor believes that he or the person by whose authority he acts or a person from whom he or such other person derives title was unlawfully dispossessed of such land or movable property and is entitled to possession, and provided, further, that:
      (i) the force is used immediately or on fresh pursuit after such dispossession; or
      (ii) the actor believes that the person against whom he uses force has no claim of right to the possession of the property and, in the case of land, the circumstances, as the actor believes them to be, are of such urgency that it would be an exceptional hardship to postpone the entry or re-entry until a court order is obtained.

(2) *Meaning of Possession.* For the purposes of Subsection (1) of this Section:

(a) a person who has parted with the custody of property to another who refuses to restore it to him is no longer in possession, unless the property is movable and was and still is located on land in his possession;

(b) a person who has been dispossessed of land does not regain possession thereof merely by setting foot thereon;

(c) a person who has a license to use or occupy real property is deemed to be in possession thereof except against the licensor acting under claim of right.

(3) *Limitations on Justifiable Use of Force.*

(a) *Request to Desist.* The use of force is justifiable under this Section only if the actor first requests the person against whom such force is used to desist from his interference with the property, unless the actor believes that:

(i) such request would be useless; or

(ii) it would be dangerous to himself or another person to make the request; or

(iii) substantial harm will be done to the physical condition of the property which is sought to be protected before the request can effectively be made.

(b) *Exclusion of Trespasser.* The use of force to prevent or terminate a trespass is not justifiable under this Section if the actor knows that the exclusion of the trespasser will expose him to substantial danger of serious bodily harm.

(c) *Resistance of Lawful Re-entry or Recaption.* The use of force to prevent an entry or re-entry upon land or the recaption of movable property is not justifiable under this Section, although the actor believes that such re-entry or recaption is unlawful, if:

(i) the re-entry or recaption is made by or on behalf of a person who was actually dispossessed of the property; and

(ii) it is otherwise justifiable under paragraph (1)(b) of this Section.

(d) *Use of Deadly Force.* The use of deadly force is not justifiable under this Section unless the actor believes that:

(i) the person against whom the force is used is attempting to dispossess him of his dwelling otherwise than under a claim of right to its possession; or

(ii) the person against whom the force is used is attempting to commit or consummate arson, burglary, robbery or other felonious theft or property destruction and either:

(1) has employed or threatened deadly force against or in the presence of the actor; or

(2) the use of force other than deadly force to prevent the commission or the consummation of the crime would expose the actor or another in his presence to substantial danger of serious bodily harm.

(4) *Use of Confinement as Protective Force.* The justification afforded by this Section extends to the use of confinement as protective force only if the actor takes all reasonable measures to terminate the confinement as soon as he knows that he can do so with safety to the property, unless the person confined has been arrested on a charge of crime.

(5) *Use of Device to Protect Property.* The justification afforded by this Section extends to the use of a device for the purpose of protecting property only if:

(a) the device is not designed to cause or known to create a substantial risk of causing death or serious bodily harm; and

(b) the use of the particular device to protect the property from entry or trespass is reasonable under the circumstances, as the actor believes them to be; and

(c) the device is one customarily used for such a purpose or reasonable care is taken to make known to probable intruders the fact that it is used.

(6) *Use of Force to Pass Wrongful Obstructor.* The use of force to pass a person whom the actor believes to be purposely or knowingly and unjustifiably obstructing the actor from going to a place to which he may lawfully go is justifiable, provided that:

(a) the actor believes that the person against whom he uses force has no claim of right to obstruct the actor; and

(b) the actor is not being obstructed from entry or movement on land which he knows to be in the possession or custody of the person obstructing him, or in the possession or custody of another person by whose authority the obstructor acts, unless the circumstances, as the actor believes them to be, are of such urgency that it would not be reasonable to postpone the entry or movement on such land until a court order is obtained; and

(c) the force used is not greater than would be justifiable if the person obstructing the actor were using force against him to prevent his passage.

Section 3.07. Use of Force in Law Enforcement.

(1) *Use of Force Justifiable to Effect an Arrest.* Subject to the provisions of this Section and of Section 3.09, the use of force upon or toward the person of another is justifiable when the actor is making or assisting in making an arrest and the actor believes that such force is immediately necessary to effect a lawful arrest.

(2) *Limitations on the Use of Force.*

(a) The use of force is not justifiable under this Section unless:

(i) the actor makes known the purpose of the arrest or believes that it is otherwise known by or cannot reasonably be made known to the person to be arrested; and

(ii) when the arrest is made under a warrant, the warrant is valid or believed by the actor to be valid.

(b) The use of deadly force is not justifiable under this Section unless:

(i) the arrest is for a felony; and

(ii) the person effecting the arrest is authorized to act as a peace officer or is assisting a person whom he believes to be authorized to act as a peace officer; and

(iii) the actor believes that the force employed creates no substantial risk of injury to innocent persons; and

(iv) the actor believes that:

(1) the crime for which the arrest is made involved conduct including the use or threatened use of deadly force; or

(2) there is a substantial risk that the person to be arrested will cause death or serious bodily harm if his apprehension is delayed.

(3) *Use of Force to Prevent Escape from Custody.* The use of force to prevent the escape of an arrested person from custody is justifiable when the force could justifiably have been employed to effect the arrest under which the person is in

custody, except that a guard or other person authorized to act as a peace officer is justified in using any force, including deadly force, which he believes to be immediately necessary to prevent the escape of a person from a jail, prison, or other institution for the detention of persons charged with or convicted of a crime.

(4) *Use of Force by Private Person Assisting an Unlawful Arrest.*

(a) A private person who is summoned by a peace officer to assist in effecting an unlawful arrest, is justified in using any force which he would be justified in using if the arrest were lawful, provided that he does not believe the arrest is unlawful.

(b) A private person who assists another private person in effecting an unlawful arrest, or who, not being summoned, assists a peace officer in effecting an unlawful arrest, is justified in using any force which he would be justified in using if the arrest were lawful, provided that (i) he believes the arrest is lawful, and (ii) the arrest would be lawful if the facts were as he believes them to be.

(5) *Use of Force to Prevent Suicide or the Commission of a Crime.*

(a) The use of force upon or toward the person of another is justifiable when the actor believes that such force is immediately necessary to prevent such other person from committing suicide, inflicting serious bodily harm upon himself, committing or consummating the commission of a crime involving or threatening bodily harm, damage to or loss of property or a breach of the peace, except that:

(i) any limitations imposed by the other provisions of this Article on the justifiable use of force in self-protection, for the protection of others, the protection of property, the effectuation of an arrest or the prevention of an escape from custody shall apply notwithstanding the criminality of the conduct against which such force is used; and

(ii) the use of deadly force is not in any event justifiable under this Subsection unless:

(1) the actor believes that there is a substantial risk that the person whom he seeks to prevent from committing a crime will cause death or serious bodily harm to another unless the commission or the consummation of the crime is prevented and that the use of such force presents no substantial risk of injury to innocent persons; or

(2) the actor believes that the use of such force is necessary to suppress a riot or mutiny after the rioters or mutineers have been ordered to disperse and warned, in any particular manner that the law may require, that such force will be used if they do not obey.

(b) The justification afforded by this Subsection extends to the use of confinement as preventive force only if the actor takes all reasonable measures to terminate the confinement as soon as he knows that he safely can, unless the person confined has been arrested on a charge of crime.

Section 3.08. Use of Force by Persons with Special Responsibility for Care, Discipline or Safety of Others.

The use of force upon or toward the person of another is justifiable if:

(1) the actor is the parent or guardian or other person similarly responsible for the general care and supervision of a minor or a person acting at the request of such parent, guardian or other responsible person and:

(a) the force is used for the purpose of safeguarding or promoting the welfare of the minor, including the prevention or punishment of his misconduct; and

(b) the force used is not designed to cause or known to create a substantial risk of causing death, serious bodily harm, disfigurement, extreme pain or mental distress or gross degradation; or

(2) the actor is a teacher or a person otherwise entrusted with the care or supervision for a special purpose of a minor and:

(a) the actor believes that the force used is necessary to further such special purpose, including the maintenance of reasonable discipline in a school, class or other group, and that the use of such force is consistent with the welfare of the minor; and

(b) the degree of force, if it had been used by the parent or guardian of the minor, would not be unjustifiable under Subsection (1)(b) of this Section; or

(3) the actor is the guardian or other person similarly responsible for the general care and supervision of an incompetent person; and:

(a) the force is used for the purpose of safeguarding or promoting the welfare of the incompetent person, including the prevention of his misconduct, or, when such incompetent person is in a hospital or other institution for his care and custody, for the maintenance of reasonable discipline in such institution; and

(b) the force used is not designed to cause or known to create a substantial risk of causing death, serious bodily harm, disfigurement, extreme or unnecessary pain, mental distress, or humiliation; or

(4) the actor is a doctor or other therapist or a person assisting him at his direction, and:

(a) the force is used for the purpose of administering a recognized form of treatment which the actor believes to be adapted to promoting the physical or mental health of the patient; and

(b) the treatment is administered with the consent of the patient or, if the patient is a minor or an incompetent person, with the consent of his parent or guardian or other person legally competent to consent in his behalf, or the treatment is administered in an emergency when the actor believes that no one competent to consent can be consulted and that a reasonable person, wishing to safeguard the welfare of the patient, would consent; or

(5) the actor is a warden or other authorized official of a correctional institution, and:

(a) he believes that the force used is necessary for the purpose of enforcing the lawful rules or procedures of the institution, unless his belief in the lawfulness of the rule or procedure sought to be enforced is erroneous and his error is due to ignorance or mistake as to the provisions of the Code, any other provision of the criminal law or the law governing the administration of the institution; and

(b) the nature or degree of force used is not forbidden by Article 303 or 304 of the Code; and

(c) if deadly force is used, its use is otherwise justifiable under this Article; or

(6) the actor is a person responsible for the safety of a vessel or an aircraft or a person acting at his direction, and

(a) he believes that the force used is necessary to prevent interference with the operation of the vessel or aircraft or obstruction of the execution of a lawful order, unless his belief in the lawfulness of the order is erroneous and his error is due to ignorance or mistake as to the law defining his authority; and

(b) if deadly force is used, its use is otherwise justifiable under this Article; or

(7) the actor is a person who is authorized or required by law to maintain order or decorum in a vehicle, train or other carrier or in a place where others are assembled, and:

(a) he believes that the force used is necessary for such purpose; and

(b) the force used is not designed to cause or known to create a substantial risk of causing death, bodily harm, or extreme mental distress.

Section 3.09. Mistake of Law as to Unlawfulness of Force or Legality of Arrest; Reckless or Negligent Use of Otherwise Justifiable Force; Reckless or Negligent Injury or Risk of Injury to Innocent Persons.

(1) The justification afforded by Sections 3.04 to 3.07, inclusive, is unavailable when:

(a) the actor's belief in the unlawfulness of the force or conduct against which he employs protective force or his belief in the lawfulness of an arrest which he endeavors to effect by force is erroneous; and

(b) his error is due to ignorance or mistake as to the provisions of the Code, any other provision of the criminal law or the law governing the legality of an arrest or search.

(2) When the actor believes that the use of force upon or toward the person of another is necessary for any of the purposes for which such belief would establish a justification under Sections 3.03 to 3.08 but the actor is reckless or negligent in having such belief or in acquiring or failing to acquire any knowledge or belief which is material to the justifiability of his use of force, the justification afforded by those Sections is unavailable in a prosecution for an offense for which recklessness or negligence, as the case may be, suffices to establish culpability.

(3) When the actor is justified under Sections 3.03 to 3.08 in using force upon or toward the person of another but he recklessly or negligently injures or creates a risk of injury to innocent persons, the justification afforded by those Sections is unavailable in a prosecution for such recklessness or negligence towards innocent persons.

Section 3.10. Justification in Property Crimes.

Conduct involving the appropriation, seizure or destruction of, damage to, intrusion on or interference with property is justifiable under circumstances which would establish a defense of privilege in a civil action based thereon, unless:

(1) the Code or the law defining the offense deals with the specific situation involved; or

(2) a legislative purpose to exclude the justification claimed otherwise plainly appears.

Section 3.11. Definitions.

In this Article, unless a different meaning plainly is required:

(1) "unlawful force" means force, including confinement, which is employed without the consent of the person against whom it is directed and the employment of which constitutes an offense or actionable tort or would constitute such offense or tort except for a defense (such as the absence of intent, negligence, or mental capacity; duress; youth; or diplomatic status) not amounting to a privilege to use the force. Assent constitutes consent, within the meaning of this Section, whether or not it otherwise is legally effective, except assent to the infliction of death or serious bodily harm;

(2) "deadly force" means force which the actor uses with the purpose of causing or which he knows to create a substantial risk of causing death or serious bodily harm. Purposely firing a firearm in the direction of another person or at a vehicle in which another person is believed to be constitutes deadly force. A threat to cause death or seriously bodily harm, by the production of a weapon or otherwise, so long as the actor's purpose is limited to creating an apprehension that he will use deadly force if necessary, does not constitute deadly force;

(3) "dwelling" means any building or structure, though movable or temporary, or a portion thereof, which is for the time being the actor's home or place of lodging.

ARTICLE 4. RESPONSIBILITY

Section 4.01. Mental Disease or Defect Excluding Responsibility.

(1) A person is not responsible for criminal conduct if at the time of such conduct as a result of mental disease or defect he lacks substantial capacity either to appreciate the criminality [wrongfulness] of his conduct or to conform his conduct to the requirements of law.

(2) As used in this Article, the terms "mental disease or defect" do not include an abnormality manifested only by repeated criminal or otherwise anti-social conduct.

Section 4.02. Evidence of Mental Disease or Defect Admissible When Relevant to Element of the Offense; [Mental Disease or Defect Impairing Capacity as Ground for Mitigation of Punishment in Capital Cases].

(1) Evidence that the defendant suffered from a mental disease or defect is admissible whenever it is relevant to prove that the defendant did or did not have a state of mind which is an element of the offense.

[(2) Whenever the jury or the Court is authorized to determine or to recommend whether or not the defendant shall be sentenced to death or imprisonment upon conviction, evidence that the capacity of the defendant to appreciate the criminality [wrongfulness] of his conduct or to conform his conduct to the requirements of law was impaired as a result of mental disease or defect is admissible in favor of sentence of imprisonment.]

Section 4.03. Mental Disease or Defect Excluding Responsibility Is Affirmative
           Defense; Requirement of Notice; Form of Verdict and Judgment
           When Finding of Irresponsibility Is Made.

(1) Mental disease or defect excluding responsibility is an affirmative defense.

(2) Evidence of mental disease or defect excluding responsibility is not admissible unless the defendant, at the time of entering his plea of not guilty or within ten days thereafter or at such later time as the Court may for good cause permit, files a written notice of his purpose to rely on such defense.

(3) When the defendant is acquitted on the ground of mental disease or defect excluding responsibility, the verdict and the judgment shall so state.

Section 4.04. Mental Disease or Defect Excluding Fitness to Proceed.

No person who as a result of mental disease or defect lacks capacity to understand the proceedings against him or to assist in his own defense shall be tried, convicted or sentenced for the commission of an offense so long as such incapacity endures.

Section 4.05. Psychiatric Examination of Defendant with Respect to Mental Disease or Defect.

(1) Whenever the defendant has filed a notice of intention to rely on the defense of mental disease or defect excluding responsibility, or there is reason to doubt his fitness to proceed, or reason to believe that mental disease or defect of the defendant will otherwise become an issue in the cause, the Court shall appoint at least one qualified psychiatrist or shall request the Superintendent of the _____ Hospital to designate at least one qualified psychiatrist, which designation may be or include himself, to examine and report upon the mental condition of the defendant. The Court may order the defendant to be committed to a hospital or other suitable facility for the purpose of the examination for a period of not exceeding sixty days or such longer period as the Court determines to be necessary for the purpose and may direct that a qualified psychiatrist retained by the defendant be permitted to witness and participate in the examination.

(2) In such examination any method may be employed which is accepted by the medical profession for the examination of those alleged to be suffering from mental disease or defect.

(3) The report of the examination shall include the following: (a) a description of the nature of the examination; (b) a diagnosis of the mental condition of the defendant; (c) if the defendant suffers from a mental disease or defect, an opinion as to his capacity to understand the proceedings against him and to assist in his own defense; (d) when a notice of intention to rely on the defense of irresponsibility has been filed, an opinion as to the extent, if any, to which the capacity of the defendant to appreciate the criminality [wrongfulness] of his conduct or to conform his conduct to the requirements of law was impaired at the time of the criminal conduct charged; and (e) when directed by the Court, an opinion as to the capacity of the defendant to have a particular state of mind which is an element of the offense charged.

If the examination can not be conducted by reason of the unwillingness of the defendant to participate therein, the report shall so state and shall include, if possible, an opinion as to whether such unwillingness of the defendant was the result of mental disease or defect.

The report of the examination shall be filed [in triplicate] with the clerk of the Court, who shall cause copies to be delivered to the district attorney and to counsel for the defendant.

Section 4.06. Determination of Fitness to Proceed; Effect of Finding of Unfitness; Proceedings if Fitness is Regained; [Post-Commitment Hearing].

(1) When the defendant's fitness to proceed is drawn in question, the issue shall be determined by the Court. If neither the prosecuting attorney nor counsel for the defendant contests the finding of the report filed pursuant to Section 4.05, the Court may make the determination on the basis of such report. If the finding is contested, the Court shall hold a hearing on the issue. If the report is received in evidence upon such hearing, the party who contests the finding thereof shall have the right to summon and to cross-examine the psychiatrists who joined in the report and to offer evidence upon the issue.

(2) If the Court determines that the defendant lacks fitness to proceed, the proceeding against him shall be suspended, except as provided in Subsection (3) [Subsections (3) and (4)] of this Section, and the Court shall commit him to the custody of the Commissioner of Mental Hygiene [Public Health or Correction] to be placed in an appropriate institution of the Department of Mental Hygiene [Public Health or Correction] for so long as such unfitness shall endure. When the Court, on its own motion or upon the application of the Commissioner of Mental Hygiene [Public Health or Correction] or the prosecuting attorney, determines, after a hearing if a hearing is requested, that the defendant has regained fitness to proceed, the proceeding shall be resumed. If, however, the Court is of the view that so much time has elapsed since the commitment of the defendant that it would be unjust to resume the criminal proceeding, the Court may dismiss the charge and may order the defendant to be discharged or, subject to the law governing the civil commitment of persons suffering from mental disease or defect, order the defendant to be committed to an appropriate institution of the Department of Mental Hygiene [Public Health].

(3) The fact that the defendant is unfit to proceed does not preclude any legal objection to the prosecution which is susceptible of fair determination prior to trial and without the personal participation of the defendant.

[Alternative: (3) At any time within ninety days after commitment as provided in Subsection (2) of this Section, or at any later time with permission of the Court granted for good cause, the defendant or his counsel or the Commissioner of Mental Hygiene [Public Health or Correction] may apply for a special post-commitment hearing. If the application is made by or on behalf of a defendant not represented by counsel, he shall be afforded a reasonable opportunity to obtain counsel, and if he lacks funds to do so, counsel shall be assigned by the Court. The application shall be granted only if the counsel for the defendant satisfies the Court by affidavit or otherwise that as an attorney he has reasonable grounds for a good faith belief that his client has, on the facts and the law, a defense to the charge other than mental disease or defect excluding responsibility.

[(4) If the motion for a special post-commitment hearing is granted, the hearing shall be by the Court without a jury. No evidence shall be offered at the hearing by either party on the issue of mental disease or defect as a defense to, or in mitigation of, the crime charged. After hearing, the Court may in an appropriate case quash the indictment or other charge, or find it to be defective or insufficient, or determine that it is not proved beyond a reasonable doubt by the evidence, or otherwise terminate the proceedings on the evidence or the law. In any such case, unless all defects in the proceedings are promptly cured, the Court shall terminate the commitment ordered under Subsection (2) of this Section and order the defendant to be discharged or, subject to the law governing the civil commitment of persons suffering from mental disease or defect, order the defendant to be committed to an appropriate institution of the Department of Mental Hygiene [Public Health].]

Section 4.07. Determination of Irresponsibility on Basis of Report; Access to Defendant by Psychiatrist of His Own Choice; Form of Expert Testimony When Issue of Responsibility Is Tried.

(1) If the report filed pursuant to Section 4.05 finds that the defendant at the time of the criminal conduct charged suffered from a mental disease or defect which substantially impaired his capacity to appreciate the criminality [wrongfulness] of his conduct or to conform his conduct to the requirements of law, and the Court, after a hearing if a hearing is requested by the prosecuting attorney or the defendant, is satisfied that such impairment was sufficient to exclude responsibility, the Court on motion of the defendant shall enter judgment of acquittal on the ground of mental disease or defect excluding responsibility.

(2) When, notwithstanding the report filed pursuant to Section 4.05, the defendant wishes to be examined by a qualified psychiatrist or other expert of his own choice, such examiner shall be permitted to have reasonable access to the defendant for the purposes of such examination.

(3) Upon the trial, the psychiatrists who reported pursuant to Section 4.05 may be called as witnesses by the prosecution, the defendant or the Court. If the issue is being tried before a jury, the jury may be informed that the psychiatrists were designated by the Court or by the Superintendent of the _____ Hospital at the request of the Court, as the case may be. If called by the Court, the witness shall be subject to cross-examination by the prosecution and by the defendant. Both the prosecution and the defendant may summon any other qualified psychiatrist or other expert to testify, but no one who has not examined the defendant shall be competent to testify to an expert opinion with respect to the mental condition or responsibility of the defendant, as distinguished from the validity of the procedure followed by, or the general scientific propositions stated by, another witness.

(4) When a psychiatrist or other expert who has examined the defendant testifies concerning his mental condition, he shall be permitted to make a statement as to the the nature of his examination, his diagnosis of the mental condition of the defendant at the time of the commission of the offense charged and his opinion as to the extent, if any, to which the capacity of the defendant to appreciate the criminality [wrongfulness] of his conduct or to conform his conduct to the requirements of law or to have a particular state of mind which is an element of the offense charged was impaired as a result of mental disease or defect at that time. He shall be permitted to make any explanation reasonably serving to clarify his diagnosis and opinion and may be cross-examined as to any matter bearing on his competency or credibility or the validity of his diagnosis or opinion.

Section 4.08. Legal Effect of Acquittal on the Ground of Mental Disease or Defect Excluding Responsibility; Commitment; Release or Discharge.

(1) When a defendant is acquitted on the ground of mental disease or defect excluding responsibility, the Court shall order him to be committed to the custody of the Commissioner of Mental Hygiene [Public Health] to be placed in an appropriate institution for custody, care and treatment.

(2) If the Commissioner of Mental Hygiene [Public Health] is of the view that a person committed to his custody, pursuant to paragraph (1) of this Section, may be discharged or released on condition without danger to himself or to others, he shall make application for the discharge or release of such person in a report to the Court by which such person was committed and shall transmit a copy of such application and report to the prosecuting attorney of the county [parish] from which the defendant was committed. The Court shall thereupon appoint at least two qualified psychiatrists to examine such person and to report within sixty days, or such longer period as the Court determines to be necessary for the purpose, their opinion as to his mental condition. To facilitate such examination and the proceedings thereon, the Court may cause such person to be confined in any institution located near the place where the Court sits, which may hereafter be designated by the Commissioner of Mental Hygiene [Public Health] as suitable for the temporary detention of irresponsible persons.

(3) If the Court is satisfied by the report filed pursuant to paragraph (2) of this Section and such testimony of the reporting psychiatrists as the Court deems necessary that the committed person may be discharged or released on condition without danger to himself or others, the Court shall order his discharge or his release on such conditions as the Court determines to be necessary. If the Court is not so satisfied, it shall promptly order a hearing to determine whether such person may safely be discharged or released. Any such hearing shall be deemed a civil proceeding and the burden shall be upon the committed person to prove that he may safely be discharged or released. According to the determination of the Court upon the hearing, the committed person shall thereupon be discharged or released on such conditions as the Court determines to be necessary, or shall be recommitted to the custody of the Commissioner of Mental Hygiene [Public Health], subject to discharge or release only in accordance with the procedure prescribed above for a first hearing.

(4) If, within [five] years after the conditional release of a committed person, the Court shall determine, after hearing evidence, that the conditions of release have not been fulfilled and that for the safety of such person or for the safety of others his conditional release should be revoked, the Court shall forthwith order him to be recommitted to the Commissioner of Mental Hygiene [Public Health], subject to discharge or release only in accordance with the procedure prescribed above for a first hearing.

(5) A committed person may make application for his discharge or release to the Court by which he was committed, and the procedure to be followed upon such application shall be the same as that prescribed above in the case of an application by the Commissioner of Mental Hygiene [Public Health]. However, no such application by a committed person need be considered until he has been confined for a period of not less than [six months] from the date of the order of commitment, and if the determination of the Court be adverse to the application, such person shall not be permitted to file a further application until [one year] has elapsed from the date of any preceding hearing on an application for his release or discharge.

Section 4.09. Statements for Purposes of Examination or Treatment Inadmissible Except on Issue of Mental Condition.

A statement made by a person subjected to psychiatric examination or treatment pursuant to Sections 4.05, 4.06 or 4.08 for the purposes of such examination or treatment shall not be admissible in evidence against him in any criminal proceeding on any issue other than that of his mental condition but it shall be admissible upon that issue, whether or not it would otherwise be deemed a privileged communication [, unless such statement constitutes an admission of guilt of the crime charged].

Section 4.10. Immaturity Excluding Criminal Conviction; Transfer of Proceedings to Juvenile Court.

(1) A person shall not be tried for or convicted of an offense if:

(a) at the time of the conduct charged to constitute the offense he was less than sixteen years of age [, in which case the Juvenile Court shall have exclusive jurisdiction]; or

(b) at the time of the conduct charged to constitute the offense he was sixteen or seventeen years of age, unless:

(i) the Juvenile Court has no jurisdiction over him, or,

(ii) the Juvenile Court has entered an order waiving jurisdiction and consenting to the institution of criminal proceedings against him.

(2) No court shall have jurisdiction to try or convict a person of an offense if criminal proceedings against him are barred by Subsection (1) of this Section. When it appears that a person charged with the commission of an offense may be of such an age that criminal proceedings may be barred under Subsection (1) of this Section, the Court shall hold a hearing thereon, and the burden shall be on the prosecution to establish to the satisfaction of the Court that the criminal proceeding is not barred upon such grounds. If the Court determines that the proceeding is barred, custody of the person charged shall be surrendered to the Juvenile Court, and the case, including all papers and processes relating thereto, shall be transferred.

ARTICLE 5. INCHOATE CRIMES

Section 5.01. Criminal Attempt.

(1) *Definition of Attempt.* A person is guilty of an attempt to commit a crime if, acting with the kind of culpability otherwise required for commission of the crime, he:

(a) purposely engages in conduct which would constitute the crime if the attendant circumstances were as he believes them to be; or

(b) when causing a particular result is an element of the crime, does or omits to do anything with the purpose of causing or with the belief that it will cause such result without further conduct on his part; or

(c) purposely does or omits to do anything which, under the circumstances as he believes them to be, is an act or omission constituting a substantial step in a course of conduct planned to culminate in his commission of the crime.

(2) *Conduct Which May Be Held Substantial Step Under Subsection (1)(c).* Conduct shall not be held to constitute a substantial step under Subsection (1)(c) of this Section unless it is strongly corroborative of the actor's criminal purpose. Without negativing the sufficiency of other conduct, the following, if strongly corroborative of the actor's criminal purpose, shall not be held insufficient as a matter of law:

(a) lying in wait, searching for or following the contemplated victim of the crime;

(b) enticing or seeking to entice the contemplated victim of the crime to go to the place contemplated for its commission;

(c) reconnoitering the place contemplated for the commission of the crime;

(d) unlawful entry of a structure, vehicle or enclosure in which it is contemplated that the crime will be committed;

(e) possession of materials to be employed in the commission of the crime, which are specially designed for such unlawful use or which can serve no lawful purpose of the actor under the circumstances;

(f) possession, collection or fabrication of materials to be employed in the commission of the crime, at or near the place contemplated for its commission, where such possession, collection or fabrication serves no lawful purpose of the actor under the circumstances;

(g) soliciting an innocent agent to engage in conduct constituting an element of the crime.

(3) *Conduct Designed to Aid Another in Commission of a Crime.* A person who engages in conduct designed to aid another to commit a crime which would establish his complicity under Section 2.06 if the crime were committed by such other person, is guilty of an attempt to commit the crime, although the crime is not committed or attempted by such other person.

(4) *Renunciation of Criminal Purpose.* When the actor's conduct would otherwise constitute an attempt under Subsection (1)(b) or (1)(c) of this Section, it is an affirmative defense that he abandoned his effort to commit the crime or otherwise prevented its commission, under circumstances manifesting a complete and voluntary renunication of his criminal purpose. The establishment of such defense does not, however, affect the liability of an accomplice who did not join in such abandonment or prevention.

Within the meaning of this Article, renunciation of criminal purpose is not voluntary if it is motivated, in whole or in part, by circumstances, not present or apparent at the inception of the actor's course of conduct, which increase the probability of detection or apprehension or which make more difficult the accomplishment of the criminal purpose. Renunciation is not complete if it is motivated by a decision to postpone the criminal conduct until a more advantageous time or to transfer the criminal effort to another but similar objective or victim.

Section 5.02. Criminal Solicitation.

(1) *Definition of Solicitation.* A person is guilty of solicitation to commit a crime if with the purpose of promoting or facilitating its commission he commands, encourages or requests another person to engage in specific conduct which would constitute such crime or an attempt to commit such crime or which would establish his complicity in its commission or attempted commission.

(2) *Uncommunicated Solicitation.* It is immaterial under Subsection (1) of this Section that the actor fails to communicate with the person he solicits to commit a crime if his conduct was designed to effect such communication.

(3) *Renunciation of Criminal Purpose.* It is an affirmative defense that the actor, after soliciting another person to commit a crime, persuaded him not to do so or otherwise prevented the commission of the crime, under circumstances manifesting a complete and voluntary renunciation of his criminal purpose.

Section 5.03. Criminal Conspiracy.

(1) *Definition of Conspiracy.* A person is guilty of conspiracy with another person or persons to commit a crime if with the purpose of promoting or facilitating its commission he:

(a) agrees with such other person or persons that they or one or more of them will engage in conduct which constitutes such crime or an attempt or solicitation to commit such crime; or

(b) agrees to aid such other person or persons in the planning or commission of such crime or of an attempt or solicitation to commit such crime.

(2) *Scope of Conspiratorial Relationship.* If a person guilty of conspiracy, as defined by Subsection (1) of this Section, knows that a person with whom he conspires to commit a crime has conspired with another person or persons to commit the same crime, he is guilty of conspiring with such other person or persons, whether or not he knows their identity, to commit such crime.

(3) *Conspiracy With Multiple Criminal Objectives.* If a person conspires to commit a number of crimes, he is guilty of only one conspiracy so long as such multiple crimes are the object of the same agreement or continuous conspiratorial relationship.

(4) *Joinder and Venue in Conspiracy Prosecutions.*

(a) Subject to the provisions of paragraph (b) of this Subsection, two or more persons charged with criminal conspiracy may be prosecuted jointly if:

(i) they are charged with conspiring with one another; or

(ii) the conspiracies alleged, whether they have the same or different parties, are so related that they constitute different aspects of a scheme of organized criminal conduct.

(b) In any joint prosecution under paragraph (a) of this Subsection:

(i) no defendant shall be charged with a conspiracy in any county [parish or district] other than one in which he entered into such conspiracy or in which an overt act pursuant to such conspiracy was done by him or by a person with whom he conspired; and

(ii) neither the liability of any defendant nor the admissibility against him of evidence of acts or declarations of another shall be enlarged by such joinder; and

(iii) the Court shall order a severance or take a special verdict as to any defendant who so requests, if it deems it necessary or appropriate to promote the fair determination of his guilt or innocence, and shall take any other proper measures to protect the fairness of the trial.

(5) *Overt Act.* No person may be convicted of conspiracy to commit a crime, other than a felony of the first or second degree, unless an overt act in pursuance of such conspiracy is alleged and proved to have been done by him or by a person with whom he conspired.

(6) *Renunciation of Criminal Purpose.* It is an affirmative defense that the actor, after conspiring to commit a crime, thwarted the success of the conspiracy, under circumstances manifesting a complete and voluntary renunciation of his criminal purpose.

(7) *Duration of Conspiracy.* For purposes of Section 1.06 (4):

(a) conspiracy is a continuing course of conduct which terminates when the crime or crimes which are its object are committed or the agreement that they be committed is abandoned by the defendant and by those with whom he conspired; and

(b) such abandonment is presumed if neither the defendant nor anyone with whom he conspired does any overt act in pursuance of the conspiracy during the applicable period of limitation; and

(c) if an individual abandons the agreement, the conspiracy is terminated as to him only if and when he advises those with whom he conspired of his abandonment or he informs the law enforcement authorities of the existence of the conspiracy and of his participation therein.

Section 5.04. Incapacity, Irresponsibility or Immunity of Party to Solicitation or Conspiracy.

(1) Except as provided in Subsection (2) of this Section, it is immaterial to the liability of a person who solicits or conspires with another to commit a crime that:

(a) he or the person whom he solicits or with whom he conspires does not occupy a particular position or have a particular characteristic which is an element of such crime, if he believes that one of them does; or

(b) the person whom he solicits or with whom he conspires is irresponsible or has an immunity to prosecution or conviction for the commission of the crime.

(2) It is a defense to a charge of solicitation or conspiracy to commit a crime that if the criminal object were achieved, the actor would not be guilty of a crime under the law defining the offense or as an accomplice under Section 2.06(5) or 2.06(6) (a) or (b).

Section 5.05. Grading of Criminal Attempt, Solicitation and Conspiracy; Mitigation in Cases of Lesser Danger; Multiple Convictions Barred.

(1) *Grading.* Except as otherwise provided in this Section, attempt, solicitation and conspiracy are crimes of the same grade and degree as the most serious offense which is attempted or solicited or is an object of the conspiracy. An attempt, solicitation or conspiracy to commit a [capital crime or a] felony of the first degree is a felony of the second degree.

(2) *Mitigation.* If the particular conduct charged to constitute a criminal attempt, solicitation or conspiracy is so inherently unlikely to result or culminate in the commission of a crime that neither such conduct nor the actor presents a public danger warranting the grading of such offense under this Section, the Court shall exercise its power under Section 6.12 to enter judgment and impose sentence for a crime of lower grade or degree or, in extreme cases, may dismiss the prosecution.

(3) *Multiple Convictions.* A person may not be convicted of more than one offense defined by this Article for conduct designed to commit or to culminate in the commission of the same crime.

Section 5.06. Possessing Instruments of Crime; Weapons.

(1) *Criminal Instruments Generally.* A person commits a misdemeanor if he possesses any instrument of crime with purpose to employ it criminally. "Instrument of crime" means:

(a) anything specially made or specially adapted for criminal use; or

(b) anything commonly used for criminal purposes and possessed by the actor under circumstances which do not negative unlawful purpose.

(2) *Presumption of Criminal Purpose from Possession of Weapon.* If a person possesses a firearm or other weapon on or about his person, in a vehicle occupied by him, or otherwise readily available for use, it shall be presumed that he had the purpose to employ it criminally, unless:

(a) the weapon is possessed in the actor's home or place of business;

(b) the actor is licensed or otherwise authorized by law to possess such weapon; or

(c) the weapon is of a type commonly used in lawful sport.

"Weapon" means anything readily capable of lethal use and possessed under circumstances not manifestly appropriate for lawful uses which it may have; the term includes a firearm which is not loaded or lacks a clip or other component to render it immediately operable, and components which can readily be assembled into a weapon.

(3) *Presumptions as to Possession of Criminal Instruments in Automobiles.* Where a weapon or other instrument of crime is found in an automobile, it shall be presumed to be in the possession of the occupant if there is but one. If there is more than one occupant, it is presumed to be in the possession of all, except under the following circumstances:

(a) where it is found upon the person of one of the occupants;

(b) where the automobile is not a stolen one and the weapon or instrument is found out of view in a glove compartment, car trunk, or other enclosed customary depository, in which case it shall be presumed to be in the possession of the occupant or occupants who own or have authority to operate the automobile;

(c) in the case of a taxicab, a weapon or instrument found in the passengers' portion of the vehicle shall be presumed to be in the possession of all the passengers, if there are any, and, if not, in the possession of the driver.

Section 5.07.   Prohibited Offensive Weapons.

A person commits a misdemeanor if, except as authorized by law, he makes, repairs, sells, or otherwise deals in, uses, or possesses any offensive weapon. "Offensive weapon" means any bomb, machine gun, sawed-off shotgun, firearm specially made or specially adapted for concealment or silent discharge, any blackjack, sandbag, metal knuckles, dagger, or other implement for the infliction of serious bodily injury which serves no common lawful purpose. It is a defense under this Section for the defendant to prove by a preponderance of evidence that he possessed or dealt with the weapon solely as a curio or in a dramatic performance, or that he possessed it briefly in consequence of having found it or taken it from an aggressor, or under circumstances similarly negating any purpose or likelihood that the weapon would be used unlawfully. The presumptions provided in Section 5.06(3) are applicable to prosecutions under this Section.

ARTICLE 6. AUTHORIZED DISPOSITION OF OFFENDERS

Section 6.01 Degrees of Felonies.

(1) Felonies defined by this Code are classified, for the purpose of sentence, into three degrees, as follows:

(a) felonies of the first degree;

(b) felonies of the second degree;

(c) felonies of the third degree.

A felony is of the first or second degree when it is so designated by the Code. A crime declared to be a felony, without specification of degree, is of the third degree.

(2) Notwithstanding any other provision of law, a felony defined by any statute of this State other than this Code shall constitute for the purpose of sentence a felony of the third degree.

Section 6.02. Sentence in Accordance with Code; Authorized Dispositions.

(1) No person convicted of an offense shall be sentenced otherwise than in accordance with this Article.

[(2) The Court shall sentence a person who has been convicted of murder to death or imprisonment, in accordance with Section 210.6.]

(3) Except as provided in Subsection (2) of this Section and subject to the applicable provisions of the Code, the Court may suspend the imposition of sentence on a person who has been convicted of a crime, may order him to be committed in lieu of sentence, in accordance with Section 6.13, or may sentence him as follows:

(a) to pay a fine authorized by Section 6.03; or

(b) to be placed on probation [, and, in the case of a person convicted of a felony or misdemeanor to imprisonment for a term fixed by the Court not exceeding thirty days to be served as a condition of probation]; or

(c) to imprisonment for a term authorized by Sections 6.05, 6.06, 6.07, 6.08, 6.09, or 7.06; or

(d) to fine and probation or fine and imprisonment, but not to probation and imprisonment [, except as authorized in paragraph (b) of this Subsection].

(4) The Court may suspend the imposition of sentence on a person who has been convicted of a violation or may sentence him to pay a fine authorized by Section 6.03.

(5) This Article does not deprive the Court of any authority conferred by law to decree a forfeiture of property, suspend or cancel a license, remove a person from office, or impose any other civil penalty. Such a judgment or order may be included in the sentence.

Section 6.03. Fines.

A person who has been convicted of an offense may be sentenced to pay a fine not exceeding:

(1) $10,000, when the conviction is of a felony of the first or second degree;

(2) $5,000, when the conviction is of a felony of the third degree;

(3) $1,000, when the conviction is of a misdemeanor;

(4) $500, when the conviction is of a petty misdemeanor or a violation;

(5) any higher amount equal to double the pecuniary gain derived from the offense by the offender;

(6) any higher amount specifically authorized by statute.

Section 6.04. Penalties Against Corporations and Unincorporated Associations; Forfeiture of Corporate Charter or Revocation of Certificate Authorizing Foreign Corporation to Do Business in the State.

(1) The Court may suspend the sentence of a corporation or an

unincorporated association which has been convicted of an offense or may sentence it to pay a fine authorized by Section 6.03.

(2) (a) The [prosecuting attorney] is authorized to institute civil proceedings in the appropriate court of general jurisdiction to forfeit the charter of a corporation organized under the laws of this State or to revoke the certificate authorizing a foreign corporation to conduct business in this State. The Court may order the charter forfeited or the certificate revoked upon finding (i) that the board of directors or a high managerial agent acting in behalf of the corporation has, in conducting the corporation's affairs, purposely engaged in a persistent course of criminal conduct and (ii) that for the prevention of future criminal conduct of the same character, the public interest requires the charter of the corporation to be forfeited and the corporation to be dissolved or the certificate to be revoked.

(b) When a corporation is convicted of a crime or a high managerial agent of a corporation, as defined in Section 2.07, is convicted of a crime committed in the conduct of the affairs of the corporation, the Court, in sentencing the corporation or the agent, may direct the [prosecuting attorney] to institute proceedings authorized by paragraph (a) of this Subsection.

(c) The proceedings authorized by paragraph (a) of this Subsection shall be conducted in accordance with the procedures authorized by law for the involuntary dissolution of a corporation or the revocation of the certificate authorizing a foreign corporation to conduct business in this State. Such proceedings shall be deemed additional to any other proceedings authorized by law for the purpose of forfeiting the charter of a corporation or revoking the certificate of a foreign corporation.

Section 6.05. Young Adult Offenders.

(1) *Specialized Correctional Treatment.* A young adult offender is a person convicted of a crime who, at the time of sentencing, is sixteen but less than twenty-two years of age. A young adult offender who is sentenced to a term of imprisonment which may exceed thirty days [alternatives: (1) ninety days; (2) one year] shall be committed to the custody of the Division of Young Adult Correction of the Department of Correction, and shall receive, as far as practicable, such special and individualized correctional and rehabilitative treatment as may be appropriate to his needs.

(2) *Special Term.* A young adult offender convicted of a felony may, in lieu of any other sentence of imprisonment authorized by this Article, be sentenced to a special term of imprisonment without a minimum and with a maximum of four years, regardless of the degree of the felony involved, if the Court is of the opinion that such special term is adequate for his correction and rehabilitation and will not jeopardize the protection of the public.

[(3) *Removal of Disabilities; Vacation of Conviction.*

(a) In sentencing a young adult offender to the special term provided by this Section or to any sentence other than one of imprisonment, the Court may order that so long as he is not convicted of another felony, the judgment shall not constitute a conviction for the purposes of any disqualification or disability imposed by law upon conviction of a crime.

(b) When any young adult offender is unconditionally discharged from probation or parole before the expiration of the maximum term thereof, the Court may enter an order vacating the judgment of conviction.]

[(4) *Commitment for Observation.* If, after pre-sentence investigation, the Court desires additional information concerning a young adult offender before imposing sentence, it may order that he be committed, for a period not exceeding ninety days, to the custody of the Division of Young Adult Correction of the Department of Correction for observation and study at an appropriate reception or classification center. Such Division of the Department of Correction and the [Young Adult Division of the] Board of Parole shall advise the Court of their findings and recommendations on or before the expiration of such ninety-day period.]

Section 6.06. Sentence of Imprisonment for Felony; Ordinary Terms.

A person who has been convicted of a felony may be sentenced to imprisonment, as follows:

(1) in the case of a felony of the first degree, for a term the minimum of which shall be fixed by the Court at not less than one year nor more than ten years, and the maximum of which shall be life imprisonment;

(2) in the case of a felony of the second degree, for a term the minimum of which shall be fixed by the Court at not less than one year nor more than three years, and the maximum of which shall be ten years;

(3) in the case of a felony of the third degree, for a term the minimum of which shall be fixed by the Court at not less than one year nor more than two years, and the maximum of which shall be five years.

Alternate Section 6.06. Sentence of Imprisonment for Felony; Ordinary Terms.

A person who has been convicted of a felony may be sentenced to imprisonment, as follows:

(1) in the case of a felony of the first degree, for a term the minimum of which shall be fixed by the Court at not less than one year nor more than ten years, and the maximum at not more than twenty years or at life imprisonment;

(2) in the case of a felony of the second degree, for a term the minimum of which shall be fixed by the Court at not less than one year nor more than three years, and the maximum at not more than ten years;

(3) in the case of a felony of the third degree, for a term the minimum of which shall be fixed by the Court at not less than one year nor more than two years, and the maximum at not more than five years.

No sentence shall be imposed under this Section of which the minimum is longer than one-half the maximum, or, when the maximum is life imprisonment, longer than ten years.

Section 6.07. Sentence of Imprisonment for Felony; Extended Terms.

In the cases designated in Section 7.03, a person who has been convicted of a felony may be sentenced to an extended term of imprisonment, as follows:

(1) in the case of a felony of the first degree, for a term the minimum of which shall be fixed by the Court at not less than five years nor more than ten years, and the maximum of which shall be life imprisonment;

(2) in the case of a felony of the second degree, for a term the minimum of which shall be fixed by the Court at not less than one year nor more than five years, and the maximum of which shall be fixed by the Court at not less than ten nor more than twenty years;

(3) in the case of a felony of the third degree, for a term the minimum of which shall be fixed by the Court at not less than one year nor more than three years, and the maximum of which shall be fixed by the Court at not less than five nor more than ten years.

Section 6.08. Sentence of Imprisonment for Misdemeanors and Petty Misdemeanors; Ordinary Terms.

A person who has been convicted of a misdemeanor or a petty misdemeanor may be sentenced to imprisonment for a definite term which shall be fixed by the Court and shall not exceed one year in the case of a misdemeanor or thirty days in the case of a petty misdemeanor.

Section 6.09. Sentence of Imprisonment for Misdemeanors and Petty Misdemeanors; Extended Terms.

(1) In the cases designated in Section 7.04, a person who has been convicted of a misdemeanor or a petty misdemeanor may be sentenced to an extended term of imprisonment, as follows:

(a) in the case of a misdemeanor, for a term the minimum of which shall be fixed by the Court at not more than one year and the maximum of which shall be three years;

(b) in the case of a petty misdemeanor, for a term the minimum of which shall be fixed by the Court at not more than six months and the maximum of which shall be two years.

(2) No such sentence for an extended term shall be imposed unless:

(a) the Director of Correction has certified that there is an institution in the Department of Correction, or in a county, city [or other appropriate political subdivision of the State] which is appropriate for the detention and correctional treatment of such misdemeanants or petty misdemeanants, and that such institution is available to receive such commitments; and

(b) the [Board of Parole] [Parole Administrator] has certified that the Board of Parole is able to visit such institution and to assume responsibility for the release of such prisoners on parole and for their parole supervision.

Section 6.10. First Release of All Offenders on Parole; Sentence of Imprisonment Includes Separate Parole Term; Length of Parole Term; Length of Recommitment and Reparole After Revocation of Parole; Final Unconditional Release.

(1) *First Release of All Offenders on Parole.* An offender sentenced to an indefinite term of imprisonment in excess of one year under Section 6.05, 6.06, 6.07, 6.09 or 7.06 shall be released conditionally on parole at or before the expiration of the maximum of such term, in accordance with Article 305.

(2) *Sentence of Imprisonment Includes Separate Parole Term; Length of Parole Term.* A sentence to an indefinite term of imprisonment in excess of one year under Section 6.05, 6.06, 6.07, 6.09 or 7.06 includes as a separate portion of the sentence a term of parole or of recommitment for violation of the conditions of parole which governs the duration of parole or recommitment after the offender's first conditional release on parole. The minimum of such term is one year and the maximum is five years, unless the sentence was imposed under Section 6.05(2) or Section 6.09, in which case the maximum is two years.

(3) *Length of Recommitment and Reparole After Revocation of Parole.* If an offender is recommitted upon revocation of his parole, the term of further imprisonment upon such recommitment and of any subsequent reparole or recommitment under the same sentence shall be fixed by the Board of Parole but shall not exceed in aggregate length the unserved balance of the maximum parole term provided by Subsection (2) of this Section.

(4) *Final Unconditional Release.* When the maximum of his parole term has expired or he has been sooner discharged from parole under Section 305.12, an offender shall be deemed to have served his sentence and shall be released unconditionally.

Section 6.11. Place of Imprisonment.

(1) When a person is sentenced to imprisonment for an indefinite term with a maximum in excess of one year, the Court shall commit him to the custody of the Department of Correction [or other single department or agency] for the term of his sentence and until released in accordance with law.

(2) When a person is sentenced to imprisonment for a definite term, the Court shall designate the institution or agency to which he is committed for the term of his sentence and until released in accordance with law.

Section 6.12. Reduction of Conviction by Court to Lesser Degree of Felony or to Misdemeanor.

If, when a person has been convicted of a felony, the Court, having regard to the nature and circumstances of the crime and to the history and character of the defendant, is of the view that it would be unduly harsh to sentence the offender in accordance with the Code, the Court may enter judgment of conviction for a lesser degree of felony or for a misdemeanor and impose sentence accordingly.

Section 6.13. Civil Commitment in Lieu of Prosecution or of Sentence.

(1) When a person prosecuted for a [felony of the third degree,] misdemeanor or petty misdemeanor is a chronic alcoholic, narcotic addict [or prostitute] or person suffering from mental abnormality and the Court is authorized by law to order the civil commitment of such person to a hospital or other institution for medical, psychiatric or other rehabilitative treatment, the Court may order such commitment and dismiss the prosecution. The order of commitment may be made after conviction, in which event the Court may set aside the verdict or judgment of conviction and dismiss the prosecution.

(2) The Court shall not make an order under Subsection (1) of this Section unless it is of the view that it will substantially further the rehabilitation of the defendant and will not jeopardize the protection of the public.

ARTICLE 7. AUTHORITY OF COURT IN SENTENCING

Section 7.01. Criteria for Withholding Sentence of Imprisonment and for Placing Defendant on Probation.

(1) The Court shall deal with a person who has been convicted of a crime without imposing sentence of imprisonment unless, having regard to the nature

and circumstances of the crime and the history, character and condition of the defendant, it is of the opinion that his imprisonment is necessary for protection of the public because:

(a) there is undue risk that during the period of a suspended sentence or probation the defendant will commit another crime; or

(b) the defendant is in need of correctional treatment that can be provided most effectively by his commitment to an institution; or

(c) a lesser sentence will depreciate the seriousness of the defendant's crime.

(2) The following grounds, while not controlling the discretion of the Court, shall be accorded weight in favor of withholding sentence of imprisonment:

(a) the defendant's criminal conduct neither caused nor threatened serious harm;

(b) the defendant did not contemplate that his criminal conduct would cause or threaten serious harm;

(c) the defendant acted under a strong provocation;

(d) there were substantial grounds tending to excuse or justify the defendant's criminal conduct, though failing to establish a defense;

(e) the victim of the defendant's criminal conduct induced or facilitated its commission;

(f) the defendant has compensated or will compensate the victim of his criminal conduct for the damage or injury that he sustained;

(g) the defendant has no history of prior delinquency or criminal activity or has led a law-abiding life for a substantial period of time before the commission of the present crime;

(h) the defendant's criminal conduct was the result of circumstances unlikely to recur;

(i) the character and attitudes of the defendant indicate that he is unlikely to commit another crime;

(j) the defendant is particularly likely to respond affirmatively to probationary treatment;

(k) the imprisonment of the defendant would entail excessive hardship to himself or his dependents.

(3) When a person who has been convicted of a crime is not sentenced to imprisonment, the Court shall place him on probation if he is in need of the supervision, guidance, assistance or direction that the probation service can provide.

Section 7.02. Criteria for Imposing Fines.

(1) The Court shall not sentence a defendant only to pay a fine, when any other disposition is authorized by law, unless having regard to the nature and circumstances of the crime and to the history and character of the defendant, it is of the opinion that the fine alone suffices for protection of the public.

(2) The Court shall not sentence a defendant to pay a fine in addition to a sentence of imprisonment or probation unless:

(a) the defendant has derived a pecuniary gain from the crime; or

(b) the Court is of opinion that a fine is specially adapted to deterrence of the crime involved or to the correction of the offender.

(3) The Court shall not sentence a defendant to pay a fine unless:

(a) the defendant is or will be able to pay the fine; and

(b) the fine will not prevent the defendant from making restitution or reparation to the victim of the crime.

(4) In determining the amount and method of payment of a fine, the Court shall take into account the financial resources of the defendant and the nature of the burden that its payment will impose.

Section 7.03. Criteria for Sentence of Extended Term of Imprisonment; Felonies.

The Court may sentence a person who has been convicted of a felony to an extended term of imprisonment if it finds one or more of the grounds specified in this Section. The finding of the Court shall be incorporated in the record.

(1) The defendant is a persistent offender whose commitment for an extended term is necessary for protection of the public.

The Court shall not make such a finding unless the defendant is over twenty-one years of age and has previously been convicted of two felonies or of one felony and two misdemeanors, committed at different times when he was over [insert Juvenile Court age] years of age.

(2) The defendant is a professional criminal whose commitment for an extended term is necessary for protection of the public.

The Court shall not make such a finding unless the defendant is over twenty-one years of age and:

(a) the circumstances of the crime show that the defendant has knowingly devoted himself to criminal activity as a major source of livelihood; or

(b) the defendant has substantial income or resources not explained to be derived from a source other than criminal activity.

(3) The defendant is a dangerous, mentally abnormal person whose commitment for an extended term is necessary for protection of the public.

The Court shall not make such a finding unless the defendant has been subjected to a psychiatric examination resulting in the conclusions that his mental condition is gravely abnormal; that his criminal conduct has been characterized by a pattern of repetitive or compulsive behavior or by persistent aggressive behavior with heedless indifference to consequences; and that such condition makes him a serious danger to others.

(4) The defendant is a multiple offender whose criminality was so extensive that a sentence of imprisonment for an extended term is warranted.

The Court shall not make such a finding unless:

(a) the defendant is being sentenced for two or more felonies, or is already under sentence of imprisonment for felony, and the sentences of imprisonment involved will run concurrently under Section 7.06; or

(b) the defendant admits in open court the commission of one or more other felonies and asks that they be taken into account when he is sentenced; and

(c) the longest sentences of imprisonment authorized for each of the defendant's crimes, including admitted crimes taken into account, if made to run consecutively would exceed in length the minimum and maximum of the extended term imposed.

Section 7.04. Criteria for Sentence of Extended Term of Imprisonment; Misdemeanors and Petty Misdemeanors.

The Court may sentence a person who has been convicted of a misdemeanor or petty misdemeanor to an extended term of imprisonment if it finds one or more of the grounds specified in this Section. The finding of the Court shall be incorporated in the record.

(1) The defendant is a persistent offender whose commitment for an extended term is necessary for protection of the public.

The Court shall not make such a finding unless the defendant has previously been convicted of two crimes, committed at different times when he was over [insert Juvenile Court age] years of age.

(2) The defendant is a professional criminal whose commitment for an extended term is necessary for protection of the public.

The Court shall not make such a finding unless:

(a) the circumstances of the crime show that the defendant has knowingly devoted himself to criminal activity as a major source of livelihood; or

(b) the defendant has substantial income or resources not explained to be derived from a source other than criminal activity.

(3) The defendant is a chronic alcoholic, narcotic addict, prostitute or person of abnormal mental condition who requires rehabilitative treatment for a substantial period of time.

The Court shall not make such a finding unless, with respect to the particular category to which the defendant belongs, the Director of Correction has certified that there is a specialized institution or facility which is satisfactory for the rehabilitative treatment of such persons and which otherwise meets the requirements of Section 6.09, Subsection (2).

(4) The defendant is a multiple offender whose criminality was so extensive that a sentence of imprisonment for an extended term is warranted.

The Court shall not make such a finding unless:

(a) the defendant is being sentenced for a number of misdemeanors or petty misdemeanors or is already under sentence of imprisonment for crime of such grades, or admits in open court the commission of one or more such crimes and asks that they be taken into account when he is sentenced; and

(b) maximum fixed sentences of imprisonment for each of the defendant's crimes, including admitted crimes taken into account, if made to run consecutively, would exceed in length the maximum period of the extended term imposed.

Section 7.05. Former Conviction in Another Jurisdiction; Definition and Proof of Conviction; Sentence Taking into Account Admitted Crimes Bars Subsequent Conviction for Such Crimes.

(1) For purposes of paragraph (1) of Section 7.03 or 7.04, a conviction of the commission of a crime in another jurisdiction shall constitute a previous conviction. Such conviction shall be deemed to have been of a felony if sentence of death or of imprisonment in excess of one year was authorized under the law of such other jurisdiction, of a misdemeanor if sentence of imprisonment in excess of thirty days but not in excess of a year was authorized and of a petty misdemeanor if sentence of imprisonment for not more than thirty days was authorized.

(2) An adjudication by a court of competent jurisdiction that the defendant committed a crime constitutes a conviction for purposes of Sections 7.03 to 7.05 inclusive, although sentence or the execution thereof was suspended, provided that the time to appeal has expired and that the defendant was not pardoned on the ground of innocence.

(3) Prior conviction may be proved by any evidence, including fingerprint records made in connection with arrest, conviction or imprisonment, that reasonably satisfies the Court that the defendant was convicted.

(4) When the defendant has asked that other crimes admitted in open court be taken into account when he is sentenced and the Court has not rejected such request, the sentence shall bar the prosecution or conviction of the defendant in this State for any such admitted crime.

Section 7.06. Multiple Sentences; Concurrent and Consecutive Terms.

(1) *Sentences of Imprisonment for More Than One Crime.* When multiple sentences of imprisonment are imposed on a defendant for more than one crime, including a crime for which a previous suspended sentence or sentence of probation has been revoked, such multiple sentences shall run concurrently or consecutively as the Court determines at the time of sentence, except that:

(a) a definite and an indefinite term shall run concurrently and both sentences shall be satisfied by service of the indefinite term; and

(b) the aggregate of consecutive definite terms shall not exceed one year; and

(c) the aggregate of consecutive indefinite terms shall not exceed in minimum or maximum length the longest extended term authorized for the highest grade and degree of crime for which any of the sentences was imposed; and

(d) not more than one sentence for an extended term shall be imposed.

(2) *Sentences of Imprisonment Imposed at Different Times.* When a defendant who has previously been sentenced to imprisonment is subsequently sentenced to another term for a crime committed prior to the former sentence, other than a crime committed while in custody:

(a) the multiple sentences imposed shall so far as possible conform to Subsection (1) of this Section; and

(b) whether the Court determines that the terms shall run concurrently or consecutively, the defendant shall be credited with time served in imprisonment on the prior sentence in determining the permissible aggregate length of the term or terms remaining to be served; and

(c) when a new sentence is imposed on a prisoner who is on parole, the balance of the parole term on the former sentence shall be deemed to run during the period of the new imprisonment.

(3) *Sentence of Imprisonment for Crime Committed While on Parole.* When a defendant is sentenced to imprisonment for a crime committed while on parole in this State, such term of imprisonment and any period of reimprisonment that the Board of Parole may require the defendant to serve upon the revocation of his parole shall run concurrently, unless the Court orders them to run consecutively.

(4) *Multiple Sentences of Imprisonment in Other Cases.* Except as otherwise provided in this Section, multiple terms of imprisonment shall run concurrently or consecutively as the Court determines when the second or subsequent sentence is imposed.

(5) *Calculation of Concurrent and Consecutive Terms of Imprisonment.*

(a) When indefinite terms run concurrently, the shorter minimum terms merge in and are satisfied by serving the longest minimum term and the shorter maximum terms merge in and are satisfied by discharge of the longest maximum term.

(b) When indefinite terms run consecutively, the minimum terms are added to arrive at an aggregate minimum to be served equal to the sum of all minimum terms and the maximum terms are added to arrive at an aggregate maximum equal to the sum of all maximum terms.

(c) When a definite and an indefinite term run consecutively, the period of the definite term is added to both the minimum and maximum of the indefinite term and both sentences are satisfied by serving the indefinite term.

(6) *Suspension of Sentence or Probation and Imprisonment; Multiple Terms of Suspension and Probation.* When a defendant is sentenced for more than one offense or a defendant already under sentence is sentenced for another offense committed prior to the former sentence:

(a) the Court shall not sentence to probation a defendant who is under sentence of imprisonment [with more than thirty days to run] or impose a sentence of probation and a sentence of imprisonment [, except as authorized by Section 6.02(3)(b)]; and

(b) multiple periods of suspension or probation shall run concurrently from the date of the first such disposition; and

(c) when a sentence of imprisonment is imposed for an indefinite term, the service of such sentence shall satisfy a suspended sentence on another count or a prior suspended sentence or sentence to probation; and

(d) when a sentence of imprisonment is imposed for a definite term, the period of a suspended sentence on another count or a prior suspended sentence or sentence to probation shall run during the period of such imprisonment.

(7) *Offense Committed While Under Suspension of Sentence or Probation.* When a defendant is convicted of an offense committed while under suspension of sentence or on probation and such suspension or probation is not revoked:

(a) if the defendant is sentenced to imprisonment for an indefinite term, the service of such sentence shall satisfy the prior suspended sentence or sentence to probation; and

(b) if the defendant is sentenced to imprisonment for a definite term, the period of the suspension or probation shall not run during the period of such imprisonment; and

(c) if sentence is suspended or the defendant is sentenced to probation, the period of such suspension or probation shall run concurrently with or consecutively to the remainder of the prior periods, as the Court determines at the time of sentence.

Section 7.07. Procedure on Sentence; Pre-sentence Investigation and Report; Remand for Psychiatric Examination; Transmission of Records to Department of Correction.

(1) The Court shall not impose sentence without first ordering a pre-sentence investigation of the defendant and according due consideration to a written report of such investigation where:

(a) the defendant has been convicted of a felony; or
(b) the defendant is less than twenty-two years of age and has been convicted of a crime; or

(c) the defendant will be [placed on probation or] sentenced to imprisonment for an extended term.

(2) The Court may order a pre-sentence investigation in any other case.

(3) The pre-sentence investigation shall include an analysis of the circumstances attending the commission of the crime, the defendant's history of delinquency or criminality, physical and mental condition, family situation and background, economic status, education, occupation and personal habits and any other matters that the probation officer deems relevant or the Court directs to be included.

(4) Before imposing sentence, the Court may order the defendant to submit to psychiatric observation and examination for a period of not exceeding sixty days or such longer period as the Court determines to be necessary for the purpose. The defendant may be remanded for this purpose to any available clinic or mental hospital or the Court may appoint a qualified psychiatrist to make the examination. The report of the examination shall be submitted to the Court.

(5) Before imposing sentence, the Court shall advise the defendant or his counsel of the factual contents and the conclusions of any pre-sentence investigation or psychiatric examination and afford fair opportunity, if the defendant so requests, to controvert them. The sources of confidential information need not, however, be disclosed.

(6) The Court shall not impose a sentence of imprisonment for an extended term unless the ground therefor has been established at a hearing after the conviction of the defendant and on written notice to him of the ground proposed. Subject to the limitation of Subsection (5) of this Section, the defendant shall have the right to hear and controvert the evidence against him and to offer evidence upon the issue.

(7) If the defendant is sentenced to imprisonment, a copy of the report of any pre-sentence investigation or psychiatric examination shall be transmitted forthwith to the Department of Correction [or other state department or agency] or, when the defendant is committed to the custody of a specific institution, to such institution.

Section 7.08. Commitment for Observation; Sentence of Imprisonment for Felony Deemed Tentative for Period of One Year; Re-sentence on Petition of Commissioner of Correction.

(1) If, after pre-sentence investigation, the Court desires additional information concerning an offender convicted of a felony or misdemeanor before imposing sentence, it may order that he be committed, for a period not exceeding ninety days, to the custody of the Department of Correction, or, in the case of a young adult offender, to the custody of the Division of Young Adult Correction, for observation and study at an appropriate reception or classification center. The Department and the Board of Parole, or the Young Adult Divisions thereof, shall advise the Court of their findings and recommendations on or before the expiration of such ninety-day period. If the offender is thereafter sentenced to imprisonment, the period of such commitment for observation shall be deducted from the maximum term and from the minimum, if any, of such sentence.

(2) When a person has been sentenced to imprisonment upon conviction of a felony, whether for an ordinary or extended term, the sentence shall be deemed tentative, to the extent provided in this Section, for the period of one year

following the date when the offender is received in custody by the Department of Correction [or other state department or agency].

(3) If, as a result of the examination and classification by the Department of Correction [or other state department or agency] of a person under sentence of imprisonment upon conviction of a felony, the Commissioner of Correction [or other department head] is satisfied that the sentence of the Court may have been based upon a misapprehension as to the history, character or physical or mental condition of the offender, the Commissioner, during the period when the offender's sentence is deemed tentative under Subsection (2) of this Section shall file in the sentencing Court a petition to re-sentence the offender. The petition shall set forth the information as to the offender that is deemed to warrant his re-sentence and may include a recommendation as to the sentence to be imposed.

(4) The Court may dismiss a petition filed under Subsection (3) of this Section without a hearing if it deems the information set forth insufficient to warrant reconsideration of the sentence. If the Court is of the view that the petition warrants such reconsideration, a copy of the petition shall be served on the offender, who shall have the right to be heard on the issue and to be represented by counsel.

(5) When the Court grants a petition filed under Subsection (3) of this Section, it shall re-sentence the offender and may impose any sentence that might have been imposed originally for the felony of which the defendant was convicted. The period of his imprisonment prior to re-sentence and any reduction for good behavior to which he is entitled shall be applied in satisfaction of the final sentence.

(6) For all purposes other than this Section, a sentence of imprisonment has the same finality when it is imposed that it would have if this Section were not in force.

(7) Nothing in this Section shall alter the remedies provided by law for vacating or correcting an illegal sentence.

Section 7.09. Credit for Time of Detention Prior to Sentence; Credit for Imprisonment Under Earlier Sentence for the Same Crime.

(1) When a defendant who is sentenced to imprisonment has previously been detained in any state or local correctional or other institution following his [conviction of] [arrest for] the crime for which such sentence is imposed, such period of detention following his [conviction] [arrest] shall be deducted from the maximum term, and from the minimum, if any, of such sentence. The officer having custody of the defendant shall furnish a certificate to the Court at the time of sentence, showing the length of such detention of the defendant prior to sentence in any state or local correctional or other institution, and the certificate shall be annexed to the official records of the defendant's commitment.

(2) When a judgment of conviction is vacated and a new sentence is thereafter imposed upon the defendant for the same crime, the period of detention and imprisonment theretofore served shall be deducted from the maximum term, and from the minimum, if any, of the new sentence. The officer having custody of the defendant shall furnish a certificate to the Court at the time of sentence, showing the period of imprisonment served under the original sentence, and the certificate shall be annexed to the official records of the defendant's new commitment.

PART II. DEFINITION OF SPECIFIC CRIMES

Offenses Against Existence or Stability of the State

[This category of offenses, including treason, sedition, espionage and like crimes, was excluded from the scope of the Model Penal Code. These offenses are peculiarly the concern of the federal government. The Constitution itself defines treason: "Treason against the United States shall consist only in levying War against them, or in adhering to their Enemies, giving them Aid and Comfort. . . ." Article III, Section 3; cf. Pennsylvania v. Nelson, 350 U.S. 497 (supersession of state sedition legislation by federal law). Also, the definition of offenses against the stability of the state is inevitably affected by special political considerations. These factors militated against the use of the Institute's limited resources to attempt to draft "model" provisions in this area. However we provide at this point in the Plan of the Model Penal Code for an Article 200, where definitions of offenses against the existence or stability of the state may be incorporated.]

Offenses Involving Danger to the Person
ARTICLE 210. CRIMINAL HOMICIDE

§ 210.0. Definitions.

In Articles 210-213, unless a different meaning plainly is required:
(1) "human being" means a person who has been born and is alive;
(2) "bodily injury" means physical pain, illness or any impairment of physical condition;
(3) "serious bodily injury" means bodily injury which creates a substantial risk of death or which causes serious, permanent disfigurement, or protracted loss or impairment of the function of any bodily member or organ;
(4) "deadly weapon" means any firearm, or other weapon, device, instrument, material or substance, whether animate or inanimate, which in the manner it is used or is intended to be used is known to be capable of producing death or serious bodily injury.

§ 210.1. Criminal Homicide.

(1) A person is guilty of criminal homicide if he purposely, knowingly, recklessly or negligently causes the death of another human being.
(2) Criminal homicide is murder, manslaughter or negligent homicide.

§ 210.2. Murder.

(1) Except as provided in Section 210.3(1)(b), criminal homicide constitutes murder when:
(a) it is committed purposely or knowingly; or
(b) it is committed recklessly under circumstances manifesting extreme indifference to the value of human life. Such recklessness and indifference are presumed if the actor is engaged or is an accomplice in the commission of, or an attempt to commit, or flight after committing or attempting to commit robbery, rape or deviate sexual intercourse by force or threat of force, arson, burglary, kidnapping or felonious escape.

(2) Murder is a felony of the first degree [but a person convicted of murder may be sentenced to death, as provided in Section 210.6].

§ 210.3. Manslaughter.

(1) Criminal homicide constitutes manslaughter when:

(a) it is committed recklessly; or

(b) a homicide which would otherwise be murder is committed under the influence of extreme mental or emotional disturbance for which there is reasonable explanation or excuse. The reasonableness of such explanation or excuse shall be determined from the viewpoint of a person in the actor's situation under the circumstances as he believes them to be.

(2) Manslaughter is a felony of the second degree.

§ 210.4. Negligent Homicide.

(1) Criminal homicide constitutes negligent homicide when it is committed negligently.

(2) Negligent homicide is a felony of the third degree.

§ 210.5. Causing or Aiding Suicide.

(1) *Causing Suicide as Criminal Homicide.* A person may be convicted of criminal homicide for causing another to commit suicide only if he purposely causes such suicide by force, duress or deception.

(2) *Aiding or Soliciting Suicide as an Independent Offense.* A person who purposely aids or solicits another to commit suicide is guilty of a felony of the second degree if his conduct causes such suicide or an attempted suicide, and otherwise of a misdemeanor.

[§ 210.6. Sentence of Death for Murder; Further Proceedings to Determine Sentence.*

(1) *Death Sentence Excluded.* When a defendant is found guilty of murder, the Court shall impose sentence for a felony of the first degree if it is satisfied that:

(a) none of the aggravating circumstances enumerated in Subsection (3) of this Section was established by the evidence at the trial or will be established if further proceedings are initiated under Subsection (2) of this Section; or

(b) substantial mitigating circumstances, established by the evidence at the trial, call for leniency; or

(c) the defendant, with the consent of the prosecuting attorney and the approval of the Court, pleaded guilty to murder as a felony of the first degree; or

(d) the defendant was under 18 years of age at the time of the commission of the crime; or

(e) the defendant's physical or mental condition calls for leniency; or

(f) although the evidence suffices to sustain the verdict, it does not foreclose all doubt respecting the defendant's guilt.

(2) *Determination by Court or by Court and Jury.* Unless the Court imposes sentence under Subsection (1) of this Section, it shall conduct a separate pro-

---

* The brackets signify that the American Law Institute has taken no position on the abolition or retention of capital punishment.

ceeding to determine whether the defendant should be sentenced for a felony of the first degree or sentenced to death. The proceeding shall be conducted before the Court alone if the defendant was convicted by a Court sitting without a jury or upon his plea of guilty or if the prosecuting attorney and the defendant waive a jury with respect to sentence. In other cases it shall be conducted before the Court sitting with the jury which determined the defendant's guilt or, if the Court for good cause shown discharges that jury, with a new jury empanelled for the purpose.

In the proceeding, evidence may be presented as to any matter that the Court deems relevant to sentence, including but not limited to the nature and circumstances of the crime, the defendant's character, background, history, mental and physical condition and any of the aggravating or mitigating circumstances enumerated in Subsections (3) and (4) of this Section. Any such evidence, not legally privileged, which the Court deems to have probative force, may be received, regardless of its admissibility under the exclusionary rules of evidence, provided that the defendant's counsel is accorded a fair opportunity to rebut such evidence. The prosecuting attorney and the defendant or his counsel shall be permitted to present argument for or against sentence of death.

The determination whether sentence of death shall be imposed shall be in the discretion of the Court, except that when the proceeding is conducted before the Court sitting with a jury, the Court shall not impose sentence of death unless it submits to the jury the issue whether the defendant should be sentenced to death or to imprisonment and the jury returns a verdict that the sentence should be death. If the jury is unable to reach a unanimous verdict, the Court shall dismiss the jury and impose sentence for a felony of the first degree.

The Court, in exercising its discretion as to sentence, and the jury, in determining upon its verdict, shall take into account the aggravating and mitigating circumstances enumerated in Subsections (3) and (4) and any other facts that it deems relevant, but it shall not impose or recommend sentence of death unless it finds one of the aggravating circumstances enumerated in Subsection (3) and further finds that there are no mitigating circumstances sufficiently substantial to call for leniency. When the issue is submitted to the jury, the Court shall so instruct and also shall inform the jury of the nature of the sentence of imprisonment that may be imposed, including its implication with respect to possible release upon parole, if the jury verdict is against sentence of death.

Alternative formulation of Subsection (2):

(2) *Determination by Court.* Unless the Court imposes sentence under Subsection (1) of this Section, it shall conduct a separate proceeding to determine whether the defendant should be sentenced for a felony of the first degree or sentenced to death. In the proceeding, the Court, in accordance with Section 7.07, shall consider the report of the pre-sentence investigation and, if a psychiatric examination has been ordered, the report of such examination. In addition, evidence may be presented as to any matter that the Court deems relevant to sentence, including but not limited to the nature and circumstances of the crime, the defendant's character, background, history, mental and physical condition and any of the aggravating or mitigating circumstances enumerated in Subsections (3) and (4) of this Section. Any such evidence, not legally privileged which the Court deems to have probative force, may be received, regardless of its admissibility under the exclusionary rules of evidence, provided that the defendant's counsel is accorded a fair opportunity to rebut such evidence. The prosecuting attorney and the defendant or his counsel shall be permitted to present argument for or against sentence of death.

The determination whether sentence of death shall be imposed shall be in the discretion of the Court. In exercising such discretion, the Court shall take into account the aggravating and mitigating circumstances enumerated in Subsections (3) and (4) and any other facts that it deems relevant but shall not impose sentence of death unless it finds one of the aggravating circumstances enumerated in Subsection (3) and further finds that there are no mitigating circumstances sufficiently substantial to call for leniency.

(3) *Aggravating Circumstances.*

(a) The murder was committed by a convict under sentence of imprisonment.

(b) The defendant was previously convicted of another murder or of a felony involving the use or threat of violence to the person.

(c) At the time the murder was committed the defendant also committed another murder.

(d) The defendant knowingly created a great risk of death to many persons.

(e) The murder was committed while the defendant was engaged or was an accomplice in the commission of, or an attempt to commit, or flight after committing or attempting to commit robbery, rape or deviate sexual intercourse by force or threat of force, arson, burglary or kidnapping.

(f) The murder was committed for the purpose of avoiding or preventing a lawful arrest or effecting an escape from lawful custody.

(g) The murder was committed for pecuniary gain.

(h) The murder was especially heinous, atrocious or cruel, manifesting exceptional depravity.

(4) *Mitigating Circumstances.*

(a) The defendant has no significant history of prior criminal activity.

(b) The murder was committed while the defendant was under the influence of extreme mental or emotional disturbance.

(c) The victim was a participant in the defendant's homicidal conduct or consented to the homicidal act.

(d) The murder was committed under circumstances which the defendant believed to provide a moral justification or extenuation for his conduct.

(e) The defendant was an accomplice in a murder committed by another person and his participation in the homicidal act was relatively minor.

(f) The defendant acted under duress or under the domination of another person.

(g) At the time of the murder, the capacity of the defendant to appreciate the criminality [wrongfulness] of his conduct or to conform his conduct to the requirements of law was impaired as a result of a mental disease or defect or intoxication.

(h) The youth of the defendant at the time of the crime.]

ARTICLE 211. ASSAULT; RECKLESS ENDANGERING; THREATS

§ 211.0. Definitions.

In this Article, the definition given in Section 210.0 apply unless a different meaning plainly is required.

§ 211.1. Assault.

(1) *Simple Assault.* A person is guilty of assault if he:

(a) attempts to cause or purposely, knowingly, or recklessly causes bodily injury to another; or

(b) negligently causes bodily injury to another with a deadly weapon; or

(c) attempts by physical menace to put another in fear of imminent serious bodily injury.

Simple assault is a misdemeanor unless committed in a fight or scuffle entered into by mutual consent, in which case it is a petty misdemeanor.*

(2) *Aggravated Assault.* A person is guilty of aggravated assault if he:

(a) attempts to cause serious bodily injury to another, or causes such injury purposely, knowingly or recklessly under circumstances manifesting extreme indifference to the value of human life; or

(b) attempts to cause or purposely or knowingly causes bodily injury to another with a deadly weapon.

Aggravated assault under paragraph (a) is a felony of the second degree; aggravated assault under paragraph (b) is a felony of the third degree.

§ 211.2. Recklessly Endangering Another Person.

A person commits a misdemeanor if he recklessly engages in conduct which places or may place another person in danger of death or serious bodily injury. Recklessness and danger shall be presumed where a person knowingly points a firearm at or in the direction of another, whether or not the actor believed the firearm to be loaded.

§ 211.3. Terroristic Threats.

A person is guilty of a felony of the third degree if he threatens to commit any crime of violence with purpose to terrorize another or to cause evacuation of a building, place of assembly, or facility of public transportation, or otherwise to cause serious public inconvenience, or in reckless disregard of the risk of causing such terror or inconvenience.

ARTICLE 212. KIDNAPPING AND RELATED OFFENSES; COERCION

§ 212.0. Definitions.

In this Article, the definitions given in Section 210.0 apply unless a different meaning plainly is required.

§ 212.1. Kidnapping.

A person is guilty of kidnapping if he unlawfully removes another from his place of residence or business, or a substantial distance from the vicinity where he is found, or if he unlawfully confines another for a substantial period in a place of isolation, with any of the following purposes:

(a) to hold for ransom or reward, or as a shield or hostage; or

---

* This provision does not negative the possibility that consent may be a complete defense under certain circumstances.

(b) to facilitate commission of any felony or flight thereafter; or

(c) to inflict bodily injury on or to terrorize the victim or another; or

(d) to interfere with the performance of any governmental or political function.

Kidnapping is a felony of the first degree unless the actor voluntarily releases the victim alive and in a safe place prior to trial, in which case it is a felony of the second degree. A removal or confinement is unlawful within the meaning of this Section if it is accomplished by force, threat or deception, or, in the case of a person who is under the age of 14 or incompetent, if it is accomplished without the consent of a parent, guardian or other person responsible for general supervision of his welfare.

§ 212.2. Felonious Restraint.

A person commits a felony of the third degree if he knowingly:

(a) restrains another unlawfully in circumstances exposing him to risk of serious bodily injury; or

(b) holds another in a condition of involuntary servitude.

§ 212.3. False Imprisonment.

A person commits a misdemeanor if he knowingly restrains another unlawfully so as to interfere substantially with his liberty.

§ 212.4. Interference with Custody.

(1) *Custody of Children.* A person commits an offense if he knowingly or recklessly takes or entices any child under the age of 18 from the custody of its parent, guardian or other lawful custodian, when he has no privilege to do so. It is an affirmative defense that:

(a) the actor believed that his action was necessary to preserve the child from danger to its welfare; or

(b) the child, being at the time not less than 14 years old, was taken away at its own instigation without enticement and without purpose to commit a criminal offense with or against the child.

Proof that the child was below the critical age gives rise to a presumption that the actor knew the child's age or acted in reckless disregard thereof. The offense is a misdemeanor unless the actor, not being a parent or person in equivalent relation to the child, acted with knowledge that his conduct would cause serious alarm for the child's safety, or in reckless disregard of a likelihood of causing such alarm, in which case the offense is a felony of the third degree.

(2) *Custody of Committed Persons.* A person is guilty of a misdemeanor if he knowingly or recklessly takes or entices any committed person away from lawful custody when he is not privileged to do so. "Committed person" means, in addition to anyone committed under judicial warrant, any orphan, neglected or delinquent child, mentally defective or insane person, or other dependent or incompetent person entrusted to another's custody by or through a recognized social agency or otherwise by authority of law.

§ 212.5. Criminal Coercion.

(1) *Offense Defined.* A person is guilty of criminal coercion if, with purpose unlawfully to restrict another's freedom of action to his detriment, he threatens to:

(a) commit any criminal offense; or

(b) accuse anyone of a criminal offense; or

(c) expose any secret tending to subject any person to hatred, contempt or ridicule, or to impair his credit or business repute; or

(d) take or withhold action as an official, or cause an official to take or withhold action.

It is an affirmative defense to prosecution based on paragraphs (b), (c) or (d) that the actor believed the accusation or secret to be true or the proposed official action justified and that his purpose was limited to compelling the other to behave in a way reasonably related to the circumstances which were the subject of the accusation, exposure or proposed official action, as by desisting from further misbehavior, making good a wrong done, refraining from taking any action or responsibility for which the actor believes the other disqualified.

(2) *Grading.* Criminal coercion is a misdemeanor unless the threat is to commit a felony or the actor's purpose is felonious, in which cases the offense is a felony of the third degree.

ARTICLE 213. SEXUAL OFFENSES

§ 213.0. Definitions.

In this Article, unless a different meaning plainly is required:

(1) the definitions given in Section 210.0 apply;

(2) "Sexual intercourse" includes intercourse per os or per anum, with some penetration however slight; emission is not required;

(3) "Deviate sexual intercourse" means sexual intercourse per os or per anum between human beings who are not husband and wife, and any form of sexual intercourse with an animal.

§ 213.1. Rape and Related Offenses.

(1) *Rape.* A male who has sexual intercourse with a female not his wife is guilty of rape if:

(a) he compels her to submit by force or by threat of imminent death, serious bodily injury, extreme pain or kidnapping, to be inflicted on anyone; or

(b) he has substantially impaired her power to appraise or control her conduct by administering or employing without her knowledge drugs, intoxicants or other means for the purpose of preventing resistance; or

(c) the female is unconscious; or

(d) the female is less than 10 years old.

Rape is a felony of the second degree unless (i) in the course thereof the actor inflicts serious bodily injury upon anyone, or (ii) the victim was not a voluntary social companion of the actor upon the occasion of the crime and had not previously permitted him sexual liberties, in which cases the offense is a felony of the first degree.

(2) *Gross Sexual Imposition.* A male who has sexual intercourse with a female not his wife commits a felony of the third degree if:

(a) he compels her to submit by any threat that would prevent resistance by a woman of ordinary resolution; or

(b) he knows that she suffers from a mental disease or defect which renders her incapable of appraising the nature of her conduct; or

(c) he knows that she is unaware that a sexual act is being committed upon her or that she submits because she mistakenly supposes that he is her husband.

§ 213.2. Deviate Sexual Intercourse by Force or Imposition.

(1) *By Force or Its Equivalent.* A person who engages in deviate sexual intercourse with another person, or who causes another to engage in deviate sexual intercourse, commits a felony of the second degree if:

(a) he compels the other person to participate by force or by threat of imminent death, serious bodily injury, extreme pain or kidnapping, to be inflicted on anyone; or

(b) he has substantially impaired the other person's power to appraise or control his conduct, by administering or employing without the knowledge of the other person drugs, intoxicants or other means for the purpose of preventing resistance; or

(c) the other person is unconscious; or

(d) the other person is less than 10 years old.

(2) *By Other Imposition.* A person who engages in deviate sexual intercourse with another person, or who causes another to engage in deviate sexual intercourse, commits a felony of the third degree if:

(a) he compels the other person to participate by any threat that would prevent resistance by a person of ordinary resolution; or

(b) he knows that the other person suffers from a mental disease or defect which renders him incapable of appraising the nature of his conduct; or

(c) he knows that the other person submits because he is unaware that a sexual act is being committed upon him.

§ 213.3. Corruption of Minors and Seduction.

(1) *Offense Defined.* A male who has sexual intercourse with a female not his wife, or any person who engages in deviate sexual intercourse or causes another to engage in deviate sexual intercourse, is guilty of an offense if:

(a) the other person is less than [16] years old and the actor is at least [4] years older than the other person; or

(b) the other person is less than 21 years old and the actor is his guardian or otherwise responsible for general supervision of his welfare; or

(c) the other person is in custody of law or detained in a hospital or other institution and the actor has supervisory or disciplinary authority over him; or

(d) the other person is a female who is induced to participate by a promise of marriage which the actor does not mean to perform.

(2) *Grading.* An offense under paragraph (a) of Subsection (1) is a felony of the third degree. Otherwise an offense under this section is a misdemeanor.

§ 213.4. Sexual Assault.

A person who has sexual contact with another not his spouse, or causes such other to have sexual conduct with him, is guilty of sexual assault, a misdemeanor, if:

(1) he knows that the contact is offensive to the other person; or

(2) he knows that the other person suffers from a mental disease or defect which renders him or her incapable of appraising the nature of his or her conduct; or

(3) he knows that the other person is unaware that a sexual act is being committed; or

(4) the other person is less than 10 years old; or

(5) he has substantially impaired the other person's power to appraise or control his or her conduct, by administering or employing without the other's knowledge drugs, intoxicants or other means for the purpose of preventing resistance; or

(6) the other person is less than [16] years old and the actor is at least [four] years older than the other person; or

(7) the other person is less than 21 years old and the actor is his guardian or otherwise responsible for general supervision of his welfare; or

(8) the other person is in custody of law or detained in a hospital or other institution and the actor has supervisory or disciplinary authority over him.

Sexual contact is any touching of the sexual or other intimate parts of the person for the purpose of arousing or gratifying sexual desire.

§ 213.5. Indecent Exposure.

A person commits a misdemeanor if, for the purpose of arousing or gratifying sexual desire of himself or of any person other than his spouse, he exposes his genitals under circumstances in which he knows his conduct is likely to cause affront or alarm.

§ 213.6. Provisions Generally Applicable to Article 213.

(1) *Mistake as to Age.* Whenever in this Article the criminality of conduct depends on a child's being below the age of 10, it is no defense that the actor did not know the child's age, or reasonably believed the child to be older than 10. When criminality depends on the child's being below a critical age other than 10, it is a defense for the actor to prove by a preponderance of the evidence that he reasonably believed the child to be above the critical age.

(2) *Spouse Relationships.* Whenever in this Article the definition of an offense excludes conduct with a spouse, the exclusion shall be deemed to extend to persons living as man and wife, regardless of the legal status of their relationship. The exclusion shall be inoperative as respects spouses living apart under a decree of judicial separation. Where the definition of an offense excludes conduct with a spouse or conduct by a woman, this shall not preclude conviction of a spouse or woman as accomplice in a sexual act which he or she causes another person, not within the exclusion, to perform.

(3) *Sexually Promiscuous Complainants.* It is a defense to prosecution under Section 213.3 and paragraphs (6), (7) and (8) of Section 213.4 for the actor to prove by a preponderance of the evidence that the alleged victim had, prior to the time of the offense charged, engaged promiscuously in sexual relations with others.

(4) *Prompt Complaint.* No prosecution may be instituted or maintained under this Article unless the alleged offense was brought to the notice of public authority within [3] months of its occurrence or, where the alleged victim was less than [16] years old or otherwise incompetent to make complaint, within [3] months after a parent, guardian or other competent person specially interested in the victim learns of the offense.

(5) *Testimony of Complainants.* No person shall be convicted of any felony under this Article upon the uncorroborated testimony of the alleged victim. Corroboration may be circumstantial. In any prosecution before a jury for an offense under this Article, the jury shall be instructed to evaluate the testimony of a victim or complaining witness with special care in view of the emotional involvement of the witness and the difficulty of determining the truth with respect to alleged sexual activities carried out in private.

Offenses Against Property

ARTICLE 220. ARSON, CRIMINAL MISCHIEF, AND OTHER PROPERTY DESTRUCTION

§ 220.1. Arson and Related Offenses.

(1) *Arson.* A person is guilty of arson, a felony of the second degree, if he starts a fire or causes an explosion with the purpose of:

(a) destroying a building or occupied structure of another; or

(b) destroying or damaging any property, whether his own or another's, to collect insurance for such loss. It shall be an affirmative defense to prosecution under this paragraph that the actor's conduct did not recklessly endanger any building or occupied structure of another or place any other person in danger of death or bodily injury.

(2) *Reckless Burning or Exploding.* A person commits a felony of the third degree if he purposely starts a fire or causes an explosion, whether on his own property or another's and thereby recklessly:

(a) places another person in danger of death or bodily injury; or

(b) places a building or occupied structure of another in danger of damage or destruction.

(3) *Failure to Control or Report Dangerous Fire.* A person who knows that a fire is endangering life or a substantial amount of property of another and fails to take reasonable measures to put out or control the fire, when he can do so without substantial risk to himself, or to give a prompt fire alarm, commits a misdemeanor if:

(a) he knows that he is under an official, contractual, or other legal duty to prevent or combat the fire; or

(b) the fire was started, albeit lawfully, by him or with his assent, or on property in his custody or control.

(4) *Definitions.* "Occupied structure" means any structure, vehicle or place adapted for overnight accommodation of persons, or for carrying on business therein, whether or not a person is actually present. Property is that of another, for the purposes of this section, if anyone other than the actor has a possessory or proprietory interest therein. If a building or structure is divided into separately occupied units, any unit not occupied by the actor is an occupied structure of another.

§ 220.2. Causing or Risking Catastrophe.

(1) *Causing Catastrophe.* A person who causes a catastrophe by explosion, fire, flood, avalanche, collapse of building, release of poison gas, radioactive material or other harmful or destructive force or substance, or by any other means of causing potentially widespread injury or damage, commits a felony of the second degree if he does so purposely or knowingly, or a felony of the third degree if he does so recklessly.

(2) *Risking Catastrophe.* A person is guilty of a misdemeanor if he recklessly creates a risk of catastrophe in the employment of fire, explosives or other dangerous means listed in Subsection (1).

(3) *Failure to Prevent Catastrophe.* A person who knowingly or recklessly fails to take reasonable measures to prevent or mitigate a catastrophe commits a misdemeanor if:

(a) he knows that he is under an official, contractual or other legal duty to take such measures; or

(b) he did or assented to the act causing or threatening the catastrophe.

§ 220.3. Criminal Mischief.

(1) *Offense Defined.* A person is guilty of criminal mischief if he:

(a) damages tangible property of another purposely, recklessly, or by negligence in the employment of fire, explosives, or other dangerous means listed in Section 220.2(1); or

(b) purposely or recklessly tampers with tangible property of another so as to endanger person or property; or

(c) purposely or recklessly causes another to suffer pecuniary loss by deception or threat.

(2) *Grading.* Criminal mischief is a felony of the third degree if the actor purposely causes pecuniary loss in excess of $5,000, or a substantial interruption or impairment of public communication, transportation, supply of water, gas or power, or other public service. It is a misdemeanor if the actor purposely causes pecuniary loss in excess of $100, or a petty misdemeanor if he purposely or recklessly causes pecuniary loss in excess of $25. Otherwise criminal mischief is a violation.

ARTICLE 221. BURGLARY AND OTHER CRIMINAL INTRUSION

§ 221.0. Definitions.

In this Article, unless a different meaning plainly is required:

(1) "occupied structure" means any structure, vehicle or place adapted for overnight accommodation of persons, or for carrying on business therein, whether or not a person is actually present.

(2) "night" means the period between thirty minutes past sunset and thirty minutes before sunrise.

§ 221.1. Burglary.

(1) *Burglary Defined.* A person is guilty of burglary if he enters a building or occupied structure, or separately secured or occupied portion thereof, with

purpose to commit a crime therein, unless the premises are at the time open to the public or the actor is licensed or privileged to enter. It is an affirmative defense to prosecution for burglary that the building or structure was abandoned.

(2) *Grading.* Burglary is a felony of the second degree if it is perpetrated in the dwelling of another at night, or if, in the course of committing the offense, the actor:

(a) purposely, knowingly or recklessly inflicts or attempts to inflict bodily injury on anyone; or
(b) is armed with explosives or a deadly weapon.

Otherwise, burglary is a felony of the third degree. An act shall be deemed "in the course of committing" an offense if it occurs in an attempt to commit the offense or in flight after the attempt or commission.

(3) *Multiple Convictions.* A person may not be convicted both for burglary and for the offense which it was his purpose to commit after the burglarious entry or for an attempt to commit that offense, unless the additional offense constitutes a felony of the first or second degree.

§ 221.2. Criminal Trespass.

(1) *Buildings and Occupied Structures.* A person commits an offense if, knowing that he is not licensed or privileged to do so, he enters or surreptitiously remains in any building or occupied structure, or separately secured or occupied portion thereof. An offense under this Subsection is a misdemeanor if it is committed in a dwelling at night. Otherwise it is a petty misdemeanor.

(2) *Defiant Trespasser.* A person commits an offense if, knowing that he is not licensed or privileged to do so, he enters or remains in any place as to which notice against trespass is given by:

(a) actual communication to the actor; or
(b) posting in a manner prescribed by law or reasonably likely to come to the attention of intruders; or
(c) fencing or other enclosure manifestly designed to exclude intruders.

An offense under this Subsection constitutes a petty misdemeanor if the offender defies an order to leave personally communicated to him by the owner of the premises or other authorized person. Otherwise it is a violation.

(3) *Defenses.* It is an affirmative defense to prosecution under this Section that:

(a) a building or occupied structure involved in an offense under Subsection (1) was abandoned; or
(b) the premises were at the time open to members of the public and the actor complied with all lawful conditions imposed on access to or remaining in the premises; or
(c) the actor reasonably believed that the owner of the premises, or other person empowered to license access thereto, would have licensed him to enter or remain.

ARTICLE 222. ROBBERY

§ 222.1. Robbery.

(1) *Robbery Defined.* A person is guilty of robbery if, in the course of committing a theft, he:

    (a) inflicts serious bodily injury upon another; or

    (b) threatens another with or purposely puts him in fear of immediate serious bodily injury; or

    (c) commits or threatens immediately to commit any felony of the first or second degree.

An act shall be deemed "in the course of committing a theft" if it occurs in an attempt to commit theft or in flight after the attempt or commission.

(2) *Grading.* Robbery is a felony of the second degree, except that it is a felony of the first degree if in the course of committing the theft the actor attempts to kill anyone, or purposely inflicts or attempts to inflict serious bodily injury.

ARTICLE 223. THEFT AND RELATED OFFENSES

§ 223.0. Definitions.

In this Article, unless a different meaning plainly is required:

(1) "deprive" means: (a) to withhold property of another permanently or for so extended a period as to appropriate a major portion of its economic value, or with intent to restore only upon payment of reward or other compensation; or (b) to dispose of the property so as to make it unlikely that the owner will recover it.

(2) "financial institution" means a bank, insurance company, credit union, building and loan association, investment trust or other organization held out to the public as a place of deposit of funds or medium of savings or collective investment.

(3) "government" means the United States, any State, county, municipality, or other political unit, or any department, agency or subdivision of any of the foregoing, or any corporation or other association carrying out the functions of government.

(4) "movable property" means property the location of which can be changed, including things growing on, affixed to, or found in land, and documents although the rights represented thereby have no physical location. "Immovable property" is all other property.

(5) "obtain" means: (a) in relation to property, to bring about a transfer or purported transfer of a legal interest in the property, whether to the obtainer or another; or (b) in relation to labor or service, to secure performance thereof.

(6) "property" means anything of value, including real estate, tangible and intangible personal property, contract rights, choses-in-action and other interests in or claims to wealth, admission or transportation tickets, captured or domestic animals, food and drink, electric or other power.

(7) "property of another" includes property in which any person other than the actor has an interest which the actor is not privileged to infringe, regardless of the fact that the actor also has an interest in the property and regardless of the fact that the other person might be precluded from civil recovery because

the property was used in an unlawful transaction or was subject to forfeiture as contraband. Property in possession of the actor shall not be deemed property of another who has only a security interest therein, even if legal title is in the creditor pursuant to a conditional sales contract or other security agreement.

§ 223.1. Consolidation of Theft Offenses; Grading; Provisions Applicable to Theft Generally.

(1) *Consolidation of Theft Offenses.* Conduct denominated theft in this Article constitutes a single offense. An accusation of theft may be supported by evidence that it was committed in any manner that would be theft under this Article, notwithstanding the specification of a different manner in the indictment or information, subject only to the power of the Court to ensure fair trial by granting a continuance or other appropriate relief where the conduct of the defense would be prejudiced by lack of fair notice or by surprise.

(2) *Grading of Theft Offenses.*

(a) Theft constitutes a felony of the third degree if the amount involved exceeds $500, or if the property stolen is a firearm, automobile, airplane, motorcycle, motorboat, or other motor-propelled vehicle, or in the case of theft by receiving stolen property, if the receiver is in the business of buying or selling stolen property.

(b) Theft not within the preceding paragraph constitutes a misdemeanor, except that if the property was not taken from the person or by threat, or in breach of a fiduciary obligation, and the actor proves by a preponderance of the evidence that the amount involved was less than $50, the offense constitutes a petty misdemeanor.

(c) The amount involved in a theft shall be deemed to be the highest value, by any reasonable standard, of the property or services which the actor stole or attempted to steal. Amounts involved in thefts committed pursuant to one scheme or course of conduct, whether from the same person or several persons, may be aggregated in determining the grade of the offense.

(3) *Claim of Right.* It is an affirmative defense to prosecution for theft that the actor:

(a) was unaware that the property or service was that of another; or

(b) acted under an honest claim of right to the property or service involved or that he had a right to acquire or dispose of it as he did; or

(c) took property exposed for sale, intending to purchase and pay for it promptly, or reasonably believing that the owner, if present, would have consented.

(4) *Theft from Spouse.* It is no defense that theft was from the actor's spouse, except that misappropriation of household and personal effects, or other property normally accessible to both spouses, is theft only if it occurs after the parties have ceased living together.

§ 223.2. Theft by Unlawful Taking or Disposition.

(1) *Movable Property.* A person is guilty of theft if he unlawfully takes, or exercises unlawful control over, movable property of another with purpose to deprive him thereof.

(2) *Immovable Property.* A person is guilty of theft if he unlawfully transfers immovable property of another or any interest therein with purpose to benefit himself or another not entitled thereto.

§ 223.3. Theft by Deception.

A person is guilty of theft if he purposely obtains property of another by deception. A person deceives if he purposely:

(1) creates or reinforces a false impression, including false impressions as to law, value, intention or other state of mind; but deception as to a person's intention to perform a promise shall not be inferred from the fact alone that he did not subsequently perform the promise; or

(2) prevents another from acquiring information which would affect his judgment of a transaction; or

(3) fails to correct a false impression which the deceiver previously created or reinforced, or which the deceiver knows to be influencing another to whom he stands in a fiduciary or confidential relationship; or

(4) fails to disclose a known lien, adverse claim or other legal impediment to the enjoyment of property which he transfers or encumbers in consideration for the property obtained, whether such impediment is or is not valid, or is or is not a matter of official record.

The term "deceive" does not, however, include falsity as to matters having no pecuniary significance, or puffing by statements unlikely to deceive ordinary persons in the group addressed.

§ 223.4. Theft by Extortion.

A person is guilty of theft if he purposely obtains property of another by threatening to:

(1) inflict bodily injury on anyone or commit any other criminal offense; or

(2) accuse anyone of a criminal offense; or

(3) expose any secret tending to subject any person to hatred, contempt or ridicule, or to impair his credit or business repute; or

(4) take or withhold action as an official, or cause an official to take or withhold action; or

(5) bring about or continue a strike, boycott or other collective unofficial action, if the property is not demanded or received for the benefit of the group in whose interest the actor purports to act; or

(6) testify or provide information or withhold testimony or information with respect to another's legal claim or defense; or

(7) inflict any other harm which would not benefit the actor.

It is an affirmative defense to prosecution based on paragraphs (2), (3) or (4) that the property obtained by threat of accusation, exposure, lawsuit or other invocation of official action was honestly claimed as restitution or indemnification for harm done in the circumstances to which such accusation, exposure, lawsuit or other official action relates, or as compensation for property or lawful services.

§ 223.5. Theft of Property Lost, Mislaid, or Delivered by Mistake.

A person who comes into control of property of another that he knows to have been lost, mislaid, or delivered under a mistake as to the nature or amount of the property or the identity of the recipient is guilty of theft if, with purpose to deprive the owner thereof, he fails to take reasonable measures to restore the property to a person entitled to have it.

§ 223.6. Receiving Stolen Property.

(1) *Receiving.* A person is guilty of theft if he purposely receives, retains, or disposes of movable property of another knowing that it has been stolen, or believing that it has probably been stolen, unless the property is received, retained, or disposed with purpose to restore it to the owner. "Receiving" means acquiring possession, control or title, or lending on the security of the property.

(2) *Presumption of Knowledge.* The requisite knowledge or belief is presumed in the case of a dealer who:

(a) is found in possession or control of property stolen from two or more persons on separate occasions; or

(b) has received stolen property in another transaction within the year preceding the transaction charged; or

(c) being a dealer in property of the sort received, acquires it for a consideration which he knows is far below its reasonable value.

"Dealer" means a person in the business of buying or selling goods including a pawnbroker.

§ 223.7. Theft of Services.

(1) A person is guilty of theft if he purposely obtains services which he knows are available only for compensation, by deception or threat, or by false token or other means to avoid payment for the service. "Services" includes labor, professional service, transportation, telephone or other public service, accommodation in hotels, restaurants or elsewhere, admission to exhibitions, use of vehicles or other movable property. Where compensation for service is ordinarily paid immediately upon the rendering of such service, as in the case of hotels and restaurants, refusal to pay or absconding without payment or offer to pay gives rise to a presumption that the service was obtained by deception as to intention to pay.

(2) A person commits theft if, having control over the disposition of services of others, to which he is not entitled, he knowingly diverts such services to his own benefit or to the benefit of another not entitled thereto.

§ 223.8. Theft by Failure to Make Required Disposition of Funds Received.

A person who purposely obtains property upon agreement, or subject to a known legal obligation, to make specified payment or other disposition, whether from such property or its proceeds or from his own property to be reserved in equivalent amount, is guilty of theft if he deals with the property obtained as his own and fails to make the required payment or disposition. The foregoing applies notwithstanding that it may be impossible to identify particular property as belonging to the victim at the time of the actor's failure to make the required payment or disposition. An officer or employee of the government or of a financial institution is presumed: (i) to know any legal obligation relevant to his criminal liability under this Section, and (ii) to have dealt with the property as his own if he fails to pay or account upon lawful demand, or if an audit reveals a shortage or falsification of accounts.

§ 223.9. Unauthorized Use of Automobiles and Other Vehicles.

A person commits a misdemeanor if he operates another's automobile, airplane, motorcycle, motorboat, or other motor-propelled vehicle without consent of the owner. It is an affirmative defense to prosecution under this Section that the actor reasonably believed that the owner would have consented to the operation had he known of it.

ARTICLE 224. FORGERY AND FRAUDULENT PRACTICE

§ 224.0. Definitions.

In this Article, the definitions given in Section 223.0 apply unless a different meaning plainly is required.

§ 224.1. Forgery.

(1) *Definition.* A person is guilty of forgery if, with purpose to defraud or injure anyone, or with knowledge that he is facilitating a fraud or injury to be perpetrated by anyone, the actor:

(a) alters any writing of another without his authority; or

(b) makes, completes, executes, authenticates, issues or transfers any writing so that it purports to be the act of another who did not authorize that act, or to have been executed at a time or place or in a numbered sequence other than was in fact the case, or to be a copy of an original when no such original existed; or

(c) utters any writing which he knows to be forged in a manner specified in paragraphs (a) or (b).

"Writing" includes printing or any other method of recording information, money, coins, tokens, stamps, seals, credit cards, badges, trade-marks, and other symbols of value, right, privilege, or identification.

(2) *Grading.* Forgery is a felony of the second degree if the writing is or purports to be part of an issue of money, securities, postage or revenue stamps, or other instruments issued by the government, or part of an issue of stock, bonds or other instruments representing interests in or claims against any property or enterprise. Forgery is a felony of the third degree if the writing is or purports to be a will, deed, contract, release, commercial instrument, or other document evidencing, creating, transferring, altering, terminating, or otherwise affecting legal relations. Otherwise forgery is a misdemeanor.

§ 224.2. Simulating Objects of Antiquity, Rarity, Etc.

A person commits a misdemeanor if, with purpose to defraud anyone or with knowledge that he is facilitating a fraud to be perpetrated by anyone, he makes, alters or utters any object so that it appears to have value because of antiquity, rarity, source, or authorship which it does not possess.

§ 224.3. Fraudulent Destruction, Removal or Concealment of Recordable Instruments.

A person commits a felony of the third degree if, with purpose to deceive or injure anyone, he destroys, removes or conceals any will, deed, mortgage, security instrument or other writing for which the law provides public recording.

§ 224.4. Tampering with Records.

A person commits a misdemeanor if, knowing that he has no privilege to do so, he falsifies, destroys, removes or conceals any writing or record, with purpose to deceive or injure anyone or to conceal any wrongdoing.

§ 224.5. Bad Checks.

A person who issues or passes a check or similar sight order for the payment of money, knowing that it will not be honored by the drawee, commits a misdemeanor. For the purposes of this Section as well as in any prosecution for theft committed by means of a bad check, an issuer is presumed to know that the check or order (other than a post-dated check or order) would not be paid, if:

(1) the issuer had no account with the drawee at the time the check or order was issued; or

(2) payment was refused by the drawee for lack of funds, upon presentation within 30 days after issue, and the issuer failed to make good within 10 days after receiving notice of that refusal.

§ 224.6. Credit Cards.

A person commits an offense if he uses a credit card for the purpose of obtaining property or services with knowledge that:

(1) the card is stolen or forged; or

(2) the card has been revoked or cancelled; or

(3) for any other reason his use of the card is unauthorized by the issuer.

It is an affirmative defense to prosecution under paragraph (3) if the actor proves by a preponderance of the evidence that he had the purpose and ability to meet all obligations to the issuer arising out of his use of the card. "Credit card" means a writing or other evidence of an undertaking to pay for property or services delivered or rendered to or upon the order of a designated person or bearer. An offense under this Section is a felony of the third degree if the value of the property or services secured or sought to be secured by means of the credit card exceeds $500; otherwise it is a misdemeanor.

§ 224.7. Deceptive Business Practices.

A person commits a misdemeanor if in the course of business he:

(1) uses or possesses for use a false weight or measure, or any other device for falsely determining or recording any quality or quantity; or

(2) sells, offers or exposes for sale, or delivers less than the represented quantity of any commodity or service; or

(3) takes or attempts to take more than the represented quantity of any commodity or service when as buyer he furnishes the weight or measure; or

(4) sells, offers or exposes for sale adulterated or mislabeled commodities.

"Adulterated" means varying from the standard of composition or quality prescribed by or pursuant to any statute providing criminal penalties for such variance, or set by established commercial usage. "Mislabeled" means varying from the standard of truth or disclosure in labeling prescribed by or pursuant to any statute providing criminal penalties for such variance, or set by established commercial usage; or

(5) makes a false or misleading statement in any advertisement addressed to the public or to a substantial segment thereof for the purpose of promoting the purchase or sale of property or services; or

(6) makes a false or misleading written statement for the purpose of obtaining property or credit; or

(7) makes a false or misleading written statement for the purpose of promoting the sale of securities, or omits information required by law to be disclosed in written documents relating to securities.

It is an affirmative defense to prosecution under this Section if the defendant proves by a preponderance of the evidence that his conduct was not knowingly or recklessly deceptive.

§ 224.8. Commercial Bribery and Breach of Duty to Act Disinterestedly.

(1) A person commits a misdemeanor if he solicits, accepts or agrees to accept any benefit as consideration for knowingly violating or agreeing to violate a duty of fidelity to which he is subject as:

(a) partner, agent, or employee of another;

(b) trustee, guardian, or other fiduciary;

(c) lawyer, physician, accountant, appraiser, or other professional adviser or informant;

(d) officer, director, manager or other participant in the direction of the affairs of an incorporated or unincorporated association; or

(e) arbitrator or other purportedly disinterested adjudicator or referee.

(2) A person who holds himself out to the public as being engaged in the business of making disinterested selection, appraisal, or criticism of commodities or services commits a misdemeanor if he solicits, accepts or agrees to accept any benefit to influence his selection, appraisal or criticism.

(3) A person commits a misdemeanor if he confers, or offers or agrees to confer, any benefit the acceptance of which would be criminal under this Section.

§ 224.9. Rigging Publicly Exhibited Contest.

(1) A person commits a misdemeanor if, with purpose to prevent a publicly exhibited contest from being conducted in accordance with the rules and usages purporting to govern it, he:

(a) confers or offers or agrees to confer any benefit upon, or threatens any injury to a participant, official or other person associated with the contest or exhibition; or

(b) tampers with any person, animal or thing.

(2) *Soliciting or Accepting Benefit for Rigging.* A person commits a misdemeanor if he knowingly solicits, accepts or agrees to accept any benefit the giving of which would be criminal under Subsection (1).

(3) *Participation in Rigged Contest.* A person commits a misdemeanor if he knowingly engages in, sponsors, produces, judges, or otherwise participates in a

publicly exhibited contest knowing that the contest is not being conducted in compliance with the rules and usages purporting to govern it, by reason of conduct which would be criminal under this Section.

§ 224.10. Defrauding Secured Creditors.

A person commits a misdemeanor if he destroys, removes, conceals, encumbers, transfers or otherwise deals with property subject to a security interest with purpose to hinder enforcement of that interest.

§ 224.11. Fraud in Insolvency.

A person commits a misdemeanor if, knowing that proceedings have been or are about to be instituted for the appointment of a receiver or other person entitled to administer property for the benefit of creditors, or that any other composition or liquidation for the benefit of creditors has been or is about to be made, he:

(1) destroys, removes, conceals, encumbers, transfers, or otherwise deals with any property with purpose to defeat or obstruct the claim of any creditor, or otherwise to obstruct the operation of any law relating to administration of property for the benefit of creditors; or

(2) knowingly falsifies any writing or record relating to the property; or

(3) knowingly misrepresents or refuses to disclose to a receiver or other person entitled to administer property for the benefit of creditors, the existence, amount or location of the property, or any other information which the actor could be legally required to furnish in relation to such administration.

§ 224.12. Receiving Deposits in a Failing Financial Institution.

An officer, manager or other person directing or participating in the direction of a financial institution commits a misdemeanor if he receives or permits the receipt of a deposit, premium payment or other investment in the institution knowing that:

(1) due to financial difficulties the institution is about to suspend operations or go into receivership or reorganization; and

(2) the person making the deposit or other payment is unaware of the precarious situation of the institution.

§ 224.13. Misapplication of Entrusted Property and Property of Government or Financial Institution.

A person commits an offense if he applies or disposes of property that has been entrusted to him as a fiduciary, or property of the government or of a financial institution, in a manner which he knows is unlawful and involves substantial risk of loss or detriment to the owner of the property or to a person for whose benefit the property was entrusted. The offense is a misdemeanor if the amount involved exceeds $50; otherwise it is a petty misdemeanor. "Fiduciary" includes trustee, guardian, executor, administrator, receiver and any person carrying on fiduciary functions on behalf of a corporation or other organization which is a fiduciary.

§ 224.14. Securing Execution of Documents by Deception.

A person commits a misdemeanor if by deception he causes another to execute any instrument affecting, purporting to affect, or likely to affect the pecuniary interest of any person.

Offenses Against the Family
ARTICLE 230. OFFENSES AGAINST THE FAMILY

§ 230.1. Bigamy and Polygamy.

(1) *Bigamy.* A married person is guilty of bigamy, a misdemeanor, if he contracts or purports to contract another marriage, unless at the time of the subsequent marriage:

(a) the actor believes that the prior spouse is dead; or

(b) the actor and the prior spouse have been living apart for five consecutive years throughout which the prior spouse was not known by the actor to be alive; or

(c) a Court has entered a judgment purporting to terminate or annul any prior disqualifying marriage, and the actor does not know that judgment to be invalid; or

(d) the actor reasonably believes that he is legally eligible to remarry.

(2) *Polygamy.* A person is guilty of polygamy, a felony of the third degree, if he marries or cohabits with more than one spouse at a time in purported exercise of the right of plural marriage. The offense is a continuing one until all cohabitation and claim of marriage with more than one spouse terminates. This section does not apply to parties to a polygamous marriage, lawful in the country of which they are residents or nationals, while they are in transit through or temporarily visiting this State.

(3) *Other Party to Bigamous or Polygamous Marriage.* A person is guilty of bigamy or polygamy, as the case may be, if he contracts or purports to contract marriage with another knowing that the other is thereby committing bigamy or polygamy.

§ 230.2. Incest.

A person is guilty of incest, a felony of the third degree, if he knowingly marries or cohabits or has sexual intercourse with an ancestor or descendant, a brother or sister of the whole or half blood [or an uncle, aunt, nephew or niece of the whole blood]. "Cohabit" means to live together under the representation or appearance of being married. The relationships referred to herein include blood relationships without regard to legitimacy, and relationship of parent and child by adoption.

§ 230.3. Abortion.

(1) *Unjustified Abortion.* A person who purposely and unjustifiably terminates the pregnancy of another otherwise than by a live birth commits a felony of the third degree or, where the pregnancy has continued beyond the twenty-sixth week, a felony of the second degree.

(2) *Justifiable Abortion.* A licensed physician is justified in terminating a preg-

nancy if he believes there is substantial risk that continuance of the pregnancy would gravely impair the physical or mental health of the mother or that the child would be born with grave physical or mental defect, or that the pregnancy resulted from rape, incest, or other felonious intercourse. All illicit intercourse with a girl below the age of 16 shall be deemed felonious for purposes of this subsection. Justifiable abortions shall be performed only in a licensed hospital except in case of emergency when hospital facilities are unavailable. [Additional exceptions from the requirement of hospitalization may be incorporated here to take account of situations in sparsely settled areas where hospitals are not generally accessible.]

(3) *Physicians' Certificates; Presumption from Non-Compliance.* No abortion shall be performed unless two physicians, one of whom may be the person performing the abortion, shall have certified in writing the circumstances which they believe to justify the abortion. Such certificate shall be submitted before the abortion to the hospital where it is to be performed and, in the case of abortion following felonious intercourse, to the prosecuting attorney or the police. Failure to comply with any of the requirements of this Subsection gives rise to a presumption that the abortion was unjustified.

(4) *Self-Abortion.* A woman whose pregnancy has continued beyond the twenty-sixth week commits a felony of the third degree if she purposely terminates her own pregnancy otherwise than by a live birth, or if she uses instruments, drugs or violence upon herself for that purpose. Except as justified under Subsection (2), a person who induces or knowingly aids a woman to use instruments, drugs or violence upon herself for the purpose of terminating her pregnancy otherwise than by a live birth commits a felony of the third degree whether or not the pregnancy has continued beyond the twenty-sixth week.

(5) *Pretended Abortion.* A person commits a felony of the third degree if, representing that it is his purpose to perform an abortion, he does an act adapted to cause abortion in a pregnant woman although the woman is in fact not pregnant, or the actor does not believe she is. A person charged with unjustified abortion under Subsection (1) or an attempt to commit that offense may be convicted thereof upon proof of conduct prohibited by this Subsection.

(6) *Distribution of Abortifacients.* A person who sells, offers to sell, possesses with intent to sell, advertises, or displays for sale anything specially designed to terminate a pregnancy, or held out by the actor as useful for that purpose, commits a misdemeanor, unless:

(a) the sale, offer or display is to a physician or druggist or to an intermediary in a chain of distribution to physicians or druggists; or

(b) the sale is made upon prescription or order of a physician; or

(c) the possession is with intent to sell as authorized in paragraphs (a) and (b); or

(d) the advertising is addressed to persons named in paragraph (a) and confined to trade or professional channels not likely to reach the general public.

(7) *Section Inapplicable to Prevention of Pregnancy.* Nothing in this Section shall be deemed applicable to the prescription, administration or distribution of drugs or other substances for avoiding pregnancy, whether by preventing implantation of a fertilized ovum or by any other method that operates before, at or immediately after fertilization.

§ 230.4. Endangering Welfare of Children.

A parent, guardian, or other person supervising the welfare of a child under 18 commits a misdemeanor if he knowingly endangers the child's welfare by violating a duty of care, protection or support.

§ 230.5. Persistent Non-Support.

A person commits a misdemeanor if he persistently fails to provide support which he can provide and which he knows he is legally obliged to provide to a spouse, child or other dependent.

Offenses Against Public Administration
ARTICLE 240. BRIBERY AND CORRUPT INFLUENCE

§ 240.0. Definitions.

In Articles 240-243, unless a different meaning plainly is required:

(1) "benefit" means gain or advantage, or anything regarded by the beneficiary as gain or advantage, including benefit to any other person or entity in whose welfare he is interested, but not an advantage promised generally to a group or class of voters as a consequence of public measures which a candidate engages to support or oppose;

(2) "government" includes any branch, subdivision or agency of the government of the State or any locality within it;

(3) "harm" means loss, disadvantage or injury, or anything so regarded by the person affected, including loss, disadvantage or injury to any other person or entity in whose welfare he is interested;

(4) "official proceeding" means a proceeding heard or which may be heard before any legislative, judicial, administrative or other governmental agency or official authorized to take evidence under oath, including any referee, hearing examiner, commissioner, notary or other person taking testimony or deposition in connection with any such proceeding;

(5) "party official" means a person who holds an elective or appointive post in a political party in the United States by virtue of which he directs or conducts, or participates in directing or conducting party affairs at any level of responsibility;

(6) "pecuniary benefit" is benefit in the form of money, property, commercial interests or anything else the primary significance of which is economic gain;

(7) "public servant" means any officer or employee of government, including legislators and judges, and any person participating as juror, advisor, consultant or otherwise, in performing a governmental function; but the term does not include witnesses;

(8) "administrative proceeding" means any proceeding, other than a judicial proceeding, the outcome of which is required to be based on a record or documentation prescribed by law, or in which law or regulation is particularized in application to individuals.

§ 240.1. Bribery in Official and Political Matters.

A person is guilty of bribery, a felony of the third degree, if he offers, confers or agrees to confer upon another, or solicits, accepts or agrees to accept from another:

(1) any pecuniary benefit as consideration for the recipient's decision, opinion, recommendation, vote or other exercise of discretion as a public servant, party official or voter; or

(2) any benefit as consideration for the recipient's decision, vote, recommendation or other exercise of official discretion in a judicial or administrative proceeding; or

(3) any benefit as consideration for a violation of a known legal duty as public servant or party official.

It is no defense to prosecution under this section that a person whom the actor sought to influence was not qualified to act in the desired way whether because he had not yet assumed office, or lacked jurisdiction, or for any other reason.

§ 240.2. Threats and Other Improper Influence in Official and Political Matters.

(1) *Offenses Defined.* A person commits an offense if he:

(a) threatens unlawful harm to any person with purpose to influence his decision, opinion, recommendation, vote or other exercise of discretion as a public servant, party official or voter; or

(b) threatens harm to any public servant with purpose to influence his decision, opinion, recommendation, vote or other exercise of discretion in a judicial or administrative proceeding; or

(c) threatens harm to any public servant or party official with purpose to influence him to violate his known legal duty; or

(d) privately addresses to any public servant who has or will have an official discretion in a judicial or administrative proceeding any representation, entreaty, argument or other communication with purpose to influence the outcome on the basis of considerations other than those authorized by law.

It is no defense to prosecution under this Section that a person whom the actor sought to influence was not qualified to act in the desired way, whether because he had not yet assumed office, or lacked jurisdiction, or for any other reason.

(2) *Grading.* An offense under this Section is a misdemeanor unless the actor threatened to commit a crime or made a threat with purpose to influence a judicial or administrative proceeding, in which cases the offense is a felony of the third degree.

§ 240.3. Compensation for Past Official Action.

A person commits a misdemeanor if he solicits, accepts or agrees to accept any pecuniary benefit as compensation for having, as public servant, given a decision, opinion, recommendation or vote favorable to another, or for having otherwise exercised a discretion in his favor, or for having violated his duty. A person commits a misdemeanor if he offers, confers or agrees to confer compensation acceptance of which is prohibited by this Section.

§ 240.4. Retaliation for Past Official Action.

A person commits a misdemeanor if he harms another by any unlawful act in retaliation for anything lawfully done by the latter in the capacity of public servant.

§ 240.5. Gifts to Public Servants by Persons Subject to Their Jurisdiction.

(1) *Regulatory and Law Enforcement Officials.* No public servant in any department or agency exercising regulatory functions, or conducting inspections or investigations, or carrying on civil or criminal litigation on behalf of the government, or having custody of prisoners, shall solicit, accept or agree to accept any pecuniary benefit from a person known to be subject to such regulation, inspection, investigation or custody, or against whom such litigation is known to be pending or contemplated.

(2) *Officials Concerned with Government Contracts and Pecuniary Transactions.* No public servant having any discretionary function to perform in connection with contracts, purchases, payments, claims or other pecuniary transactions of the government shall solicit, accept or agree to accept any pecuniary benefit from any person known to be interested in or likely to become interested in any such contract, purchase, payment, claim or transaction.

(3) *Judicial and Administrative Officials.* No public servant having judicial or administrative authority and no public servant employed by or in a court or other tribunal having such authority, or participating in the enforcement of its decisions, shall solicit, accept or agree to accept any pecuniary benefit from a person known to be interested in or likely to become interested in any matter before such public servant or a tribunal with which he is associated.

(4) *Legislative Officials.* No legislator or public servant employed by the legislature or by any committee or agency thereof shall solicit, accept or agree to accept any pecuniary benefit from any person known to be interested in a bill, transaction or proceeding, pending or contemplated, before the legislature or any committee or agency thereof.

(5) *Exceptions.* This Section shall not apply to:

(a) fees prescribed by law to be received by a public servant, or any other benefit for which the recipient gives legitimate consideration or to which he is otherwise legally entitled; or

(b) gifts or other benefits conferred on account of kinship or other personal, professional or business relationship independent of the official status of the receiver; or

(c) trivial benefits incidental to personal, professional or business contacts and involving no substantial risk of undermining official impartiality.

(6) *Offering Benefits Prohibited.* No person shall knowingly confer, or offer or agree to confer, any benefit prohibited by the foregoing Subsections.

(7) *Grade of Offense.* An offense under this Section is a misdemeanor.

§ 240.6. Compensating Public Servant for Assisting Private Interests in Relation to Matters Before Him.

(1) *Receiving Compensation.* A public servant commits a misdemeanor if he solicits, accepts or agrees to accept compensation for advice or other assistance in preparing or promoting a bill, contract, claim, or other transaction or proposal as to which he knows that he has or is likely to have an official discretion to exercise.

(2) *Paying Compensation.* A person commits a misdemeanor if he pays or offers or agrees to pay compensation to a public servant with knowledge that acceptance by the public servant is unlawful.

§ 240.7. Selling Political Endorsement; Special Influence.

(1) *Selling Political Endorsement.* A person commits a misdemeanor if he solicits, receives, agrees to receive, or agrees that any political party or other person shall receive, any pecuniary benefit as consideration for approval or disapproval of an appointment or advancement in public service, or for approval or disapproval of any person or transaction for any benefit conferred by an official or agency of government. "Approval" includes recommendation, failure to disapprove, or any other manifestation of favor or acquiescence. "Disapproval" includes failure to approve, or any other manifestation of disfavor or nonacquiescence.

(2) *Other Trading in Special Influence.* A person commits a misdemeanor if he solicits, receives or agrees to receive any pecuniary benefit as consideration for exerting special influence upon a public servant or procuring another to do so. "Special influence" means power to influence through kinship, friendship or other relationship, apart from the merits of the transaction.

(3) *Paying for Endorsement or Special Influence.* A person commits a misdemeanor if he offers, confers or agrees to confer any pecuniary benefit receipt of which is prohibited by this Section.

ARTICLE 241. PERJURY AND OTHER FALSIFICATION IN OFFICIAL MATTERS

§ 241.0. Definitions.

In this Article, unless a different meaning plainly is required:

(1) the definitions given in Section 240.0 apply; and

(2) "statement" means any representation, but includes a representation of opinion, belief or other state of mind only if the the representation clearly relates to state of mind apart from or in addition to any facts which are the subject of the representation.

§ 241.1. Perjury.

(1) *Offense Defined.* A person is guilty of perjury, a felony of the third degree, if in any official proceeding he makes a false statement under oath or equivalent affirmation, or swears or affirms the truth of a statement previously made, when the statement is material and he does not believe it to be true.

(2) *Materiality.* Falsification is material, regardless of the admissibility of the statement under rules of evidence, if it could have affected the course or outcome of the proceeding. It is no defense that the declarant mistakenly believed the falsification to be immaterial. Whether a falsification is material in a given factual situation is a question of law.

(3) *Irregularities No Defense.* It is not a defense to prosecution under this Section that the oath or affirmation was administered or taken in an irregular manner or that the declarant was not competent to make the statement. A document purporting to be made upon oath or affirmation at any time when the actor presents it as being so verified shall be deemed to have been duly sworn or affirmed.

(4) *Retraction.* No person shall be guilty of an offense under this Section if he retracted the falsification in the course of the proceeding in which it was made before it became manifest that the falsification was or would be exposed and before the falsification substantially affected the proceeding.

(5) *Inconsistent Statements.* Where the defendant made inconsistent statements under oath or equivalent affirmation, both having been made within the period of the statute of limitations, the prosecution may proceed by setting forth the inconsistent statements in a single count alleging in the alternative that one or the other was false and not believed by the defendant. In such case it shall not be necessary for the prosecution to prove which statement was false but only that one or the other was false and not believed by the defendant to be true.

(6) *Corroboration.* No person shall be convicted of an offense under this Section where proof of falsity rests solely upon contradiction by testimony of a single person other than the defendant.

§ 241.2 False Swearing.

(1) *False Swearing in Official Matters.* A person who makes a false statement under oath or equivalent affirmation, or swears or affirms the truth of such a statement previously made, when he does not believe the statement to be true, is guilty of a misdemeanor if:

(a) the falsification occurs in an official proceeding; or

(b) the falsification is intended to mislead a public servant in performing his official function.

(2) *Other False Swearing.* A person who makes a false statement under oath or equivalent affirmation, or swears or affirms the truth of such a statement previously made, when he does not believe the statement to be true, is guilty of a petty misdemeanor, if the statement is one which is required by law to be sworn or affirmed before a notary or other person authorized to administer oaths.

(3) *Perjury Provisions Applicable.* Subsections (3) to (6) of Section 241.1 apply to the present Section.

§ 241.3. Unsworn Falsification to Authorities.

(1) *In General.* A person commits a misdemeanor if, with purpose to mislead a public servant in performing his official function, he:

(a) makes any written false statement which he does not believe to be true; or

(b) purposely creates a false impression in a written application for any pecuniary or other benefit, by omitting information necessary to prevent statements therein from being misleading; or

(c) submits or invites reliance on any writing which he knows to be forged, altered or otherwise lacking in authenticity; or

(d) submits or invites reliance on any sample, specimen, map, boundary-mark, or other object which he knows to be false.

(2) *Statements "Under Penalty."* A person commits a petty misdemeanor if he makes a written false statement which he does not believe to be true, on or pursuant to a form bearing notice, authorized by law, to the effect that false statements made therein are punishable.

(3) *Perjury Provisions Applicable.* Subsections (3) to (6) of Section 241.1 apply to the present section.

§ 241.4. False Alarms to Agencies of Public Safety.

A person who knowingly causes a false alarm of fire or other emergency to be transmitted to or within any organization, official or volunteer, for dealing with emergencies involving danger to life or property commits a misdemeanor.

§ 241.5. False Reports to Law Enforcement Authorities.

(1) *Falsely Incriminating Another.* A person who knowingly gives false information to any law enforcement officer with purpose to implicate another commits a misdemeanor.

(2) *Fictitious Reports.* A person commits a petty misdemeanor if he:

(a) reports to law enforcement authorities an offense or other incident within their concern knowing that it did not occur; or

(b) pretends to furnish such authorities with information relating to an offense or incident when he knows he has no information relating to such offense or incident.

§ 241.6. Tampering with Witnesses and Informants; Retaliation Against Them.

(1) *Tampering.* A person commits an offense if, believing that an official proceeding or investigation is pending or about to be instituted, he attempts to induce or otherwise cause a witness or informant to:

(a) testify or inform falsely; or

(b) withhold any testimony, information, document or thing; or

(c) elude legal process summoning him to testify or supply evidence; or

(d) absent himself from any proceeding or investigation to which he has been legally summoned.

The offense is a felony of the third degree if the actor employs force, deception, threat or offer of pecuniary benefit. Otherwise it is a misdemeanor.

(2) *Retaliation Against Witness or Informant.* A person commits a misdemeanor if he harms another by any unlawful act in retaliation for anything lawfully done in the capacity of witness or informant.

(3) *Witness or Informant Taking Bribe.* A person commits a felony of the third degree if he solicits, accepts or agrees to accept any benefit in consideration of his doing any of the things specified in clauses (a) to (d) of Subsection (1).

§ 241.7. Tampering with or Fabricating Physical Evidence.

A person commits a misdemeanor if, believing that an official proceeding or investigation is pending or about to be instituted, he:

(1) alters, destroys, conceals or removes any record, document or thing with purpose to impair its verity or availability in such proceeding or investigation; or

(2) makes, presents or uses any record, document or thing knowing it to be false and with purpose to mislead a public servant who is or may be engaged in such proceeding or investigation.

§ 241.8. Tampering with Public Records or Information.

(1) *Offense Defined.* A person commits an offense if he:

(a) knowingly makes a false entry in, or false alteration of, any record, document or thing belonging to, or received or kept by, the government for information or record, or required by law to be kept by others for information of the government; or

(b) makes, presents or uses any record, document or thing knowing it to be false, and with purpose that it be taken as a genuine part of information or records referred to in paragraph (a); or

(c) purposely and unlawfully destroys, conceals, removes or otherwise impairs the verity or availability of any such record, document or thing.

(2) *Grading.* An offense under this Section is a misdemeanor unless the actor's purpose is to defraud or injure anyone, in which case the offense is a felony of the third degree.

§ 241.9. Impersonating a Public Servant.

A person commits a misdemeanor if he falsely pretends to hold a position in the public service with purpose to induce another to submit to such pretended official authority or otherwise to act in reliance upon that pretense to his prejudice.

ARTICLE 242. OBSTRUCTING GOVERNMENTAL OPERATIONS; ESCAPES

§ 242.0. Definitions.

In this Article, unless another meaning plainly is required, the definitions given in Section 240.0 apply.

§ 242.1. Obstructing Administration of Law or Other Governmental Function.

A person commits a misdemeanor if he purposely obstructs, impairs or perverts the administration of law or other governmental function by force, violence, physical interference or obstacle, breach of official duty, or any other unlawful act, except that this Section does not apply to flight by a person charged with crime, refusal to submit to arrest, failure to perform a legal duty other than an official duty, or any other means of avoiding compliance with law without affirmative interference with governmental functions.

§ 242.2. Resisting Arrest or Other Law Enforcement.

A person commits a misdemeanor if, for the purpose of preventing a public servant from effecting a lawful arrest or discharging any other duty, the person creates a substantial risk of bodily injury to the public servant or anyone else, or employs means justifying or requiring substantial force to overcome the resistance.

§ 242.3. Hindering Apprehension or Prosecution.

A person commits an offense if, with purpose to hinder the apprehension, prosecution, conviction or punishment of another for crime, he:

(1) harbors or conceals the other; or

(2) provides or aids in providing a weapon, transportation, disguise or other means of avoiding apprehension or effecting escape; or

(3) conceals or destroys evidence of the crime, or tampers with a witness, informant, document or other source of information, regardless of its admissibility in evidence; or

(4) warns the other of impending discovery or apprehension, except that this paragraph does not apply to a warning given in connection with an effort to bring another into compliance with law; or

(5) volunteers false information to a law enforcement officer.

The offense is a felony of the third degree if the conduct which the actor knows has been charged or is liable to be charged against the person aided would constitute a felony of the first or second degree. Otherwise it is a misdemeanor.

§ 242.4. Aiding Consummation of Crime.

A person commits an offense if he purposely aids another to accomplish an unlawful object of a crime, as by safeguarding the proceeds thereof or converting the proceeds into negotiable funds. The offense is a felony of the third degree if the principal offense was a felony of the first or second degree. Otherwise it is a misdemeanor.

§ 242.5. Compounding.

A person commits a misdemeanor if he accepts or agrees to accept any pecuniary benefit in consideration of refraining from reporting to law enforcement authorities the commission or suspected commission of any offense or information relating to an offense. It is an affirmative defense to prosecution under this Section that the pecuniary benefit did not exceed an amount which the actor believed to be due as restitution or indemnification for harm caused by the offense.

§ 242.6. Escape.

(1) *Escape.* A person commits an offense if he unlawfully removes himself from official detention or fails to return to official detention following temporary leave granted for a specific purpose or limited period. "Official detention" means arrest, detention in any facility for custody of persons under charge or conviction of crime or alleged or found to be delinquent, detention for extradition or deportation, or any other detention for law enforcement purposes; but "official detention" does not include supervision of probation or parole, or constraint incidental to release on bail.

(2) *Permitting or Facilitating Escape.* A public servant concerned in detention commits an offense if he knowingly or recklessly permits an escape. Any person who knowingly causes or facilitates an escape commits an offense.

(3) *Effect of Legal Irregularity in Detention.* Irregularity in bringing about or maintaining detention, or lack of jurisdiction of the committing or detaining authority, shall not be a defense to prosecution under this Section if the escape is from a prison or other custodial facility or from detention pursuant to commit-

ment by official proceedings. In the case of other detentions, irregularity or lack of jurisdiction shall be a defense only if:

(a) the escape involved no substantial risk of harm to the person or property of anyone other than the detainee; or

(b) the detaining authority did not act in good faith under color of law.

(4) *Grading of Offenses.* An offense under this Section is a felony of the third degree where:

(a) the actor was under arrest for or detained on a charge of felony or following conviction of crime; or

(b) the actor employs force, threat, deadly weapon or other dangerous instrumentality to effect the escape; or

(c) a public servant concerned in detention of persons convicted of crime purposely facilitates or permits an escape from a detention facility.

Otherwise an offense under this section is a misdemeanor.

§ 242.7. Implements for Escape; Other Contraband.

(1) *Escape Implements.* A person commits a misdemeanor if he unlawfully introduces within a detention facility, or unlawfully provides an inmate with, any weapon, tool or other thing which may be useful for escape. An inmate commits a misdemeanor if he unlawfully procures, makes, or otherwise provides himself with, or has in his possession, any such implement of escape. "Unlawfully" means surreptitiously or contrary to law, regulation or order of the detaining authority.

(2) *Other Contraband.* A person commits a petty misdemeanor if he provides an inmate with anything which the actor knows it is unlawful for the inmate to possess.

§ 242.8. Bail Jumping; Default in Required Appearance.

A person set at liberty by court order, with or without bail, upon condition that he will subsequently appear at a specified time and place, commits a misdemeanor if, without lawful excuse, he fails to appear at that time and place. The offense constitutes a felony of the third degree where the required appearance was to answer to a charge of felony, or for disposition of any such charge, and the actor took flight or went into hiding to avoid apprehension, trial or punishment. This Section does not apply to obligations to appear incident to release under suspended sentence or on probation or parole.

ARTICLE 243. ABUSE OF OFFICE

§ 243.0. Definitions.

In this Article, unless a different meaning plainly is required, the definitions given in Section 240.0 apply.

§ 243.1. Official Oppression.

A person acting or purporting to act in an official capacity or taking advantage of such actual or purported capacity commits a misdemeanor if, knowing that his conduct is illegal, he:

(1) subjects another to arrest, detention, search, seizure, mistreatment, dispossession, assessment, lien or other infringement of personal or property rights; or

(2) denies or impedes another in the exercise or enjoyment of any right, privilege, power or immunity.

§ 243.2. Speculating or Wagering on Official Action or Information.

A public servant commits a misdemeanor if, in contemplation of official action by himself or by a governmental unit with which he is associated, or in reliance on information to which he has access in his official capacity and which has not been made public, he:

(1) acquires a pecuniary interest in any property, transaction or enterprise which may be affected by such information or official action; or
(2) speculates or wagers on the basis of such information or official action; or
(3) aids another to do any of the foregoing.

Offenses Against Public Order and Decency

ARTICLE 250. RIOT, DISORDERLY CONDUCT, AND RELATED OFFENSES

§ 250.1. Riot; Failure to Disperse.

(1) *Riot.* A person is guilty of riot, a felony of the third degree, if he participates with [two] or more others in a course of disorderly conduct:

(a) with purpose to commit or facilitate the commission of a felony or misdemeanor;
(b) with purpose to prevent or coerce official action; or
(c) when the actor or any other participant to the knowledge of the actor uses or plans to use a firearm or other deadly weapon.

(2) *Failure of Disorderly Persons to Disperse Upon Official Order.* Where [three] or more persons are participating in a course of disorderly conduct likely to cause substantial harm or serious inconvenience, annoyance or alarm, a peace officer or other public servant engaged in executing or enforcing the law may order the participants and others in the immediate vicinity to disperse. A person who refuses or knowingly fails to obey such an order commits a misdemeanor.

§ 250.2. Disorderly Conduct.

(1) *Offense Defined.* A person is guilty of disorderly conduct if, with purpose to cause public inconvenience, annoyance or alarm, or recklessly creating a risk thereof, he:

(a) engages in fighting or threatening, or in violent or tumultuous behavior; or
(b) makes unreasonable noise or offensively coarse utterance, gesture or display, or addresses abusive language to any person present; or
(c) creates a hazardous or physically offensive condition by any act which serves no legitimate purpose of the actor.

"Public" means affecting or likely to affect persons in a place to which the public or a substantial group has access; among the places included are highways, transport facilities, schools, prisons, apartment houses, places of business or amusement, or any neighborhood.

(2) *Grading.* An offense under this section is a petty misdemeanor if the actor's purpose is to cause substantial harm or serious inconvenience, or if he persists in disorderly conduct after reasonable warning or request to desist. Otherwise disorderly conduct is a violation.

§ 250.3. False Public Alarms.

A person is guilty of a misdemeanor if he initiates or circulates a report or warning of an impending bombing or other crime or catastrophe, knowing that the report or warning is false or baseless and that it is likely to cause evacuation of a building, place or assembly, or facility of public transport, or to cause public inconvenience or alarm.

§ 250.4. Harassment.

A person commits a petty misdemeanor if, with purpose to harass another, he:

(1) makes a telephone call without purpose of legitimate communication; or

(2) insults, taunts or challenges another in a manner likely to provoke violent or disorderly response; or

(3) makes repeated communications anonymously or at extremely inconvenient hours, or in offensively coarse language; or

(4) subjects another to an offensive touching; or

(5) engages in any other course of alarming conduct serving no legitimate purpose of the actor.

§ 250.5. Public Drunkenness; Drug Incapacitation.

A person is guilty of an offense if he appears in any public place manifestly under the influence of alcohol, narcotics or other drug, not therapeutically administered, to the degree that he may endanger himself or other persons or property, or annoy persons in his vicinity. An offense under this Section constitutes a petty misdemeanor if the actor has been convicted hereunder twice before within a period of one year. Otherwise the offense constitutes a violation.

§ 250.6. Loitering or Prowling.

A person commits a violation if he loiters or prowls in a place, at a time, or in a manner not usual for law-abiding individuals under circumstances that warrant alarm for the safety of persons or property in the vicinity. Among the circumstances which may be considered in determining whether such alarm is warranted is the fact that the actor takes flight upon appearance of a peace officer, refuses to identify himself, or manifestly endeavors to conceal himself or any object. Unless flight by the actor or other circumstances makes it impracticable, a peace officer shall prior to any arrest for an offense under this section afford the actor an opportunity to dispel any alarm which would otherwise be warranted, by requesting him to identify himself and explain his presence and conduct. No person shall be convicted of an offense under this Section if the peace officer did not comply with the preceding sentence, or if it appears at trial that the explanation given by the actor was true and, if believed by the peace officer at the time, would have dispelled the alarm.

§ 250.7. Obstructing Highways and Other Public Passages.

(1) A person, who, having no legal privilege to do so, purposely or recklessly obstructs any highway or other public passage, whether alone or with others, commits a violation, or, in case he persists after warning by a law officer, a petty misdemeanor. "Obstructs" means renders impassable without unreasonable inconvenience or hazard. No person shall be deemed guilty of recklessly obstructing in violation of this Subsection solely because of a gathering of persons to hear him speak or otherwise communicate, or solely because of being a member of such a gathering.

(2) A person in a gathering commits a violation if he refuses to obey a reasonable official request or order to move:

(a) to prevent obstruction of a highway or other public passage; or

(b) to maintain public safety by dispersing those gathered in dangerous proximity to a fire or other hazard.

An order to move, addressed to a person whose speech or other lawful behavior attracts an obstructing audience, shall not be deemed reasonable if the obstruction can be readily remedied by police control of the size or location of the gathering.

§ 250.8. Disrupting Meetings and Processions.

A person commits a misdemeanor if, with purpose to prevent or disrupt a lawful meeting, procession or gathering, he does any act tending to obstruct or interfere with it physically, or make any utterance, gesture or display designed to outrage the sensibilities of the group.

§ 250.9. Desecration of Venerated Objects.

A person commits a misdemeanor if he purposely desecrates any public monument or structure, or place of worship or burial, or if he purposely desecrates the national flag or any other object of veneration by the public or a substantial segment thereof in any public place. "Desecrate" means defacing, damaging, polluting or otherwise physically mistreating in a way that the actor knows will outrage the sensibilities of persons likely to observe or discover his action.

§ 250.10. Abuse of Corpse.

Except as authorized by law, a person who treats a corpse in a way that he knows would outrage ordinary family sensibilities commits a misdemeanor.

§ 250.11. Cruelty to Animals.

A person commits a misdemeanor if he purposely or recklessly:

(1) subjects any animal to cruel mistreatment; or

(2) subjects any animal in his custody to cruel neglect; or

(3) kills or injures any animal belonging to another without legal privilege or consent of the owner.

Subsections (1) and (2) shall not be deemed applicable to accepted veterinary practices and activities carried on for scientific research.

§ 250.12. Violation of Privacy.

(1) *Unlawful Eavesdropping or Surveillance.* A person commits a misdemeanor if, except as authorized by law, he:

    (a) trespasses on property with purpose to subject anyone to eavesdropping or other surveillance in a private place; or

    (b) installs in any private place, without the consent of the person or persons entitled to privacy there, any device for observing, photographing, recording, amplifying or broadcasting sounds or events in such place, or uses any such unauthorized installation; or

    (c) installs or uses outside a private place any device for hearing, recording, amplifying or broadcasting sounds originating in such place which would not ordinarily be audible or comprehensible outside, without the consent of the person or persons entitled to privacy there.

"Private place" means a place where one may reasonably expect to be safe from casual or hostile intrusion or surveillance, but does not include a place to which the public or a substantial group thereof has access.

(2) *Other Breach of Privacy of Messages.* A person commits a misdemeanor if, except as authorized by law, he:

    (a) intercepts without the consent of the sender or receiver a message by telephone, telegraph, letter or other means of communicating privately; but this paragraph does not extend to (i) overhearing of messages through a regularly installed instrument on a telephone party line or on an extension, or (ii) interception by the telephone company or subscriber incident to enforcement of regulations limiting use of the facilities or incident to other normal operation and use; or

    (b) divulges without the consent of the sender or receiver the existence or contents of any such message if the actor knows that the message was illegally intercepted, or if he learned of the message in the course of employment with an agency engaged in transmitting it.

ARTICLE 251. PUBLIC INDECENCY

§ 251.1. Open Lewdness.

A person commits a petty misdemeanor if he does any lewd act which he knows is likely to be observed by others who would be affronted or alarmed.

§ 251.2. Prostitution and Related Offenses.

(1) *Prostitution.* A person is guilty of prostitution, a petty misdemeanor, if he or she:

    (a) is an inmate of a house of prostitution or otherwise engages in sexual activity as a business; or

    (b) loiters in or within view of any public place for the purpose of being hired to engage in sexual activity.

"Sexual activity" includes homosexual and other deviate sexual relations. A "house of prostitution" is any place where prostitution or promotion of prostitution is regularly carried on by one person under the control, management or supervision of another. An "inmate" is a person who engages in prostitution in or through the agency of a house of prostitution. "Public place" means any place to which the public or any substantial group thereof has access.

(2) *Promoting Prostitution.* A person who knowingly promotes prostitution of another commits a misdemeanor or felony as provided in Subsection (3). The following acts shall, without limitation of the foregoing, constitute promoting prostitution:

(a) owning, controlling, managing, supervising or otherwise keeping, alone or in association with others, a house of prostitution or a prostitution business; or

(b) procuring an inmate for a house of prostitution or a place in a house of prostitution for one who would be an inmate; or

(c) encouraging, inducing, or otherwise purposely causing another to become or remain a prostitute; or

(d) soliciting a person to patronize a prostitute; or

(e) procuring a prostitute for a patron; or

(f) transporting a person into or within this state with purpose to promote that person's engaging in prostitution, or procuring or paying for transportation with that purpose; or

(g) leasing or otherwise permitting a place controlled by the actor, alone or in association with others, to be regularly used for prostitution or the promotion of prostitution, or failure to make reasonable effort to abate such use by ejecting the tenant, notifying law enforcement authorities, or other legally available means; or

(h) soliciting, receiving, or agreeing to receive any benefit for doing or agreeing to do anything forbidden by this Subsection.

(3) *Grading of Offenses Under Subsection (2).* An offense under Subsection (2) constitutes a felony of the third degree if:

(a) the offense falls within paragraph (a), (b) or (c) of Subsection (2); or

(b) the actor compels another to engage in or promote prostitution; or

(c) the actor promotes prostitution of a child under 16, whether or not he is aware of the child's age; or

(d) the actor promotes prostitution of his wife, child, ward or any person for whose care, protection or support he is responsible.

Otherwise the offense is a misdemeanor.

(4) *Presumption from Living off Prostitutes.* A person, other than the prostitute or the prostitute's minor child or other legal dependent incapable of self-support, who is supported in whole or substantial part by the proceeds of prostitution is presumed to be knowingly promoting prostitution in violation of Subsection (2).

(5) *Patronizing Prostitutes.* A person commits a violation if he hires a prostitute to engage in sexual activity with him, or if he enters or remains in a house of prostitution for the purpose of engaging in sexual activity.

(6) *Evidence.* On the issue whether a place is a house of prostitution the following shall be admissible evidence: its general repute; the repute of the persons who reside in or frequent the place; the frequency, timing and duration of visits by non-residents. Testimony of a person against his spouse shall be admissible to prove offenses under this Section.

§ 251.3. Loitering to Solicit Deviate Sexual Relations.

A person is guilty of a petty misdemeanor if he loiters in or near any public place for the purpose of soliciting or being solicited to engage in deviate sexual relations.

§ 251.4. Obscenity.

(1) *Obscene Defined.* Material is obscene if, considered as a whole, its predominant appeal is to prurient interest, that is, a shameful or morbid interest, in nudity, sex or excretion, and if in addition it goes substantially beyond customary limits of candor in describing or representing such matters. Predominant appeal shall be judged with reference to ordinary adults unless it appears from the character of the material or the circumstances of its dissemination to be designed for children or other specially susceptible audience. Undeveloped photographs, molds, printing plates, and the like, shall be deemed obscene notwithstanding that processing or other acts may be required to make the obscenity patent or to disseminate it.

(2) *Offenses.* Subject to the affirmative defense provided in Subsection (3), a person commits a misdemeanor if he knowingly or recklessly:

(a) sells, delivers or provides, or offers or agrees to sell, deliver or provide, any obscene writing, picture, record or other representation or embodiment of the obscene; or

(b) presents or directs an obscene play, dance or performance, or participates in that portion thereof which makes it obscene; or

(c) publishes, exhibits or otherwise makes available any obscene material; or

(d) possesses any obscene material for purposes of sale or other commercial dissemination; or

(e) sells, advertises or otherwise commercially disseminates material, whether or not obscene, by representing or suggesting that it is obscene.

A person who disseminates or possesses obscene material in the course of his business is presumed to do so knowingly or recklessly.

(3) *Justifiable and Non-Commercial Private Dissemination.* It is an affirmative defense to prosecution under this Section that dissemination was restricted to:

(a) institutions or persons having scientific, educational, governmental or other similar justification for possessing obscene material; or

(b) non-commercial dissemination to personal associates of the actor.

(4) *Evidence; Adjudication of Obscenity.* In any prosecution under this Section evidence shall be admissible to show:

(a) the character of the audience for which the material was designed or to which it was directed;

(b) what the predominant appeal of the material would be for ordinary adults or any special audience to which it was directed, and what effect, if any, it would probably have on conduct of such people;

(c) artistic, literary, scientific, educational or other merits of the material;

(d) the degree of public acceptance of the material in the United States;

(e) appeal to prurient interest, or absence thereof, in advertising or other promotion of the material; and

(f) the good repute of the author, creator, publisher or other person from whom the material originated.

Expert testimony and testimony of the author, creator, publisher or other person from whom the material originated, relating to factors entering into the determination of the issue of obscenity, shall be admissible. The Court shall dismiss a prosecution for obscenity if it is satisfied that the material is not obscene.

APPENDIX B

SELECTED PORTIONS OF COMMENTARY TO THEFT AND RELATED OFFENSES
American Law Institute Model Penal Code (1981)

COMMENT TO § 220.1

1. *Antecedent Legislation.* At common law, the felony of arson was defined as the wilful and malicious burning of the dwelling of another or adjacent structures. The principal objective of the offense was protection of the lives of persons who might be within the structure burned. It was not necessary that the building actually be occupied at the time of the fire, so long as it was normally used as a dwelling. Similarly, the "of another" element was not designed so much to refer to ownership of the property by another as to occupancy by another. Thus, the owner who burned his own property when it was occupied by a tenant committed common-law arson. Some actual burning of the building was required, although this element was satisfied by any consumption of the material of which the structure was built. Conduct short of an actual burning was prosecuted as an attempt, which under the common law required conduct very near to completion of the final act and was punished as a misdemeanor.

Prior to the drafting of the Model Penal Code, a vast legislative development of the offense had occurred in the United States. In many jurisdictions, the burning of almost any property was denominated arson of some degree or was punishable with greater severity than if the property were damaged or destroyed by means other than fire. As is noted below, the statutory development was haphazard in nature and led to intolerable irrationalities in the imposition of criminal sanctions.

It was common, for example, for arson offenses to establish serious penalties for the burning of crops, timber, or other designated classes of personal property, however small in value. Before the recent revision in Alabama, the authorized sentence was one to five years for setting fire to a shock of corn or a "pile" of straw, grass, or lumber. Setting fire to a pile of coal or a tank of gasoline worth more than $25, on the other hand, was not punishable as arson at all. In California, burning a pile of coal or a tank of gasoline was third-degree arson and carried a maximum imprisonment up to three years, but burning a pile of "potatoes, or beans, or vegetables, or produce, or fruit of any kind, whether sacked, boxed, crated, or not, or any fence" could result in imprisonment for up to 10 years. A disgruntled employee of a grocer who set fire to several crates of vegetables would have been subject to more than three times the maximum penalty applicable if he had chosen to burn canned goods or wrapping paper. The penalties for burning vegetables were the same as those for burning a church, school, warehouse, or bridge and more serious than the sanctions authorized for burning a ship or for theft of the vegetables.

At least three discernible patterns existed in arson legislation that was in effect when the Model Penal Code was drafted. The first can be illustrated by the law of New York, which classified the offense in relation to the types of property involved but introduced additional criteria designed to discriminate among burnings according to the likelihood of endangering life. Thus, the fact that the burning occurred at night or while a person was in the building aggravated the offense. The fact, whether or not known to the actor, that a person entered or left the building while it was burning might determine whether the actor could receive a maximum sentence of 15, 25, or 40 years. Similar discriminations turned on the exact moment of the burning, since the statute defined nighttime as the period between sunset and sunrise.

A second type of statute discarded reference to the type of property involved and made danger to persons the explicit criterion in grading arson. The Louisiana Criminal Code was an example. It defined aggravated arson as "the intentional damaging by any explosive substance or the setting fire to any structure, water craft or movable, wherein it is foreseeable that human life might be endangered." Simple arson encompassed burnings without attendant danger to life. Similarly, federal law provided a maximum of five years imprisonment for burning certain structures and personal property but raised the maximum to 20 years "if the building be a dwelling or if the life of any person be placed in jeopardy," and the former Connecticut code authorized life imprisonment for endangering "the life of another by wilfully burning any building or vessel." It was also common to use the criterion of danger to others in defining an offense involving the burning of one's own property. The Swiss and other foreign codes graded property offenses according to whether the offender "knowingly endangered life, or bodily integrity," though they added "or the property of another." Legislation that aggravated property offenses where bodily injury or death actually resulted must likewise be regarded as an instance of grading according to danger.

The most influential factor in the pre-Model Code development of the arson offense was the Model Arson Law proposed by the National Board of Fire Underwriters in 1953. The Model Arson Law departed from explicit reference to the life-endangering qualities of the burning by classifying the offense into three degrees according to the type of property burned. The burning of dwellings and adjacent structures, whether the property of another or of the actor, was classified as first degree and was punishable by a maximum of 20 years. The burning of any other type of structure, again no matter by whom owned, was arson of the second degree, punishable by a 10-year maximum. Third-degree arson encompassed the burning of any type of personal property owned by another and exceeding $25 in value. The maximum penalty was three years. In addition, a fourth degree of arson was created to cover attempts to commit any of the types of arson described, carrying a maximum sentence of two years. A fine of up to $1000 was authorized for the attempt offense, though fines were not provided for the principal offenses themselves. Finally, a separate provision, carrying a five-year maximum, covered the burning of any property of any type, no matter by whom owned, for the purpose of defrauding an insurer.

This scheme is subject to obvious criticism on the ground that its system of classifying offenses is arbitrary. For example, the burning of an empty, isolated dwelling could lead to a 20-year sentence, while setting fire to a crowded church, theater, or jail was a lesser offense with a 10-year maximum. The destruction of a dam, factory, or public service facility was regarded as less serious than destruction of a private garage on the grounds of a suburban home. It also makes little sense to treat the burning of miscellaneous personal property, whether out of malice or to defraud insurers, as a special category of crime apart from the risks associated with burning. To destroy a valuable painting or manuscript by burning it in a hearth or furnace cannot be distinguished criminologically from any other method of property destruction. Moreover, the treatment of attempt as the same two-year felony no matter what the nature of the crime attempted seriously undercuts the grading scheme. Such an approach to attempt makes crucial the question of when an actual burning has occurred. The taking of preparatory steps up to the actual moment of igniting a dwelling is treated as a two-year felony, but once ignition and some slight consumption of the structure has occurred, even though the fire is immediately extinguished, the penalty for the offense escalates to 20 years. The Model Arson Law thus placed too much emphasis on whether the physical act of burning had occurred. The distinction is largely irrelevant to the purposes of criminal punishment and certainly cannot justify such a wide disparity in punishment.

2. *Rationale and Grading.* Existing law instructed that grading according to the type of property involved, the probability of danger to a person, or some combination of the two was the proper course to follow in drafting an appropriate arson offense. It also was clear that careful attention to the grading of arson was necessary in order to avoid the absurdities of prior law.

A course intermediate between the New York and the Louisiana approaches was selected in the drafting of the Model Penal Code offense. The crime is graded partly according to the kind of property destroyed or imperiled and partly according to danger to persons. There was a reluctance to rest entirely on danger to persons in view of the fact that almost any illegal or careless burning endangers life to some extent, as fire fighters and onlookers are drawn to the scene. To make any dangerous burning a second-degree felony would be inconsistent, moreover, with the grading policies embodied in the Model Code assault provision, where the second-degree felony classification requires that serious bodily injury actually be inflicted and that the actor either intend such injury or be so reckless with respect thereto as to manifest "extreme indifference to the value of human life." On the other hand, the old New York law with its elaborate references to various types of property burned, time of burning, presence of a human being in the burned structure, etc., was also rejected. Instead, a single class of more serious burnings, viz., of a "building or occupied structure," was selected. Within this broad category, the sentencing agencies can do better than the legislature in proportioning punishment to the actor's demonstrated indifference to human life and other variables in his personality and behavior. The example of statutes that enlarged the concept of arson to include exploding as well as burning was also followed.

As a second-degree felony, arson carries an ordinary maximum sentence of 10 years under the Model Code. It is worth noting, however, that the prosecution of other offenses, such as murder, manslaughter, or aggravated assault will be permitted [28] and that the provisions of the Model Code on consecutive sentences will permit cumulation up to the extended term limit for the most serious offense that is committed. Thus if the arson results in serious bodily injury to one person, an aggravated assault charge can be added if the circumstances of the offense manifest "extreme indifference to the value of human life." Conviction would authorize an increase in the maximum sentence to a term of 20 years. . . .

---

[28] *See* Section 1.07 *supra.* The only offense in Articles 210 and 211 that would seem not to be chargeable in addition to arson is reckless endangering, which is defined in Section 211.2 Section 1.07(1)(d) prohibits conviction of more than one offense if "the offenses differ only in that one is defined to prohibit a designed kind of conduct generally and the other to prohibit a specific instance of such conduct." This would seem to describe the relationship between reckless endangering and arson. The grading of arson as a second-degree felony is in large part justified by the fact that danger to life is threatened by such conduct. The principal ingredient of the reckless-endangerment offense is thus already taken into account in defining the arson offense.

3. *Principal Conduct.* The offense of arson was generally formulated in prior law as "setting fire to" or "burning" another's property, or one's own property if done in order to defraud an insurer. Similarly, Section 220.1(1) is framed in terms of starting a fire or causing an explosion. Thus the actor is guilty of arson even though the fire is extinguished before any significant damage occurs or, in the case of explosions, irrespective of the amount of damage that results. In effect, the attempt to destroy by fire or explosion is punishable as severely as the completed offense of destruction.

The Model Penal Code goes far beyond the common law and the Model Arson Law of the National Board of Fire Underwriters in dealing with preparation and attempt to destroy by fire. At common law, even the most elaborate and danger-ous preparation for arson would not have been punishable at all if it were interrupted short of the final effort to set the fire. The final effort itself would, as a mere attempt, have been punishable only as a misdemeanor. It was therefore a matter of extreme importance whether fire or burning had begun. The Model Arson Law and many prior laws partially corrected this situation by extending the definition of attempt in relation to arson to include the assembling of com-bustible materials near the property to be burned, but they preserved an extraor-dinary disparity of authorized sentence between an attempt as so defined and the "completed" offense signaled by the first tiny flame.

The attempt provisions of the Model Code solve the problem by broad coverage of dangerous preparatory behavior an by penalizing attempts to commit second-degree felonies as severely as the completed offense. Thus, the words "starts a fire or causes an explosion" in Section 220.1(1) effectively serve merely to identify the kind of behavior subject to penalties for arson, not the point at which criminal liability begins or the line between lesser and more serious offenses. Any legislature inclined to adopt substantive provisions pat-terned after Section 220.1(1) should, if it is not at the same time enacting general attempt provisions based on the Model Code approach to that subject, insert the words "or attempts to start" after the word "starts" and "or attempts to cause" after the word "causes" in Subsection (1) and should define "attempt" for these purposes to include preparatory acts evidencing a settled purpose to destroy by fire or explosion.

Finally, it should be noted that most recently drafted codes and proposals have followed the Model Code by including explosion as well as burning within the coverage of arson. Only Hawaii, which defines the offense in terms of damaging property, and Puerto Rico, which includes the use of explosive material as an aggravating factor, do not use "explosion" in the basic arson statute. The penological considerations concerning the use of fire or explosive material are quite similar and argue persuasively for uniform treatment. Both entail the likelihood of extensive property destruction accompanied by danger to life. Also, explosions frequently lead to fires, just as fires sometimes cause explosions.

4. *Purpose to Destroy or Damage.* The requirement of a purpose to destroy under Paragraph (1)(a) or of a purpose to destroy or damage under Paragraph (1)(b) makes it clear that the mere employment of fire with more limited objec-tives does not fall within the second-degree felony defined by Subsection (1). Thus, for example, the use of an acetylene torch to detach metal fixtures from a structure or to gain entry to a building or safe would not be penalized by this subsection, although it might well lead to liability for reckless burning under Subsection (2).

The requirement of purpose also accords with a determination not to select a precise point in time for the escalation of criminal penalties associated with arson-type conduct. Integration of the provisions of Section 5.01 with the provisions of the arson offense will reach a continuum of conduct that has as its objective a settled purpose to destroy a building or occupied structure of another or to destroy or damage to collect insurance.

The same result, it should be noted, would have been reached had the arson offense been defined in terms of actual destruction or damage, as some recent codes and proposals have done, so long as the approach to attempt reflected in Section 5.01 is maintained. For example, the proposed federal criminal code defines the counterpart offense to Paragraph (1)(a) by providing that "a person is guilty of an offense if, by fire or explosion, he ... damages substantially a building or a public structure." In combination with a broadly drafted attempt provision that grades attempts at the same level as the completed offense, the net effect of such an approach is the same as under the Model Code. Conduct that falls short of actual destruction or substantial damage, but that is performed with a purpose to effect that objective would be prosecuted as an attempt, whereas under the Model Code it might be prosecuted as the offense of arson itself if the fire were started or the explosion caused.

5. *Building or Occupied Structure.* Paragraph (1)(a) of Section 220.1 confines the second-degree felony of arson to the starting of a fire or causing of an explosion with the purpose to destroy a "building or occupied structure." The intent of this language, in accordance with the rationale developed in Comment 2 *supra,* is to confine the arson offense to specially cherished property whose burning or endangering by explosion would typically endanger life. The term "occupied structure" is defined in Subsection (4) to mean any structure, vehicle, or place adapted for overnight accommodation of persons, or for carrying on business therein, whether or not a person is actually present. The language is the same as the definition of "occupied structure" in Section 221.0(1) relating to burglary, and the intent is that the words be read in the same manner. Again as in the case with burglary, the word "building" in the definition of the offense is designed to refer to structures that are capable of occupancy. An obviously abandoned shack located in an isolated area should not be the subject of a prosecution for arson, although a prosecution for the lesser criminal mischief offense dealt with in Section 220.3 may well be appropriate.

There is no requirement in Section 220.1(1)(a) that there be proof that persons were actually present in the building or occupied structure in order for an arson prosecution to go forward. The probability that a building or occupied structure is actually being used in ways that make fire or explosion dangerous to life is so high that it might well be pointless to require the prosecution to charge and prove occupancy. It is clear, moreover, that the degree of criminality should not turn on such fortuity. The offense is aimed at the risk to life that is threatened by fire or explosion aimed at normally occupied structures. That risk should not be judged on the basis of the presence or absence of persons on the particular occasion.

A closely related rationale for the same result is that extraordinary rescue efforts are likely to be undertaken in the case of a fire or explosion that endangers a place where people might be present. Those who combat the fire or the effects of the explosion are unlikely to know whether persons are present within the structure. The resulting risk to putative rescuers is sufficiently related to the purpose of the arson offense so as to give significant support to the conclusion that the actual presence of people should not be determinative of the degree of the offense.

The conclusion on which Section 220.1(1)(a) is based, therefore, is that arson should deal with structures where the probability of people being present on any given occasion is substantial. It should be added that most recently enacted criminal codes have evidenced agreement with this conclusion by confining at least the most serious forms of arson to the burning of structures where there is high probability of occupancy. . . .

6. *Property of Another.* The traditional law of arson does not apply to the burning of one's own property or to other lawful burning. This result was accomplished in older legislation by use of the term "of another" in describing the property that can be the subject of arson or by use of the term "malicious" to describe the culpability with which the act must be done. Culpability terms such as "malicious" have been avoided in the Model Penal Code because of the uncertain meaning acquired by such terms, ranging from intent to recklessness or even gross negligence. Paragraph (1)(a) does adopt the conclusion, however, that second-degree felony sanctions should be reserved for a purpose to destroy the property "of another." This result should obtain except where culpability can be said to rest on other factors such as the intent to defraud covered by Paragraph (1)(b).

To burn down a structure owned and occupied by the actor may or may not be reckless in relation to other people's safety or property. Of course, there may be cases where it is the objective of the actor to kill people who are present inside a structure of his own that he sets out to destroy. The offense of arson is not necessary, however, to reach such attempts to kill. In cases where the actor has more benign motives when he sets out to destroy his own property, the risk to other people or property will depend on the isolation of the premises and the degree of care taken. The actor's poor choice of means in such an instance does not mark him with the same degree of culpability as one who burns his own building to defraud an insurer or who sets out to destroy another's building by fire or explosion in order to wreak vengeance. Accordingly, the offender who is merely reckless as to life or property in this situation is classified as a third-degree felon under Subsection (2).

The distinction between destroying one's own property and destroying the property of another makes it necessary to refine the notion of what is one's own. In the law of arson, property has been regarded as that "of another" if someone other than the actor is the lawful occupant, notwithstanding that the actor may have legal title. Accordingly, the term is defined in Subsection (4) to include a structure as to which "anyone other than the actor has a possessory or proprietary interest . . . ." The last sentence of Subsection (4) deals with cases where the property is subdivided into separately occupied units by providing that any unit not occupied by the actor is to be considered an "occupied structure of another." The offense of burglary deals with the same problem, and it may therefore be instructive to read the two offenses together in this regard. . . .

7. *Arson to Defraud Insurers.* Subsection (1)(b) makes it a felony of the second degree to start a fire or cause an explosion with the purpose of "destroying or damaging any property, whether his own or another's, to collect insurance for such loss." Such conduct could be regarded only as part of a scheme to defraud by filing false claims and therefore within the theft-by-deception provisions of Section 223.3 of the Model Code. Theft by deception, however, is graded as, at most, a third-degree felony. Subsection (1)(b) is based on the judgment that insurance fraud in this context merits the more severe sanctions of a second-degree felony in view of the great danger of bodily injury from the extensive fires often planned and executed by professionals. . . .

It should be noted that Subsection (1)(b) is not limited to the destruction of a "building or occupied structure of another" but includes "any property" no matter by whom owned. The property may thus be a stock of merchandise belonging to the actor. The rationale is that the property that will normally be the subject of destructive efforts for purposes of insurance fraud will generally be found in the types of buildings covered by Subsection (1)(a). However, the purpose of the burning or explosion in such cases may not be to destroy the building or occupied structure and hence may not fall within the coverage of Subsection (1)(a). The language of Subsection (1)(b) has thus been broadened with respect to the type of property involved to encompass property destruction that poses the same dangers as the general arson provision but that, strictly speaking, may not have the same objective.

The last sentence of Subsection (1)(b) is designed to restrict the effect of broadening the kinds of property included to the contexts described above. It provides a defense if the burning or explosion neither recklessly endangered any building or occupied structure of another nor recklessly placed any other person in danger of death or bodily injury. This is designed to insure that the heavy penalties of arson are not imposed for behavior that, while objectionable as part of a fraudulent scheme, reflects no element of personal danger. There is no reason to penalize the burning of an insured camera in a furnace more severely than any other form of destruction or concealment incidental to the filing of a fraudulent claim. The sentences authorized for theft by deception in Section 223.3 are adequate to take account of the varieties of such conduct that may occur. On the other hand, where the fraudulent burning of one's own property entails the danger typical of other arson, it is properly graded in the most severely punished category of arson. . . .

8. *Reckless Burning.* Subsection (2) is in effect a reckless-endangering provision designed to deal with danger to life or limb caused by starting a fire or causing an explosion. It differs from the arson offense dealt with in Subsection (1)(a) in that there is no requirement of a purpose to destroy a structure. The actor's purpose in the case of a violation of Subsection (2) might be quite benign. He may intend, for example, to destroy his own property, or he may be engaged in legitimate property destruction in other forms, as by razing a building that has been condemned. The actor is therefore in quite a different category of culpability than one who deliberately sets out to destroy an occupied dwelling of another.

The offense of reckless endangering defined in Section 211.2 of the Model Code is designed to protect the same interests as Subsection (2) of the arson offense but is graded as a misdemeanor. The judgment underlying Subsection (2) is that third-degree felony treatment is appropriate in cases where the method of endangering is particularly dangerous, *i.e.,* starting a fire or causing an explosion. A provision analogous to Subsection (2) will be unnecessary, of course, in those codes that grade the basic reckless-endangering provision more severely.

There are three situations dealt with in prior law that should be considered in connection with Subsection (2). The first is burning one's own property in circumstances where there is high risk that the fire will spread to the property of another. At the time of the drafting of the Model Penal Code, this was usually treated as severely as directly setting fire to the other's property. Section 220.1(2) is based on the judgment, however, that there is a clear difference between the two offenses and that such fires should be treated as a form of reckless endangering graded less severely than the general arson offense.

The second type of offense, which was also generally treated as first-degree arson, relates to the burning of lesser types of property in proximity to the specially valued categories. Here too it seems that the gravamen of the offense is recklessness with respect to the values that the general arson offense is designed to protect. It is appropriate to distinguish between reckless endangering and purposeful destruction in this context as well.

The third kind of offense concerns recklessness with regard to special categories of property that have been highly regarded from time to time, for example, setting fire to a haystack or a pile of trash near a dwelling where no burning of the dwelling itself occurs. This situation, which is analytically indistinguishable from the second category described above, was rarely covered by arson legislation except as third-degree arson dealt with the burning of any property of another valued at more than $25.

The Model Penal Code divides such offenses into three categories: Subsection (2) covers those instances where the actor manifests by burning or explosion a recklessness toward life or limb or toward those kinds of property where people are likely to be present; the reckless-endangering offense, as noted, grades less severely other instances of recklessness towards life or limb; and the criminal-mischief offense, set forth in Section 220.3, covers general property destruction in cases where life or limb is not endangered. A gap that existed in prior law has thus been closed by treating generally in Subsection (2)(a) the placing of another person in danger of death or injury rather than classifying the offenses in accordance with the type of property burned.

Considering that recklessness as to personal safety unaccompanied by actual injury is punishable in Section 211.2 as a misdemeanor, it would be hard to justify extreme severity in Subsection (2) of the arson offense. Even if harm is actually caused, classification of the offense as a second-degree felony would be excessive, for example, in the case of a workman who accidentally sets fire to a shop by taking unjustified risks with heating tools, electrical equipment, or explosives. Third-degree felony treatment for the offense of reckless burning has accordingly been provided. As explained above, the offense is regarded as more serious than simple reckless endangering but less serious than general arson itself. . . .

9. *Negligent Burning.* The question whether negligence, as distinguished from recklessness, should be penalized when fire or explosives are involved arises in view of the fact that a number of recent codes and proposals include types of negligent burning. The question is especially important under the Model Code because the recklessness offense defined in Subsection (2) requires a high degree of culpability, namely a "conscious disregard" of a substantial and unjustifiable risk that involves "a gross deviation from the standard of conduct that a law-abiding person would observe in the actor's situation." The issue has been resolved by defining criminal mischief in Section 220.3(1)(a) to include "negligence in the employment of fire, explosives, or other dangerous means listed in Section 220.2(1)," with minimal penalties when no harm is done.

Implicit in this conclusion is the rejection of any liability for arson based upon negligence, either as to the burning itself or the consequences of the burning. It is unfortunate as a matter of policy that this judgment has not been followed in recent arson enactments, most particularly with respect to negligently endangering another person or the property of another. As is developed elsewhere, negligence is rarely an appropriate basis for criminal liability. This is especially the case when the severe penalties normally authorized for arson are involved.

10. *Special Fire Regulations.* Following the general standards of the Model Code, Section 220.1 is limited to behavior condemned by the prevailing norms of the community. The innumerable special statutes and regulations requiring observance of specified precautions against fire, or relating to the handling of explosives and other dangerous materials, belong outside the penal code in bodies of law such as housing codes, fire codes, and forest codes. Any imprisonment sanctions should be moderate and ordinarily preserved for cases of intentional defiance of public authority or violation accompanied by manifest danger. The role of a penal code is adequately performed by the range of offenses included in Article 220.

11. *Failure to Control or Report Fire.* In general, the Model Penal Code, adhering to traditional Anglo-American law, does not penalize omissions. The need for modifying this position with respect to highly dangerous situations with which the actor is associated, such as fire, is evidenced by occasional legislation penalizing one's failure to control a fire originating on his own premises, whether or not he had a culpable connection with the starting of the fire.

Subsection (3) is patterned after such legislation, requiring affirmative action in two situations: (i) where the actor knows that he is under some legal duty to combat the fire; and (ii) where the fire was started by him, with his assent, or on his property. The offense, graded as a misdemeanor, is appropriately limited to situations where the actor knows of the fire and fails to take one of two affirmative actions, namely, giving a prompt alarm or, if he can do so without substantial risk to himself, taking reasonable measures to extinguish or control the fire. . . .

COMMENT TO § 220.2

1. *Background.* Section 220.2 introduces a new concept in Anglo-American penal law. It is patterned on European legislation dealing with activity creating a "common danger." The major principle on which it is based is that fire, explosion, flood, avalanche, and similar calamities are properly the subject of the criminal law in situations where they are purposely, knowingly, or recklessly created by human agencies. By analogy to the treatment of arson, the reckless creation of the risk of such a disaster is also included, as is the failure to take reasonable measures to prevent such harm in certain cases. . . .

2. *Catastrophe.* The word "catastrophe" is not defined in the Model Code but is designed to refer to mishaps of disastrous extent, affecting directly or indirectly the safety or property of many people. There is case law in other contexts to the effect that the plain and ordinary meaning of the term is "a notable disaster; a more serious calamity than might ordinarily be understood from the term 'casualty.'" This sense of the term can be drawn from the context of Subsection (1), which refers generically to any "means of causing potentially widespread injury or damage" and which specifically illustrates this concept by including catastrophe caused by "explosion, fire, flood, avalanche, collapse of building, release of poison gas, radioactive material or other harmful or destructive force or substance." . . .

3. *Causing Catastrophe.* Second-degree felony penalties are authorized by Subsection (1) for cases where the actor purposely or knowingly causes a catastrophe by one of the specified means or by any other means of causing potentially widespread injury or damage. By analogy to arson, which is punishable as a second-degree felony when fire or explosion is caused with the purpose of destroying a building or occupied structure, this classification seems appropriate for such conduct. In cases of actual death of one or more persons, it is likely that

a murder prosecution could be based on Section 210.2(1)(b) and that penalties at the first-degree felony level would thus be available. Consistent with the grading judgment reflected in Section 5.05(1), one who purposely or knowingly causes a catastrophe that does not result in death is properly treated at the same level as one who has, in effect, attempted murder. The fortuity that a death does not occur puts the actor in the same situation as most offenders who are subject to a charge of attempt based on completed conduct that, for reasons entirely apart from their motivations and desires, does not result in the harm ultimately feared.

Subsection (1) grades the offense as a third-degree felony when the catastrophe is caused recklessly. The offense in this instance is in effect an aggravated form of the misdemeanor of reckless endangerment, as defined in Section 211.2. Where the actor's recklessness is of such proportions as are contemplated by Section 220.2, grading the offense at the felony level seems entirely appropriate. And although the conduct proscribed by Subsection (1) may result primarily in widespread property damage, it is the danger to human life that is threatened or risked by widespread disaster that justifies the high penalties for the offense. . . .

4. *Risking Catastrophe.* Subsection (2) deals with instances in which the catastrophe does not actually take place but where the actor recklessly creates a risk of its occurrence. The offense is graded as a misdemeanor, a classification that is consistent with the grading of Section 211.2 on recklessly endangering the life or safety of others. Indeed, in most cases the risks covered by Subsection (2) could be adequately prosecuted under such a provision. Presumably this is the reason that some recent codification efforts have not included this branch of the offense. There will be rare cases, however, where the risk involved is limited to extensive property damage, and a separate provision is therefore necessary. . . .

5. *Failure to Prevent Catastrophe.* Subsection (3) imposes a duty to prevent or mitigate catastrophes and parallels the similar provision in Section 220.1(3) with respect to arson. The commentary on this aspect of the arson offense explains the rationale for this provision, as well as the reasons for the omission of a proposed Paragraph (c) that would have imposed an affirmative duty on anyone who was in a peculiarly favorable position to act without risk or inconvenience to himself. . . .

COMMENT TO § 220.3

1. *Background.* This offense is derived from the common-law misdemeanor of malicious mischief. The common-law offense, as well as statutory derivatives from it, was limited to damage or destruction of the tangible property of another. Typical legislation at the time the Model Penal Code was drafted consisted of numerous specifically prohibited types of harm to particular property, often supplemented by a catch-all offense dealing with injury or destruction to real or personal property in cases not specifically covered by other provisions. In some states this approach led to case law precluding application of the catch-all provision to any offense that was specifically defined elsewhere. Thus, an unwary prosecutor who filed a charge under the general provision based on conduct that was specifically prohibited elsewhere ran the risk of dismissal for charging the wrong offense.

Section 220.3 consolidates all forms of malicious mischief into a single generic offense. Subsection (1)(a) reaches purposeful or reckless damage to the tangible property of another, as well as negligent damage caused by dangerous instrumentalities listed in Section 220.2(1), such as fire, explosion, or flood. Subsections (1)(b) and (1)(c) represent an expansion of the traditional offense to include, respectively, tampering with another's property in a manner that endangers person or property and causing another to suffer pecuniary loss by deception or threat. Section 220.3 is thus a residual treatment of various forms of damage to property interests that are not encompassed by the laws of theft, arson, forgery, fraud, etc. It differs from the theft, forgery, and fraud provisions in that the focus is not upon the misappropriation of property but rather upon its destruction. It differs from arson in the sense that it is a lesser included offense to the most serious forms of property destruction. . . .

4. *Damaging Property.* There are two additional points about the coverage of Subsection (1)(a) that should be mentioned. The first relates to the term "damages," which, as noted above, is designed to refer to actual physical destruction or harm to the tangible property. Cases where the harm does not occur would have to be prosecuted as an attempt or as a form of tampering under Subsection (1)(b).

The second point relates to culpability. Recklessness is the minimum that ordinarily must be proved, although negligence is substituted in the case of fire, explosion, and other especially dangerous instrumentalities listed in Section 220.2(1). This is not inconsistent with the general position of the Model Code against the imposition of serious criminal sanctions for negligent conduct. Subsection (2) grades negligent conduct as a violation, a classification carrying no authorized term of imprisonment. Of course, in instances of the purposeful or reckless use of fire, etc., the sanctions of Subsection (2) would be available. But in the absence of at least recklessness, the arguments against criminal liability for negligent conduct were thought to prevail.

5. *Tampering with Property.* Subsection (1)(b) extends the traditional malicious-mischief offense to situations where the defendant tampers with the property of another in a way that may not itself cause damage but that creates a risk of danger to person or property. Examples would be the unauthorized moving of a railroad switch, or the unauthorized setting of a control lever in an industrial plant in a way that endangers workmen or the quality of the product. The offense requires that the actor purposely or recklessly tamper with the tangible property of another "so as to endanger person or property." The quoted phrase describes an actual risk of danger that must exist, as to which the defendant must at least be reckless. Actual harm need not occur. . . .

6. *Causing Pecuniary Loss by Deception or Threat.* No general provision corresponding to Subsection (1)(c) was found in prevailing law at the time the Model Code was drafted. The subsection is directed at such possibilities as expensive "practical jokes" — *e.g.,* sending a false telegram notifying the victim that his mother is dying in a distant city so that he spends several hundred dollars on a vain trip, or spitefully misinforming a neighboring farmer that local tests of a particular seed variety have been highly successful, so that he wastes money and a year's work planting that seed. Such conduct is distinguishable from theft, since the actor has made no appropriation to his own use. The employment of deception or threat to cause pecuniary loss is, however, a kind of property destruction that is appropriately treated as a form of criminal mischief. It is virtually indistinguishable from the spiteful destruction of personal property that will constitute most of the prosecutions under Section 220.3.

Reference to the offenses of theft by deception and theft by extortion should be made in order to determine the content of the terms "deception" and "threat." It is worth noting as well that the conduct here is limited by design to those forms of causing pecuniary loss. As noted above, the term "tangible property" is used in Subsections (1)(a) and (1)(b) rather than "property" in the broad usage of that term for purposes of theft. The reason was to exclude legitimate competition, contract breach, and other similar forms of "harm" to property interests from the property-destruction offense. Similar reasoning leads to the limitation of Subsection (1)(c) to cases of causing pecuniary loss by deception or by threat rather than broadening it to include pecuniary loss inflicted by any means. . . .

7. *Interruption of Public Service.* Criminal mischief is made a felony of the third degree if the actor purposely causes a substantial interruption or impairment of public communication, transportation, supply of water, gas or power, or other public service. Legislation in effect when the Model Code was under consideration discriminated on the basis of this circumstance, often by treating with special severity tampering with property belonging to railroads, telegraph companies, and the like, or damaging highways, bridges, or other public facilities.

However, the mere fact that property is owned by an enterprise furnishing a public service is not the proper test of danger to the public or of the degree of the defendant's culpability. Utility property includes office buildings with the usual contents, supplies of various kinds, etc. Ordinarily, only interferences with functional equipment such as power lines or tracks involve the sort of public mischief that warrants special aggravation independent of the amount of damage done. Similarly, aesthetic damage to highways and bridges does not justify special aggravation of the offense. Accordingly, it is the purposeful causing of a substantial interruption or impairment of public service on which Subsection (2) focuses. . . .

COMMENT TO § 221.1

1. *Antecedent Legislation.* The common-law concept of burglary encompassed breaking and entering the dwelling house of another at night with the intent to commit a felony therein. The scope of the offense had been enlarged by judicial interpretation and legislation, however, with the result that, at least under the most comprehensive of the statutes in force at the time the Model Penal Code was drafted, the offense could be committed by entry alone, in the daytime as well as at night, in any building, structure, or vehicle, with the intent to commit any criminal offense. Enlargement of the offense in this manner was accompanied by the adoption of various grading distinctions. Generally, the most serious penalties were reserved for situations involving actual or potential danger to persons, and misdemeanor or lesser felony sanctions were provided for less aggravated conduct.

The initial development of the offense of burglary, as well as much of the later expansion of the offense, probably resulted from an effort to compensate for defects of the traditional law of attempt. The common law of attempt ordinarily did not reach a person who embarked on a course of criminal behavior unless he came very close to his goal. Sometimes it was stated that to be guilty of attempt one had to engage in the final act which would have accomplished his object but for the intervention of circumstances beyond his control. Under that view of the law of attempt, a person apprehended while breaking into a dwelling with intent to commit a felony therein would not have committed an attempt, for he would not have arrived at the scene of his projected theft, rape, or murder. Moreover, even when the actor's conduct reached the stage where an attempt was committed, penalties for attempt were disproportionately low as compared to the penalties for the completed offense.

The development and expansion of the offense of burglary provided a partial solution to these problems. Making entry with criminal intent an independent substantive offense carrying serious sanctions moved back the moment when the law could intervene in a criminal design and authorized penalties more nearly in accord with the seriousness of the actor's conduct. The surface logic of this solution, however, tended to obscure the anomalies introduced by later expansion of the burglary concept to include non-dangerous situations and new target offenses, especially when concomitant adjustments in the penalty structure were not made.

Since every burglary is by hypothesis an attempt to commit some other crime, it is appropriate to consider the sanction for the completed offense that is the objective of the burglary in evaluating the propriety of the sentence that is authorized for the burglary itself. In some cases, it is of course quite proper for the burglary to be graded severely. Thus, entry into a home at night in order to commit a theft is surely a more aggravated offense than an attempted theft standing alone, because of the additional element of personal danger that attends such conduct. On the other hand, a greatly expanded burglary statute authorizes the prosecutor and the courts to treat as burglary behavior that is distinguishable from theft or attempted theft only on purely artificial grounds.

This point can be illustrated by examination of some of the consequences of burglary laws in effect at the time the Model Penal Code was drafted. In California, a boy who broke into an automobile to steal the contents of the glove compartment would have subjected himself to imprisonment for up to 15 years, although a successful theft of the automobile itself together with its contents would have been punishable by a maximum of only 10 years. Entering a henhouse to steal a chicken became a serious offense, while stealing a chicken at the henhouse door was merely petty larceny. A person who went into an open department store and stole something from the counter would be a burglar or a minor misdemeanant depending upon the largely immaterial question of whether he intended to steal when he entered the store. A person who entered a structure by invitation might have been classified as a burglar rather than a thief if he moved from one room to another in order to steal. The language of some statutes appeared to be broad enough to make a burglar out of one who entered his own house or office with the purpose of committing a crime, whether it be to prepare a fraudulent income tax return or to commit an assault upon his wife. The ultimate absurdity was the provision in some statutes making it burglary to commit an offense "in" a building, regardless of the lawfulness of the actor's entry or the intent with which he entered.

An entirely separate difficulty was caused by the fact that burglary generally was regarded as an offense distinct and independent from the other crime which the actor contemplated or carried out. As a result, cumulative penalties could be imposed, for example, for entering with intent to steal and for either attempted stealing or stealing. Thus, even if there was a rationale for using the burglary offense as an aggravating device because of defects in the law of attempt, the aggravation was excessive. Not only was burglary often more serious than its target offense, but there was the opportunity for consecutive sentences as well. This is to be contrasted with the normal rule that forbids conviction for both the attempt and the completed offense.

It is also worth noting that a haphazardly defined burglary offense impedes scientific study of crime and its treatment by making statistical studies based on this categorization virtually meaningless. The possibilities of arbitrary classification of offenses were so numerous under typical burglary legislation in effect when the Model Code was drafted that it was impossible to understand or evaluate even the limited crime statistics that were available.

2. *Rationale.* In view of the difficulties with the burglary offense in prior law, it is right to ask whether there remains a need for a separate burglary provision in a modern penal code. The Model Penal Code remedies the defects of attempt law that may have led to the development of the burglary offense, both by moving the point of criminality back into the area of preparation to commit a crime and by assimilating the penalty for the attempt to the penalty for the completed offense. The case for an independent burglary offense must rest on the gains that are perceived from aggravated grading of offenses that under ordinary circumstances would be punished adequately by other provisions of the Code. It is noteworthy that the civil-law countries know of no such offense, being content to penalize crimes involving intrusion by adding a minor term of imprisonment for criminal trespass to the appropriate sentence for the other crime committed or attempted. This approach could be pursued, or other offenses could be graded more severely in cases where they are accompanied by an intrusion of the sort that burglary offenses normally reach. With the crime of theft, for example, an intrusion into home or office could be made an element of aggravation, or a robbery-burglary section could be drafted to deal with the circumstances of violence or potential violence that should raise theft from a third- to a second-degree felony. Although rape, kidnapping, and infliction of serious bodily harm are already graded as first- or second-degree felonies and attempts to commit these offenses are graded as second-degree felonies, the imposition of extended sentences could be authorized for these offenses in situations where they are accomplished by intrusion.

It may be, therefore, that burglary could be eliminated as a distinct offense and the issues that are raised could be pursued as a grading matter, perhaps with the addition of a relatively minor criminal trespass provision to take account of the less serious cases. Centuries of history and a deeply imbedded Anglo-American conception such as burglary, however, are not easily discarded. The notable severity of burglary penalties is accounted for by the fact that the offense was originally confined to violent nighttime assault on a dwelling. The dwelling was and remains each man's castle, the final refuge from which he need not flee even if the alternative is to take the life of an assailant. It is the place of security for his family, as well as his most cherished possessions. Thus it is perhaps understandable that the offense should have been a capital felony at common law and that public fear of the burglar should continue to some extent even after the offense has been broadened beyond its original objective. These factors may suitably be reflected in a separate burglary provision. The needed reform should take the direction of narrowing the offense to reflect more appropriately the distinctive situation for which it was originally devised. The offense has thus been limited in the Model Code to the invasion of premises under circumstances especially likely to terrorize occupants. Most of the extensions of the offense that have been added by legislation over the years have been discarded.

There is a second point that is worth some emphasis as a part of the decision to retain a separate burglary offense. It is not uncommon for surreptitious entry to occur under circumstances where law enforcement officials are hard pressed to establish precisely what crime the actor contemplated within the premises. A serious penalty may be justified whether it is assault or theft that is the object of the entry, though the facts of the case may make it difficult to establish beyond a reasonable doubt that it was the one rather than the other. An attempt prosecution would require just such specific proof, whereas prosecution under a burglary statute requires only that it be established that the intrusion was made as a conscious step toward the accomplishment of one of a number of possible criminal objectives. Flexibility to the prosecutor in proving a target crime is thus provided by a separate provision defined in terms that approximate the traditional elements of burglary. This flexibility is a significant advantage of the approach reflected in Section 221.1.

3. *Elements of the Offense.* There are four issues to be addressed in determining the scope of a burglary offense that proceeds on this rationale: the nature of the entry, the place of entry, the objective or purpose that accompanies the entry, and a description of factors accompanying the entry that aggravate the degree of the offense. The fourth of these factors will be considered below in relation to the grading criteria established in Subsection (2). The first three are dealt with in Subsection (1) and are elaborated here.

(a) *Unprivileged Entry.* The conduct proscribed by Subsection (1) is entry at a time when the premises are not open to the public and the actor is not licensed or privileged to enter. The language referring to "premises . . . open to the public" makes it clear that entry into premises accessible to the public cannot be prosecuted as burglary even if the proprietor sought to restrict the implied license to enter, for example, by posting a notice at the door of a department store that loiterers and shoplifters are forbidden to enter. The words "licensed or privileged to enter" thus need not take account of cases where there is a general public privilege to enter but rather are designed for those cases where one's employment or ownership interest in the premises warrant his entry or where there are other circumstances where a privilege to enter should be inferred.

This definition takes a middle ground between the common-law requirement of "breaking and entering" and the complete elimination of that requirement in some statutes. Even at common law, the "breaking" had become little more than symbolic, leading to absurd distinctions. "Raising a closed window was a breaking, but raising a partly open one was not; entering through an aperture in a wall or roof was not a constructive breaking, but crawling down a chimney was; breaking open a cupboard within a dwelling was not a breaking for the purposes of burglary, whereas entering a closed room was." Entries accomplished by intimidation, trick, or collusion with a servant were likewise held to be breakings.

Subsection (1) retains the core of the common-law conception. At least this much of the concept of "breaking" should be retained in order to exclude from burglary situations such as the following: a servant enters his employer's house as he normally is privileged to do, intending on the occasion to steal some silver; a shoplifter enters a department store during business hours to steal from the counters; a litigant enters the courthouse with intent to commit perjury; a fireman called on to put out a fire resolves, as he breaks down the door of the burning house, to misappropriate some of the householder's belongings. Such situations involve no surreptitious intrusion, no element of aggravation of the crime that the actor proposes to carry out. Statutes that purport to include any entry with criminal purpose have thus not been followed.

There are a number of states that have followed the Model Code approach with respect to the elements of an unprivileged entry. The most significant departure among the recent revisions is illustrated by the inclusion in New York of language designed to deal with one who remains unlawfully on premises. New York has three degrees of burglary and defines each to include one who "knowingly enters or remains unlawfully" in prescribed premises. The quoted phrase is then defined to include one who is not "licensed or privileged" to enter or remain and to exclude premises that are open to the public.

There are at least two arguments for the inclusion in a burglary statute of language encompassing one who unlawfully remains upon property. The first is that the fact of lawful entry does not necessarily foreclose the kind of intrusion that burglary is designed to reach. This can be illustrated by the case of a customer who hides in a bank until after closing hours and then undertakes his criminal activity or by the case of a guest invited to a home who hides in a closet and engages in criminal activity when the homeowner believes that all his guests have gone. Such cases cannot be reached under the formulation in Subsection (1), since it requires an unprivileged entry. It would be possible to hold that the unlawful intent vitiated the license or consent to enter but the consequence of this would be to reintroduce an essentially fictive concept of entry.

The second reason for covering unlawful remaining relates to an unnecessary complexity that a prosecutor may face when an intruder is discovered upon premises that were open to him lawfully not long before the discovery. If evidence of forcible breaking is not available, an intruder discovered at the safe of a bank an hour after closing time may well be able to argue that he entered before closing time and remained hidden on the premises until the time of his discovery. Yet, as noted above, such an argument is hardly relevant to the proper classification of the actor as one who has or has not invaded the interests which the burglary statute is designed to protect. The explicit inclusion in the language of the burglary provision of one who unlawfully remains obviates any concern that may arise over this point.

There is a difficulty with the New York language, however, that should lead to its rejection. As the Brown Commission pointed out, it literally would include "a visitor to one's home . . . who becomes involved in an argument with his host, threatens to punch him in the nose, and is asked to leave; if he does not leave, but continues his threatening argument, he would . . . be guilty of burglary." For this reason, the Final Report of the Brown Commission included in the burglary offense one who entered or "surreptitiously" remained without license or privilege. The concept of surreptitious remaining has been carried forward in the proposed federal code as enacted by the Senate, and has been adopted in several other recently drafted codes. Most of the recently drafted statutes and proposals that have spoken to the issue have followed the New York provision, although, as noted above, some follow the Model Code and are silent on the point.

(b) *Building or Occupied Structure.* The premises protected by the burglary provision are described as "a building or occupied structure, or separately secured or occupied portion thereof." "Occupied structure" is defined in Section 221.0(1). The second sentence of Section 221.1(1) deals with cases where the building or structure was abandoned by providing in that instance an affirmative defense.

The important notion that ties these provisions together is that of occupancy. Use of this concept results in considerably narrower coverage than was achieved by many of the statutes in effect at the time the Model Code was drafted, which often extended burglary law to any structure or vehicle. Restricting the offense to buildings and other occupied structures confines it to those intrusions that are typically the most alarming and dangerous. Occupancy is also to be distinguished from the actual presence of a person. The essential notion is apparent potential for regular occupancy. Actual presence is not required because the presence or absence of a person in a structure that is normally occupied will often be purely a matter of chance so far as the intruder is concerned. The intruder is ordinarily well able to judge whether the structure is a dwelling, store, factory, warehouse, or other place where people might normally be present. It is enough to require that the structure be one that is normally occupied and that the defendant be reckless as to its character as such. If these requirements are satisfied, the fortuity of a person's actual presence or absence is irrelevant.

Subsection (1) speaks of a "building *or* occupied structure" and thus does not explicitly require that a building be occupied or adopted for occupancy. The phrase was drafted in this way because buildings are generally employed by human beings in ways that amount to occupancy. It therefore seemed unnecessary to require that the prosecutor prove the adaptability of a building for occupancy in the normal case. The final sentence of Subsection (1), however, provides an affirmative defense that would bar prosecution for burglary of abandoned or derelict buildings unsuited (and in fact unused) for human occupancy. In the case of structures other than buildings, *e.g.,* mines or ships, the prosecution would have to allege and prove occupancy as defined in Section 221.0(1) as part of its case in chief. The structure would thus have to be a place that is adapted for overnight accommodation or for the ordinary carrying on of business. This requirement is significant chiefly in relation to vehicles. It serves to exclude from burglary intrusions into freight cars, motor vehicles other than home trailers or mobile offices, ordinary small watercraft, and the like. The fact that a person *could* sleep or conduct business in such a place is not determinative. Such places are nevertheless not the sorts of facilities that ordinarily would put an intruder on notice that they may be in use for such purposes.

The provision in Subsection (1) as to separately secured or occupied portions of buildings and occupied structures takes care of the situation of apartment houses, office buildings, hotels, steamships with a series of private cabins, etc., where occupancy is by unit. It is the individual unit as well as the overall structure that must be safeguarded. Thus, while it would violate this section for a person to make an unprivileged entry into an apartment house for the purpose of stealing money or other valuables from a common safe, it would also violate the burglary provision if an intrusion is made into a single unit, even by an occupant of another unit in the same structure. . . .

(c) *Criminal Purpose.* The purpose that must accompany the intrusion is described as a "purpose to commit a crime therein." The word "crime" is defined in Section 1.04 to include any offense for which a sentence of imprisonment is authorized, thus applying the burglary provision to one who acts with a purpose to commit any offense designated as a felony, a misdemeanor, or a petty misdemeanor. Only violations are excluded. The effect of the provision is thus to enhance the penalties in some cases of what would otherwise be an attempt to commit a misdemeanor or a petty misdemeanor. In addition, some attempts to commit felonies of the third degree are raised to second-degree felonies.

There are three aspects of the offense justifying this expansive specification of the intent that suffices for burglary. The first is the requirement of an intrusive or unprivileged entry; the second is the restriction of burglary to buildings or other occupied structures; the third is the moderation of penalties except in circumstances of special danger. The first two of these factors, as described in the commentary above, are designed to isolate those situations where an intrusion for any criminal purpose creates elements of alarm and danger to persons who may be present in a place where they should be entitled to freedom from intrusion. Their perception of alarm and danger, moreover, will not depend on the particular purpose of the intruder. The fact that he may be contemplating a minor offense will be no solace to those who may reasonably fear the worst and who may react with measures that may well escalate the criminal purposes of the intruder.

The broad purpose provision of this section also reflects the realities of law enforcement more accurately than would a narrower formulation. The burglar is often apprehended, if at all, in the process of entering, when it may be difficult to establish more than the fact that he hopes to accomplish any one of a number of possible criminal objectives. As pointed out above, one of the reasons for retaining a separate burglary provision is the special difficulty that would be posed if the prosecutor were required to prove an attempt to commit a specific offense. Similarly, if the range of attempted offenses that would suffice for a burglary conviction were narrowed to felonies or to particular classes of felonies, the prosecutor would be placed in much the same dilemma.

The formulation would carry forward those cases which hold that the specific criminal purpose need not be pleaded and proved with the same particularity in prosecuting burglary as in prosecuting the crime which the burglar had in mind or an attempt to commit that crime. Some statutes and judicial decisions, on the other hand, go so far as to create a presumption that an unexplained breaking and entering is made with intent to commit a crime. This step however, does not seem desirable. The circumstances of an entry will normally lead the jury to the proper inference as to the purposes of the intruder. If there is reasonable doubt as to his criminal objective, it should be enough to convict him of criminal trespass under Section 221.2. Certainly an intrusion for such innocent purposes as sleep, escape from inclement weather, or to secure an interview should not entail the possibility of felony penalties based on a presumption of criminal intent.

There is, however, one type of crime that should be excluded from the range of offenses that will satisfy the purpose requirement of burglary, namely other trespassory offenses designed solely to protect the interests that are invaded by the unprivileged entry that the burglar necessarily makes. The proposed federal criminal code expresses this idea by describing the purpose requirement as "with intent to engage in conduct constituting a crime other than a crime set forth in this subchapter." The word "therein" in Subsection (1) of the Model Code provision performs the same function by requiring that the intent be to commit an offense after the entry has been effected. The offense of trespass will thus have already been committed and a purpose to violate Section 221.2 will be excluded from the range of illegal purposes that will suffice for a burglary conviction. . . .

4. *Grading and Multiple Convictions.* The grading of burglary presents complex questions that will be dealt with below in some detail. Basically, Section 221.1 adopts third-degree felony penalties for all burglaries as the floor, with the potential of escalating the penalties to the second-degree level if certain aggravating factors dealt with in Subsection (2) are established or if penalties for burglary and its object offense can be cumulated under Subsection (3). Each of these possibilities will be considered below. . . .

(a) *Second-Degree Felony.* Subsection (2) lists three aggravating factors that can result in the imposition of second-degree felony sanctions for the offense of burglary. The maximum sentence in such cases thus is 10 years, a term that may be extended to 20 years in the cases of the most serious offenders.

(i) *Dwelling of Another at Night.* The considerations that are significant in making the occurrence of an offense at "night" a grading criterion are that darkness facilitates commission of the offense, increases the alarm of the victims, and hampers identification of suspects. Similarly, the dwelling is the place where intrusions, particularly at night, create the greatest alarm and invoke the most justifiable claims to privacy.

Darkness does not occur at sunset but at some time during the ensuing hour. It also does not become light precisely at sunrise but at some time during the preceding hour. The selection of an interval of 30 minutes in the definition of "night" in Section 221.0(2), though necessarily arbitrary, seem desirable because it provides a measure of certainty to the law in this respect. It had some measure of support in legislation that was current at the time Section 221.1 was drafted, including safety regulations under the motor vehicle codes and the Federal Avaition Act. . . .

It should be noted finally that the phrase "dwelling of another at night" relates to the "harm or evil . . . sought to be prevented by the law defining the offense" and is thus a "material element" of the offense of burglary as that term is used in Sections 1.13(9), 1.13(10), and 2.02. The consequence is that a culpability level of recklessness is established by Section 2.02(3) for this element and that mistakes by the defendant will be governed by the general provisions of Section 2.04.

(ii) *Bodily Injury.* Subsection (2)(a) provides that second-degree felony penalties are available in cases where "in the course of committing the offense" the actor inflicts or attempts to inflict bodily injury on anyone. The quoted phrase is defined in the last sentence of Subsection (2) to apply to conduct that occurs between the period beginning with an attempt to commit the offense of burglary and ending with the conclusion of immediate flight after the attempt or commission of the offense. The term "bodily injury" is defined in Section 210.0(2), and though the definition is not explicitly made applicable to burglary, it is intended nevertheless to apply. Similarly, the notion of "attempt" contained both in Subsection (2)(a) and in the last sentence of the subsection should be interpreted consistently with the use of the term in Section 5.01.

The infliction or attempt to inflict bodily injury on another person is isolated as an aggravating factor in a number of recently drafted codes and proposals on burglary. It seems justified on the ground that intrusions accompanied by violence or the threat of violence present the most serious instances of the offense of burglary.

(iii) *Armed with Explosives or Deadly Weapon.* Subsection (2)(b) permits second-degree felony sentences in the case where the actor is armed with explosives or with a deadly weapon during "the course of committing the offense," as that term is defined in the last sentence of the subsection. This grading factor is also used in several recently drafted burglary provisions. As with Subsection (2)(a), it is justified because it evidences a willingness to engage in violence. The term "deadly weapon" is defined in Section 210.0(4).

(iv) *Other Aggravating Factors.* Recently drafted codes and proposals have included a number of additional aggravating factors beyond those used in the Model Code. Some states provide a higher penalty for entry into a dwelling house, an inhabited house, or a residential structure, regardless of whether entry is at night. Other states consider the presence of an individual inside the building as an aggravating factor. In a few states, the presence of an accomplice may result in a longer prison term. There are also a few states that have advanced unique criteria. Oregon considers being armed with a burglar's tool an aggravating factor. Puerto Rico provides a higher penalty when force is used to enter. Minnesota's burglary statute provides a higher penalty when the portion of the building entered contains a banking business and when force is used or threatened to obtain entry. South Dakota considers the unlocking of an outer door by false keys or by picking the lock as an aggravating factor.

(b) *Multiple Offenses.* Subsection (3) precludes cumulation of penalties for burglary and its object offense in all circumstances except where the object offense is itself a felony of the first or the second degree. In cases where the object offense is a third-degree felony or is a crime of unspecified degree, the burglary itself is graded at a sufficiently high level so that additional aggravation is unwarranted. Where the object offense is a felony of the first or second degree, the cumulation permitted by Subsection (3) provides a method of authorizing sufficiently long sentences in all cases. Thus, an attempted murder or rape accomplished by commission of a burglary can result in consecutive sentences for two second-degree felonies, within the limits on consecutive sentencing established by Section 7.06 of the Model Code. There are, however, a few codes that have followed the Model Code in this respect.

(c) *Third-Degre Felony.* Subsection (2) establishes all burglary at least at the third-degree felony level. Where the object offense is a misdemeanor or a petty misdemeanor, a prosecution for attempting that offense would result in sanctions no more severe than if the attempt was successful. Such attempts accompanied by an intrusion of the sort contemplated by Subsection (1), however, are properly regarded more seriously than the attempts standing alone because of the nature of the alarm that is created by such intrusions and the fact that the relatively minor criminal objectives of the intruder are unlikely to be known to any persons who may be present in the invaded premises. Thus, in the absence of the aggravating factors discussed above, treatment of all burglary as a third-degree felony carrying a maximum sentence of five years is warranted. Unaggravated burglary is generally treated at this level in most recently drafted codes and proposals, although there are a number of provisions that establish a higher maximum for the least serious form of the offense.

COMMENT TO § 221.2

1. *Background.* There was a wide variation in the statutes defining criminal trespass that were in force at the time this provision was drafted. Generally, one or more of the following factors had to be shown in order to prove the offense: notice against trespass, whether by personal communication or posting of signs; intention of the trespasser to take or destroy anything on the land or to hunt or shoot; entry by force or in the face of previous legal ejectment; the fact that the land was of particular ownership or use, *e.g.,* state land, mining or manufacturing property, railroad property, planted or cultivated land, orchards, or gardens; the fact that the trespass was in a building or structure rather than on open land.

The common thread running through these provisions is the element of unwanted intrusion, usually coupled with some sort of notice to would-be intruders that they may not enter. Most people do not object to strangers tramping through woodland or over pasture or open range. On the other hand, intrusions into buildings, onto property fenced in a manner manifestly designed to exclude intruders, or onto any private property in defiance of actual notice to keep away is generally considered objectionable and under some circumstances frightening.

Section 221.2 accordingly prohibits various forms of intrusion into a place where the actor knows he is not licensed or privileged to be. Broader penal prohibitions found in some legislation at the time the Model Code was drafted are rejected — *e.g.*, "entering and occupying real property or structures of any kind" without the owner's consent, going upon or passing over "any cultivated or enclosed land in this state, without the consent of the owner," allowing "domestic animals . . . upon the lands of another within a city." It suffices to prohibit situations involving defiance of the owner's request or notice to desist from trespass, without making every incursion on lands of another a penal offense. On the other hand, Section 221.2 is broader than many laws in effect when it was drafted insofar as it extends to an "occupied structure" as that term is defined in Section 221.0(1). This formulation embraces boats and other vehicles adapted to habitation or business.

2. *Elements of the Offense and Grading.* Section 221.2 creates three levels of criminal trespass. The offense may be punished as a misdemeanor, a petty misdemeanor, or a violation. Each will be considered in turn, following a discussion of several factors that relate to all levels of the offense.

(a) *Culpable Intrusion.* Each offense under Section 221.2 must be accompanied by the actor's knowledge that he is not privileged or licensed to enter or remain upon the property. This reflects the common requirement of criminal trespass that the actor be aware of the fact that he is making an unwarranted intrusion.

The knowledge requirement is designed primarily to exclude from criminal liability both the inadvertent trespasser and the trespasser who believes that he has received an express or implied permission to enter or remain. There is, moreover, an affirmative defense in Subsection (3) (c) to account for the case where the actor knows that he does not have a license or privilege to enter or remain upon premises but believes that he could have obtained permission had he sought it. The defense is available if the actor's belief is reasonable, and that requirement is defined in Section 1.13(16) as a belief which the actor is not reckless or negligent in holding. . . .

(b) *Public Premises.* Subsection (3) (b) provides an affirmative defense to all violations of Section 221.2. It applies where "the premises were at the time open to members of the public and the actor complied with all lawful conditions inposed on access to or remaining in the premises." This provision parallels the conception of "at the time open to the public" which was excluded from the offense of burglary under Section 221.1, though here the element has been designated as an affirmative defense.

The primary objective of the defense is to exclude criminal prosecution for mere presence of a person in a place where the public generally is invited. Persons who become undesirable due to disorderly conduct or other misbehavior may, of course, be prosecuted if the behavior itself amounts to another criminal offense. As with other provisions of the Code, moreover, the section is not intended to preclude resort to civil remedies for trespass, including the occupant's privilege, whatever it may be, of barring entry or ejecting.

In controversies that have arisen over the issue of equal access to places of public accommodation, the effect of this provision is explicitly to raise the issue whether the conditions imposed on access to premises otherwise open to the public were "lawful." Thus, in situations where federal law guarantees access without racial discrimination, no criminal trespass could occur as a result of a restriction as to race. The same analysis would apply whatever the reason for declaring unlawful the occupant's conditions on entry or remaining, whether by virtue of other federal or state law guaranteeing access to certain facilities or by virtue of other statutory or common-law requirements of non-discrimination in places open to the public. . . .

(c) *Misdemeanor.* Subsection (1) provides that it is a misdemeanor for one to enter or surreptitiously to remain in any building or occupied structure if the structure is a dwelling and if the offense is committed at night. "Occupied structure" and "night" are defined in Section 221.0 and are discussed in the commentary to Section 221.1.

As in the case of burglary, the concept of "building or occupied structure" explicitly includes a "separately secured or occupied portion thereof," such as a hotel room or a separate apartment unit. And again as in burglary, it is an affirmative defense under Subsection (3) (a) that the building or occupied structure was abandoned. Both of these issues are discussed in the commentary to Section 221.1. The Model Code language has been followed substantially in revised trespass statutes, both in the inclusion of separately secured premises and in the exclusion of abandoned premises.

A comparison of Subsections (1) and (2) will reveal that the surreptitious character of the actor's conduct has grading consequences only. A general criminal trespass statute clearly must allow the occupant or owner of property to withdraw permission once granted. Subsection (2) deals generally with the actor who remains on property under such circumstances and provides for petty misdemeanor treatment of the defiant trespasser, *i.e.,* one who "defies an order to leave personally communicated to him by the owner of the premises or other authorized person." The question addressed in Subsection (1) is whether it is appropriate to provide for more serious treatment in the case of someone who remains in a building or occupied structure under conditions that can be characterized as "surreptitious," *i.e.,* under conditions where the actor hides or otherwise conceals his presence.

Subsection (1) is based on the judgment that such treatment is appropriate. It classifies as a misdemeanor the conduct of one who, without criminal purpose but knowing that he is not licensed or privileged to do so, enters the dwelling of another at night. This is, in effect, a lesser included offense of burglary. It occurs under circumstances where the lack of criminal intent of the actor appropriately reduces the grade of his criminality though it may not reduce the fear or apprehension that will result from his conduct. Because the fear or apprehension may still remain, such conduct is properly treated as the most serious form of criminal trespass. For similar reasons, surreptitiously remaining within the dwelling of another at night under the same circumstances warrants misdemeanor classification. Even though entry may have been lawful, one who secretes himself within a dwelling at night is likely to cause the same fear and apprehension that an intruder would cause, and while the lack of criminal intent justifies lowering the grade of the offense below that of burglary, there seems to be no case for distinguishing the two situations of entry without license and surreptitious remaining without license. On the other hand, where one openly remains on property after his license to be there has expired, whether the property is a dwelling or any other kind of private premises, the same fears and apprehensions will not be present — or at least will not be caused by the trespass as opposed to other independently punishable threatening behavior — and the offense is appropriately classified, as in Subsection (2), as a lesser offense.

(d) *Petty Misdemeanor.* Subsection (1) classifies as a petty misdemeanor the conduct of one who enters or remains surreptitiously in a building or occupied structure that is not a dwelling. It also treats as a petty misdemeanor or trespasses into a dwelling that do not occur at night. Subsection (2) treats as a petty misdemeanor the conduct of one who has actually received notice to leave that has been personally communicated by someone in authority.

The invasion in these instances is serious enough to warrant criminal treatment, either because of the special sense of privacy that one should be able to associate with a building or other occupied structure or because of the open defiance of an order to leave privately owned premises. Because any other criminal conduct that the actor engages in or threatens can be reached under other sections and because the privacy interest is the only one that is reached by this section, the lowest category of criminal conduct is the appropriate level at which to place the offense. . . .

(e) *Violation.* Subsection (2) also classifies as a violation trespassory conduct that occurs if any one of three conditions obtains *i.e.,* where notice against trespass is given by actual communication to the actor, by posting in a pre-scribed manner, or by fencing or some other enclosure manifestly designed to exclude intruders.

Most instances of actual communication will become petty misdemeanors, unless the actor enters in the face of an actual communication and leaves immediately upon its renewal after entry. The major thrust of the violation offense will thus be to cover cases of the second two categories, which surely do not present serious instances of intrusion warranting criminal penalty.

Section 2.05(a) provides, it should be noted, for the enforcement of culpability provisions included within the definition of an offense classified as a violation. Thus, although strict liability is contemplated for many violations, the requirement of Subsection (2) that the actor know that he is acting without license or privilege remains an element of this offense. Thus, the case of purely inadvertent trespass is not treated as an offense by any provision of Section 221.2. . . .

COMMENT TO § 222.1

1. *Background and Rationale.* At common law, the theft of property under circumstances calculated to terrorize the victim was denominated the more serious offense of robbery. These circumstances were described as a taking from a person or in his presence by force or by putting the victim in fear of immediate bodily injury, arson of a dwelling, or accusation of sodomy. The offense was a capital felony. Gradually, most legislatures eliminated the death penalty [2] and introduced grading schemes that restricted imposition of the most severe sentences of imprisonment. Among the factors that were given grading significance were the actual infliction of bodily harm, the use or possession of "deadly" or "dangerous" weapons, the presence of an accomplice at the scene of the offense,

---

[2] At the time of the drafting of the Model Penal Code, some categories of robbery remained subject to capital punishment in about a dozen states. See T. Sellin, The Death Penalty 4, 7 (1959), reproduced in MPC T.D. 9, after p. 220 (1959). The death penalty may be unconstitutional for robbery today, at least where no one is killed. See Coker v. Georgia, 433 U.S. 584 (1977). See also Section 210.6 Comment 3 *supra.*

the use of an automobile to facilitate escape, and the special attractiveness or vulnerability of the victim, *e.g.,* a bank.

New York, for example, defined the offense in three levels at the time the Model Penal Code was drafted. Third-degree robbery consisted of taking property from the person or presence of another, or from the person of anyone in his company, and it carried a maximum sentence of 10 years. If the actor used "violence" or subjected the victim or his companion to fear of *immediate* injury to the person, the offense became second-degree robbery, with a maximum penalty of 15 years. Finally, if the robber was armed, used an accomplice or an automobile, or inflicted grievous bodily harm, the offense became first-degree robbery, and the potential maximum sentence increased to 30 years.[3]

California, Louisiana, and Wisconsin employed a different and much simpler structure. These states reached the taking of property from the person or presence of the victim by force, fear, threat, or intimidation and aggravated the offense only if the actor were armed with a deadly or dangerous weapon.[4] The authorized penalties varied considerably, with maxima for the aggravated offense of life in California, 30 years in Wisconsin, and 15 in Louisiana, and for the lesser offense of life in California, 10 years in Wisconsin, and five in Louisiana.[5]

Whatever grading scheme is followed, the core of the robbery offense is the combination of theft and the fact or threat of immediate injury. The initial question that must be faced is whether there is a continuing need for such an offense in a modern penal code. The elements of robbery could be separated so that prosecution would go forward for theft and for a separate crime relating to the infliction or threat of injury, with cumulation of punishment where appropriate. This approach might be adequate in some instances, as in a case of actual infliction of death or serious bodily injury. There are two reasons, however, why this course was not adopted in the Model Code. The first is that the combination of some types of assault with theft is properly regarded as a more serious offense than the gradation yielded by the cumulation of penalties for the two offenses viewed separately. The second is that long tradition reinforces this judgment.

The violent petty thief operating in the streets and alleys of big cities — the "mugger" — is one of the main sources of insecurity and concern in the population at large. There is a special element of terror in this kind of depredation. The ordinary citizen does not feel particularly threatened by surreptitious larceny, embezzlement, or fraud. But there is understandable abhorrence of the robber who accosts on the streets and who menaces his victims with actual or threatened violence against which there is a general sense of helplessness. In proportion as the ordinary person fears and detests such behavior, the offender

---

[3] *See* N.Y. §§ 2124-2129 (repealed 1967). Since the drafting of the Model Penal Code, New York has changed its grading scheme. Under the new structure, first-degree robbery occurs when the actor uses a dangerous instrument, is armed with a deadly weapon, causes serious injury, or displays what appears to be a firearm (with the affirmative defense that it was unworkable). A second-degree robbery takes place where the robber has a confederate, causes injury, or displays a firearm (with no affirmative defense). One is guilty of third-degree robbery if he "forcibly steals property." N.Y. §§ 160.05 to .15.

[4] Cal. § 211a; La. § 14:64(A); Wis. § 943.32. California also included robbery by "torture" in the aggravated category and still does.

[5] *See* Cal. §§ 211a, 213 (penalty structure changed in 1976); La. §§ 14.64(B) (amended in 1966 to imprisonment up to 99 years), :65; Wis. § 943.32(2).

exhibits himself as seriously deviated from community norms, thus justifying more serious sanctions. In addition, the robber may be distinguished from the stealthy thief by the hardihood that enables him to carry out his purpose in the presence of his victim and over his opposition — obstacles that might deter ordinary sneak thieves and that justify the feeling of special danger evoked by robbery.

There is, therefore, a special case for the treatment of robbery as a serious and distinct offense. The chief remaining questions concern the development of a rational robbery statute and a sensible grading structure. As indicated, the offense of robbery deals with theft under special circumstances. The critical problem of definition concerns the specification of these special circumstances. Three such issues must be addressed: the time span during which the special circumstances must occur; the nature of the special circumstances that must take place; and the culpability required for each of these elements. Each of these issues is discussed in succeeding comments.

2. *In the Course of Committing a Theft.* This phrase has been used to describe the time during which the threatening conduct must occur in order to constitute robbery. On its face, the phrase includes the period during which an actual theft occurs. Subsection (1) of Section 222.1 adds a definition that extends robbery to include conduct that "occurs in an attempt to commit theft or in flight after the attempt or commission." Thus, a robbery is committed if the required special circumstances exist at any point from the beginning of an attempt to commit a theft through the end of the flight following its attempt or commission. Separate attention to attempts and to flight is warranted.

(a) *Attempted Theft.* Since common-law larceny and robbery required asportation, the severe penalties for robbery were avoided if the victim had no property to hand over or if the theft were interrupted before the accused laid hold of the goods. Moreover, the penalties for attempted robbery were considerably milder than those authorized for the completed crime. The perception that one who attempts a robbery poses essentially the same dangers as the successful robber led legislatures to develop more serious sanctions for various forms of attempt. The offense of assault with intent to rob was one response and redefining robbery to include an assault with intent to rob was another. Often some distinctions in penalty were preserved.

There is, however, no penological justification for distinctions on this basis. The same dangers are posed by the actor who is interrupted or who is foiled by an empty pocket as by the actor who succeeds in effecting the theft. The same correctional dispositions are justified as well. The primary concern is with the physical danger or threat of danger to the citizen rather than with the property aspects of the crime. By including attempted thefts within the time span during which robbery can occur, Section 222.1 therefore makes it immaterial whether property is obtained.

At least 18 states follow the Model Penal Code in clearly including attempted theft within the coverage of the robbery offense. At least three proposed codes also follow the Model Code in this respect. Other recently drafted statutes seem ambiguous on the point. New York, for example, defines robbery as "forcible stealing." This phrase is described to include conduct that occurs "in the course of committing a larceny; and that is for the purpose of circumventing "resistance to the taking" of property, or retaining the property immediately after taking, or "compelling the owner . . . to deliver up the property," or forcing the owner "to engage in other conduct which aids in the commission of the larceny." This formulation may or may not be read to require that an actual larceny occur.

Some pre-Model Code statutes much more clearly adhered to a narrower conception of robbery by requiring a completed theft. Of these statutes, some merely provided statutory penalties for robbery and left its definition to common-law principles, which required a "taking" as an "essential element" of the crime. Other older statutes explicitly defined the offense so that a "taking" had to occur. California, for example, provided in part that robbery was "the felonious taking of personal property in the possession of another." Similarly, New Jersey defined this aspect of the offense to reach one "who forcibly takes from the person of another." Some recent revisions also follow this narrow approach. The proposed federal criminal code as enacted by the Senate applies to one who "takes property of another." Also, several states require a taking for the offense of simple robbery but include an attempted taking in more aggravated forms of the offense. For example, Utah defines robbery as the "taking of personal property" and aggravated robbery as the use of a firearm or the infliction of serious bodily injury "in the course of committing robbery," which is defined as including an "attempt to commit" a theft.

Those jurisdictions that focus upon an actual "taking" as a prerequisite for robbery must rely upon general provisions on attempt to deal with cases where the taking is not completed. This scheme has two potential consequences which are avoided by the approach of Section 222.1. First, there may be a grading difference. If a state requiring an actual "taking" were to punish an attempt less severely than the completed offense, the effect would be disparate punishment of conduct that should be treated in the same manner. On the other hand, if attempt is generally graded at the same level as the completed offense, the result reached by the Model Code could be achieved by a prosecution for attempted robbery.

The second potential consequence of focusing upon a completed taking concerns culpability. Most, if not all, attempt prosecutions require a showing of culpability substantially higher than that required for the completed offense. It is at least possible, therefore, that prosecution would be hampered if an attempt is all that can be charged. For example, while the reckless infliction of serious bodily injury may suffice for robbery itself, an incomplete taking may well require proof of a purpose to inflict such injury in order to convict of attempt. Under Section 222.1, on the other hand, the required culpability with respect to the force and fear elements of robbery is not affected by whether the property aspect of the crime is completed. The problem is avoided completely by treating attempted theft as within the completed robbery offense. The actor who engages in the violence required for robbery will thus be treated the same so long as his conduct is "in the course of committing a theft" as those terms are used in this provision.

(b) *Flight.* The Model Code definition of "in the course of committing a theft" is unusual insofar as it includes behavior after the theft has been accomplished as a determinant of robbery. Section 222.1 thus includes as robbery the conduct of a person who, having obtained or attempted to obtain the property, threatens or uses the specified force to retain the property, to escape, or to prevent pursuit. The thief's willingness to use force against those who would restrain him in flight suggests that he would have employed force to effect the theft had the need arisen. Thus, such an actor is presumably a person who presents the special dangers that the robbery statute is designed to reach and who is an appropriate subject for the sanctions designed for that offense.

No rule-of-thumb is proposed to delimit the time and space of "flight." This concept should be interpreted in accordance with the rationale for its inclusion within the robbery offense. The concept of "fresh pursuit" may be helpful in suggesting realistic boundaries between the occasion of the theft and a later distinct occasion when the escaped thief is apprehended.

Prior law was in general narrower than the Model Code on this point and did not include force during flight within the offense of robbery. Statutes that defined the offense as a "taking" accompanied by force were most likely to be interpreted to exclude flight after the taking. Some statutes still follow the old New York provision:

[T]o constitute robbery, the force or fear must be employed either to obtain or retain possession of the property or to prevent or to overcome resistance to the taking. If employed merely as a means of escape it does not constitute robbery.

The revised New York statute also seems narrower than the Model Code. It applies to the use of force for the purpose of preventing or overcoming resistance "to the retention . . . [of the property] immediately after the taking."

There are, however, several recent revisions that include flight within the aggravated form of robbery though not within the least serious form of the offense. Moreover, since the drafting of the Model Penal Code, at least 13 states have included provisions encompassing flight within all forms of the robbery offense. At least four proposed state criminal codes also include flight in terms that are comparable to the Model Code in scope. Some revisions are worded in a manner that may lead to subtle differences in interpretation. The Minnesota statute, for example, includes the use of force in the "carrying away" of the property, and Washington encompasses the use of force to "retain possession" of the property. . . .

3. *Nature of the Threatening Conduct.* Subsection (1) provides that a robbery has occurred if, in the course of committing a theft as described above, the actor "(a) inflicts serious bodily injury upon another; or (b) threatens another with or purposely puts him in fear of immediate serious bodily injury; or (c) commits or threatens immediately to commit any felony of the first or second degree." The common thread in these provisions is the seriousness of the harm that is inflicted or threatened, coupled with its imminence or immediacy. There are a number of separate issues that need to be discussed concerning the nature of these special circumstances that distinguish robbery from ordinary theft.

(a) *Serious Bodily Injury.* Both Paragraphs (a) and (b) refer to "serious" bodily injury. The term is undefined in Article 222, but the definition in Section 210.0(3) is intended to be applicable. That definition includes "bodily injury which creates a substantial risk of death or which causes serious, permanent disfigurement, or protracted loss or impairment of the function of any bodily member or organ." "Bodily injury," on the other hand, is defined in Section 210.0(2) to mean "physical pain, illness or any impairment of physical condition." Section 222.1 thus is meant to require more than "physical pain" or "any impairment" of physical condition.

Nearly all current statutes disagree with the Model Code on this point and permit a robbery prosecution on the basis of any degree of force or fear. The California statute is typical of older statutes that define robbery as the taking of property "accomplished by means of force or fear." Of the new statutes, those in Montana and New Jersey are examples of an approach virtually identical to the Model Penal Code, with the exception that "bodily injury" is substituted for "serious bodily injury." The revised New York statute reaches one who "uses or threatens the immediate use of physical force upon another person." Virtually all of the recently drafted codes and proposals include inflicted or threatened harm that falls considerably short of the Model Code's definition of "serious bodily injury." Pennsylvania was one of the few states that adopted the "serious bodily injury" formula, and even that state has since amended its statute to require serious injury only for the most aggravated form of robbery.

Departure from the Model Code's requirement of serious injury was defended in the Working Papers of the Brown Commission on the ground that "limitation of the crime to threats or infliction of serious bodily injury would eliminate from the scope of the crime forceful takings from the person such as 'muggings,' acts which are ordinarily and properly considered as robbery." The requirement that the harm inflicted or threatened to be "serious" bodily injury was not intended, however, to exclude muggings and other similar conduct from the offense of robbery. It is fear of *serious* injury that characterizes the apprehension that is excited by the prospect of a street mugging and that justifies the serious sanctions for robbery. Robbery includes threats as well as actual harm caused and without the threat of serious harm it is difficult to justify regarding the offense as a felony of the first or the second degree.

Moreover, robbery must be distingushed from ordinary theft from the person. Section 223.1(2) provides that theft from the person is at least a misdemeanor, no matter what the amount involved, and that any theft of more than $500 or of certain specified items will be a felony of the third degree. Any taking from the person will involve some use of "force" and perhaps "fear" in some general sense of being startled. But it is force or threat of force directed at placing the victim in serious fear for his safety that justifies the escalated penalties of the robbery offense. The word "serious" was added in Section 222.1 to avoid the result of making a "robber out of a man who snatches a bag and thus inflicts some pain or wrench in running off with the bag." If fear of "any impairment of physical condition" were included as robbery, it would be hard to distinguish most purse-snatching from truly dangerous robbery and difficult to justify a raising of the sanction from what, separately viewed, might be a misdemeanor or a petty misdemeanor theft coupled with, at most, a minor assault.

(b) *Actual or Threatened Injury.* All robbery statutes deal both with the actual infliction of injury and with the threat to inflict injury. Subsection (1)(a) follows this tradition by speaking to the actual injury, while Subsection (1)(b) covers threats. Subsection (1)(b) uses the language "threatens another with . . . immediate serious bodily injury" to include verbal or other express offers of serious harm. Alternatively, Subsection (1)(b) applies to one who "purposely puts him in fear of immediate serious bodily injury," by which is meant to be included menacing or other implied threat sought to be communicated to the victim by the actor's conduct. This latter language would thus apply to cases where the actor brandishes a weapon or otherwise displays the ability and the intention to use force if his wishes are not honored. The intent of the subsection is thus to reach all forms of express or implied threat immediately to inflict serious bodily injury.

Most recently drafted robbery provisions use only the term "threaten" to convey the idea sought to be reached by Subsection (1)(b). The New York statute, for example, employs the language "uses or threatens" force. There are some codes that have followed more closely the approach of the Model Code. For example, the proposed federal criminal code applies to a taking "by force and violence" or "by threatening or placing another person in fear" that force will be immediately used. Both approaches seem adequate, so long as the term "threaten" is broadly interpreted to apply to implicit as well as explicit threats.

(c) *Other Types of Harm.* In addition to the infliction or threatened infliction of serious bodily harm, Paragraph (c) includes the commission or threatened commission of any felony of the first or the second degree. There is thus no requirement that the threats be directed against the personal safety of the victim. For example, a robbery would occur under this formulation if the offender obtained property from one person by threatening an immediate rape of another, whether or not the other person were present and whoever that person might be. It may even be that the threat does not concern injury to the person at all. Obtaining property by a threat immediately to commit arson would also be robbery.

The revisions in Iowa, Pennsylvania, and Montana include a threat to commit the most serious categories of felony within the definition of robbery, as does the recent enactment in New Jersey. The remaining recent enactments and proposals have retained the traditional scope of robbery by focusing only upon the infliction or threat of personal violence to the victim of the theft or to some other person.

(d) *Immediacy of Harm.* Apart from the type of personal injury that must be caused or threatened, attention must be focused upon the timing of the harm in order to distinguish it from ordinary theft. Only certain types of threats suffice to constitute robbery, and it is the actual execution of the threat or the immediate possibility of its execution that is the unique feature of this offense. Section 223.4 of the Model Code defines as theft by extortion obtaining the property of another by any one of a series of specified threats. These include a threat to inflict bodily injury or to commit any other criminal offense. Extortion is to be distinguished from robbery both because it lacks the immediacy of execution of the threat and because the seriousness of the threat may not cause the types of apprehension at which the robbery offense is aimed.

There are some statutes derived from the old New York provision that obscure the difference between robbery and extortion. New York defined robbery as:

> the unlawful taking of personal property, from the person or in the presence of another, against his will, by means of force, or violence, or fear or injury, immediate or future, to his person or property, or the person or property of a relative or member of his family, or of anyone in his company at the time of the robbery.

There is agreement with the Model Code among the majority of the recently enacted and proposed robbery provisions, however, that any reference to "future" harm is inappropriate in a robbery offense. Though the formulas vary, these statutes recognize that actual infliction or threat of immediate or imminent infliction is the essence of the offense. The immediacy and seriousness of the threats are therefore the essential grading factors that are regarded as escalating theft by extortion to the higher sanctions provided for robbery.

There is also general agreement among the newer codes and proposals that there should be no requirement that the taking be from the person or in the presence of the victim. Though this traditional basis for classifying theft as robbery is not explicit in Section 222.1, it would ordinarily be the case since the circumstances of violence or threat of violence imply the presence of the victim. There are a few situations, however, where Section 222.1 would apply to the theft of property other than from the person or in the presence of the victim. For example, an offender might threaten to shoot the victim in order to compel him to telephone directions for the disposition of property located elsewhere or the threat may be to one person in order to secure property from another who is not then present. The traditional requirement of a taking from the person has not been included in Section 222.1 in order to encompass such cases. It is enough that there be actual force or the threat of immediate force. The additional requirement that the taking be from the person or in the presence of the victim excludes some cases that should be covered and adds little by way of narrowing the scope of the offense in any appropriate manner.

Though most of the recently drafted codes and proposals have excluded this element, there are some that have retained it. There are also a number of older statutes that still include this traditional element. . . .

4. *Culpability.* Discussion of the culpability components of robbery will be facilitated by focusing separately upon the different elements of the offense.

(a) *In the Course of Committing a Theft.* As explained above, this language describes the time span of the larcenous conduct during which the specified injuries or threats will constitute a robbery. There are three successive stages: an attempt to commit a theft, the theft itself, and flight after the attempt or theft. With respect to the attempt, the elements of culpability and conduct that must be shown can be derived from Section 5.01 and from the comprehensive theft offense described in Article 223. It is a defense to robbery that no attempted theft was committed in this sense. With respect to the theft itself, the culpability and conduct components are supplied by Article 223. Prosecution based on flight after the attempt or commission must satisfy the culpability and conduct requirements of either the attempted theft or the completed theft and must show a culpability of recklessness as to the flight itself under Section 2.02(3). This latter element should not be difficult to satisfy.

(b) *Inflicts Serious Bodily Injury.* Subsection (1)(a) was initially drafted to read "recklessly" inflicts serious bodily injury upon another. The word "recklessly" was omitted in the final draft because Section 2.02(3) makes purpose, knowledge, or recklessness the applicable culpability in the absence of any specification. The change is thus not intended to alter the culpability for this provision.

State codes in existence at the time of the drafting of the Model Code were, as a rule, interpreted to require intention for each element of the robbery offense. Since the publication of the Model Code, however, at least eight state codes have been enacted that require only recklessness for the actual infliction of bodily harm. Of the proposed codes, at least one agrees with this conclusion.

(c) *Threat of Serious Bodily Injury.* Subsection (1)(b) applies when the actor has not actually inflicted serious bodily injury but where he threatens another with such injury or purposely puts him in fear that such injury will result. The term "threaten" implies purposeful behavior. It covers explicit verbal threats that are designed to put the victim in fear that serious bodily injury will immediately result if the property is not relinquished. It is not the victim's reaction to the actor's conduct that controls, but the purposeful behavior by the actor in communicating the threat of injury. Similarly, the language "purposely puts him in fear of immediate serious bodily injury" is designed to focus upon the actor's purposeful conduct in conveying, albeit implicitly, that harm will result if resistance is encountered.

Focus upon the actor's purposeful behavior is designed to assure that the robbery offense properly identifies those offenders who pose the risks of serious harm to which the crime is addressed. When injury is actually inflicted, even though recklessly, the willingness of the actor to expose the victim to serious harm is sufficiently demonstrated. When no harm is actually caused, however, a higher culpability standard is justified much on the same theory that the crime of attempt employs a higher culpability in most instances than the completed offense. Where the conduct is not completed, the higher culpability serves to assure that the actor is one who is fully prepared to complete the conduct. A lesser standard, for example recklessly placing another in fear, runs the risk that an overreaction by the victim to conduct no more serious than pickpocketing or other minor theft from the person will unjustifiably escalate the offense from a misdemeanor to the level of second-degree felony.

It should also be noted that there will be cases, appropriately reached by a charge of attempted robbery, where the actor does not actually harm anyone or even threaten harm. If, for example, the defendant is apprehended before he reaches his robbery victim and thus before he has actually engaged in threatening conduct, proof of his purpose to engage in such conduct will justify a conviction of attempted robbery if the standards of Subsections (1)(c) and (2) of Section 5.01 are met. Section 5.01(2)(a) was drafted in large part with the offense of robbery in mind, applying as it does to one who is "lying in wait, searching for or following the contemplated victim of the crime." This provision was designed to indicate disagreement with the reversal of the conviction in *People v. Rizzo,* where the defendants were armed, were planning to rob a payroll carrier, and were searching for the victim when they were apprehended.

In summary, therefore, it is the theory of Section 222.1 that the violence aspects of the offense of robbery are the determinative elements that justify the special seriousness with which it is regarded. The offense includes actually inflicted injury as well as threats immediately to inflict injury. Where the threats are not actually communicated, a prosecution for attempt may still be appropriate if the purpose to engage in the offending conduct can be shown together with a substantial step towards its commission. On the other hand, the failure of the actor to complete a theft is not regarded as significant; robbery has occurred whenever the actor has at least attempted theft and violence is inflicted or threatened during the attempt or in flight after the attempt.

5. *Grading.* Subsection (2) provides that robbery will ordinarily be a felony of the second degree. It can be a felony of the first degree, however, "if in the course of committing the theft the actor attempts to kill anyone, or purposely inflicts or attempts to inflict serious bodily injury."

What appears to be a marked reduction to 10 years of the typical maximum penalty for robbery that was prevalent when the Model Penal Code was drafted is not as drastic as it seems, when account is taken of periods actually served by convicted robbers under then-existing laws. At that time, 90 per cent of all convicted robbers were released after fewer than eight years of imprisonment, the median period of detention for the middle 80 per cent being approximately three years. Under the Model Code sentencing structure, extended sentences up to 20 years can be imposed on persistent, professional, psychopathic, or multiple offenders. Moreover, to take most robbery beyond the second-degree felony category is to move into the realm of life imprisonment, an extreme sanction reserved in this Code for murder, aggravated rape, and aggravated kidnapping. Even attempted murder is classified as a felony of the second-degree.

As noted above, Section 222.1 punishes one class of robbery as a first-degree felony. It may seem anomalous that an attempt to kill in the context of robbery has been made a first-degree felony, while an attempt to kill out of vengeance or to remove a rival in love or business would be only a second-degree felony. The justification lies in the considerations discussed in Comment 1 above. The robber generates severe and widespread insecurity by indiscriminately assailing anyone who may be despoiled of property. In addition, the requirement here that the assault be "in the course of committing a theft" should have the effect of restricting the first-degree penalty to a narrow class of attempted killings and injuries, namely those which come close to accomplishment. Even though an attempted theft is included within that language, the offense of robbery cannot be made out, as discussed in Comment 3(b) above, unless the actual or threatened violence is in fact committed in the presence of the victim. This is in contrast to the ordinarily broad reach of Section 5.01, which defines attempts in general, including attempted murder, to include many acts previously regarded as mere preparation. Attempted killings in the course of robbery thus are classified at the highest felony level. The same reasoning applies to the case of one who purposely inflicts or attempts to inflict serious bodily injury, conduct which in itself is typically life endangering and which justifiably arouses the highest feelings of insecurity and apprehension.

It should also be explained why reference to other factors that have frequently been used to aggravate ordinary theft to robbery or to aggravate the level of robbery have been omitted. The factor of being "armed with a deadly weapon" which has been so commonly used is dropped in favor of the language in Paragraph (b) of Subsection (1), which requires threat or menace of serious bodily harm. Most cases of armed robbery will fall within this category and will be graded as a second-degree felony unless the actor satisfies the first-degree criteria of Subsection (2). Only where the robbery does not exhibit his weapon would this definition of robbery operate more narrowly than the typical armed-robbery statute. It is the employment of a weapon that should be significant in the grading of robbery, rather than the discovery, for example, of a switchblade knife in the culprit's pocket. Second-degree felony treatment is adequate in the absence of an actual attempt to use the weapon to kill or to inflict serious bodily injury.

Subsection (1)(b) clearly encompasses use of a toy pistol or unloaded gun, since such a device can be employed to threaten serious injury and may be effective to create the fear of such an injury. It has often been contended, usually unsuccessfully, that such objects are not "dangerous" or "deadly." The argument has been properly rejected, though no case for classifying robbery by such means in the highest category of felony appears to exist.

There is no good reason to include use of an automobile among the factors that would raise a theft that would otherwise amount to no more than a misdemeanor or a felony of the third degree under the provisions of Section 223.1(2) to the level of a second-degree felony. There is an even less persuasive case for using that factor, as in the former New York law, to escalate a robbery to the first-degree felony level. Use of an automobile may make it more difficult to catch the thief, but for that very reason thieves are not likely to be deterred from using cars by additional increments of punishment over five years. In any event, only caught thieves are prosecuted and to distinguish among them according to whether they rode horses, automobiles, or airplanes is to abandon the basis upon which the robbery offense is constructed, namely terroristic property aggression. Perhaps use of the automobile has been supposed to betoken organization or professionalism. These factors are dealt with explicitly, however, in other provisions of this Code dealing with extended sentences for professionals. Adequate conspiracy provisions, moreover, should provide additional leverage against crime involving confederates.

A more difficult question is posed by the fairly common statutes penalizing with special severity robbery or burglary of banks or trains. These contain particularly desirable but well-defended prizes, and are presumably chosen as targets by the most desperate and well-organized criminals. On the other hand, one reads of pathetic attempts of clumsy amateurs to rob banks. Moreover, the criteria that would lead to designating bank robbery for special treatment would lead logically to the inclusion of building and loan companies, credit unions, express companies, paymasters, post offices, jewelry stores, and truck loads of whiskey, silk, or other valuable commodities. It is difficult, if not impossible, to draft an acceptable legislative definition of this category of unusually tempting targets. This, plus the fact that most states get along without special laws on the subject, supports the judgment against making exceptional provisions here. . . .

With respect to grading criteria, all of the recently enacted codes have considerably streamlined the former law. Of the recent enactments, there remain no provisions treating train or bank robbery specially. The proposed South Carolina code would eliminate special provisions that are still in existence in that state for robbery of banks, trains, and motor vehicles for hire. The criteria employed in these recent provisions are much more associated with special indicators of dangerousness than idiosyncratic characteristics of the victim. There are a great number of provisions that differentiate degrees of robbery based on the seriousness of the injury that has been caused. Other aggravate the offense based on the infliction of *any* bodily harm. Commonly used criteria in addition to those specified in the Model Code include being armed with a deadly weapon or dangerous instrument, appearing to be or representing oneself as being armed with a deadly weapon or dangerous instrument, and having an accomplice present.

COMMENT TO § 223.1(2)

3. *Grading of Theft Offenses.* Subsection (2) advances a comprehensive grading scheme for all forms of the theft offense defined in succeeding sections of this article. Distinctions based on the value of the property stolen are supplemented by other criteria regarding as aggravating what would otherwise be minor theft. Grading by amount will be considered first, after which these other criteria will be elaborated.

(a) *Grading by Amount Stolen.* Except for certain special categories of theft, most jurisdictions classify thefts according to the monetary value of the property stolen. Before the promulgation of the Model Code, the traditional distinction adopted by most states was between grand and petty theft, with $100 being the most common dividing line and $50 the next most frequent figure. At that time, six states had three levels marked by amount, and one state had four. The maximum imprisonment for petty theft during this period was commonly one year; the range was from 30 days to five years. The typical maximum for grand larceny not accompanied by aggravating circumstances was 10 years; the range was from five to 21 years.

Subsection (2) adopts the principle of distinction based on amount. Putting a ceiling on punishment of petty theft accords with the almost universal present practice and with popular feeling. The ordinary individual feels a lesser repugnance to the taking of smaller rather than larger amounts. Thus, the petty thief evinces a lesser departure from normal standards of respect for others' property; he is presumably not as hardened or dangerous. Shorter sentences should be sufficient to deter those who have not as much to gain. On the other hand, longer sentences are called for in the case of offenders who realize greater sums. Escalation of penalty according to amount stolen decreases the incentive for crime that greater profits might induce.

Subsection (2) adopts a three-step classification on the ground that the attitudes that justify discrimination by amount probably recognize three groups of transactions: those involving really petty values, those at the opposite end of the scale relating to very substantial amounts, and a third group that falls between these two. There is a necessary measure of arbitrariness in selecting the dollar values to mark the different categories. The top of the petty class is fixed at $50, which will authorize a sentence of up to 30 days for the ordinary offender and two years for the persistent or multiple offender. The bottom of the most serious category is set at $500, which will authorize a third-degree felony conviction carrying a maximum term of five years for the ordinary offender and 10 years for the persistent, professional, dangerous, or multiple offender. The middle category between $50 and $500 is classified as a misdemeanor, which carries a maximum punishment of one year for the ordinary offender and three years for the persistent or multiple offender.

Recent penal-code revisions have accepted classification of theft by amount stolen, but there is no consensus on the number of classifications or the dollar amount. Some states have continued the traditional two-step classification. Other states have accepted the Model Code's three-step classification, while still others have four or even five levels. There is likewise little uniformity over the monetary level at which the classifications are divided, although it is notable that almost all jurisdictions set the dollar limit where felony penalties are invoked at a lower level than the $500 figure selected in the Model Code.

(b) *Methods of Valuation.* Subsection (2)(c) governs the method by which these dollar amounts are to be determined, stated as "the highest value, by any reasonable standard, of the property or services which the actor stole or attempted to steal." The purpose is to put the transaction in a higher rather than a lower category where any one of several possible criteria of value justifies the higher classification. For penal purposes, the amount stolen is not so significant as to warrant legislative or judicial refinement of methods of valuation. The system is designed to authorize a conviction of the highest category that is reasonable for a given case, with the results that appropriate penalties will be authorized for aggravated cases and that mitigation of either the category or the sentence will be possible where warranted in the individual case. If, for example, the "highest value, by any reasonable standard," results in a felony classification that is regarded as "unduly harsh," Section 6.12 of the Model Code gives the court adequate discretion to scale the offense down to a misdemeanor and impose sentence accordingly. The same considerations animate the provision in Subsection (2)(b) that a theft shall be classified in the middle (misdemeanor) category unless the defendant satisfies the tribunal that the amount involved was less than $50. It will not be necessary formally to reduce the conviction from the misdemeanor to the petty misdemeanor class, since no civil consequence turns on one or the other category and since a petty misdemeanor sentence can be imposed, if appropriate, in any misdemeanor case. The valuation provisions of Subsection (2) thus make it possible to treat a case with severity if warranted and to mitigate the effect of a high valuation if that is the desirable result.

The degree of the actor's disregard of property rights cannot always be judged by looking at the amount which he takes at a single moment from a single person. The bank teller who day after day steals $20 from his employer will have $600 at the end of a month and clearly should be regarded as engaged in felonious theft. The driver of a department store delivery truck containing hundreds of parcels, each worth less than $50, ought not to be regarded as a petty thief who is guilty of multiple offenses when he sells the contents of the truck to a "fence" and makes off with the proceeds. A swindler who moves along the street cheating housewives out of individually petty amounts similarly ought to be punished for the aggregate misconduct, even though both the place and the victim change with each transaction. Subsection (2)(c) adopts a unity of scheme or course of conduct as the basis for aggravating a series of thefts for grading purposes. In doing so, it steers a middle ground between the rigid common-law requirement of unity of place, time, and victim and the apparently unlimited aggregation offered by the Louisiana Code. . . .

(c) *Mistake as to Valuation.* Since valuation is related to "the harm or evil . . . sought to be prevented by the law defining the offense," the dollar amounts that are specified in Subsections (2)(a) and (2)(b) are "material elements of the offense" as that term is defined in Section 1.13(9) and (10) *supra.* The culpability provisions of Section 2.02 thus are fully applicable to the values used to differentiate grades of theft. Since no culpability is explicitly stated in Subsection (2), the consequence under Section 2.02(3) of the Model Code is a minimum culpability standard of recklessness. It follows that a mistake that negatives the required recklessness with respect to the value of property stolen constitutes a defense under Section 2.04(1). There are, however, two qualifications to this result applicable in most cases, as well as several other points that should be made with respect to mistakes as to amount.

The problem can best be analyzed by taking as an illustration a thief who sets out to steal what he thinks is costume jewelry worth $100 but who actually steals real jewels worth $1000. It is likely in such a case that the prosecutor will charge felony theft and that the defendant's belief that the jewels were only worth $100 would be introduced as a defense. The question is what the effect of such a defense would be under the provisions of the Model Code.

The starting point, as noted above, is that the prosecution must show that the defendant was reckless as to amount and that he therefore was reckless as to the question of valuation at $1000. This the prosecutor normally would do by proving the actual value of the jewels and asking the jury to infer the requisite reckelessness, either by not believing the defendant's story that he thought the jewels worth only $100 or by believing that the defendant never addressed the question of valuation but was seeking jewels of whatever value he could find. In most cases, it can be expected that the matter will rest on such proof. There are, however, two qualifications.

First, some cases will arise where the defendant first realized the value of the stolen goods at a time after the initial taking. In most instances of this sort, the defendant will seek to capitalize on the real value. The effect of such conduct will be to defeat the defense of mistake, either on the theory that the unlawful appropriation occurred at the time he realized the true value or on the theory that his effort to capitalize on the real value shows that he meant all along to get as much as he could. Moreover, if the mistake defense hypothesized is pressed by the defendant, the prosecutor should be able to explore the defendant's conduct subsequent to the taking for the inferences of this character that can be drawn.

Second, even if the defense is believable in the context in which it is asserted, the fact that the prosecution charged felony theft will not prevent a conviction of the lesser included offense of misdemeanor theft. This result will obtain either on the general theory that a lesser included offense conviction is always possible or on the principle of Section 2.04(2) *supra*. In no event, therefore, would the culpability defense hypothesized require a complete acquittal.

Before turning to the rationale for this result, one should note one additional variation in the operation of Subsection (2)(c). The first sentence of the subsection provides that the amount involved shall be the highest reasonable value of the property or services "which the actor stole or attempted to steal." Thus, in the converse of the situation hypothesized above, where the defendant intends to take real jewels but in fact takes costume jewelry, the appropriate valuation will turn on what the defendant intended to take. An elaborate scheme to steal valuable jewels from a museum or a safe can thus be prosecuted for what it was, even though the plan was frustrated by the substitution of fakes for the originals. This result will follow both because of the inclusion of the language "attempted to steal" in Subsection (2)(c) and because of the general posture of the attempt provisions in Section 5.01 of the Model Code relating to the so-called "impossibility" defense.

This structure represents a change from the common-law view of mistakes as to valuation, both with respect to the requirement of culpability as to value and with respect to the abandonment of the impossibility defense. The commentary to Section 5.01 adequately sets forth the general state of the law and the rationale for the Model Code position on the latter point. With respect to the former, the traditional position is that "a person who intentionally commits an unlawful act, and in so doing inflicts an unforeseen injury, is criminally liable for such injury." As applied to the situation under discussion, the defendant would be held by this view to take the jewels as he found them and thus to be guilty of felony theft even though he held the non-reckless belief that the jewels were worth only $100. It is thus a fair statement of the existing law at the time the Model Code was drafted that the amount actually stolen determined whether the offense was grand or petty theft.

This view is rejected by the Model Code for the same reasons that strict liability has generally been rejected in the plan of the Code. The amount involved in a theft has criminological significance only if it corresponds with what the thief expected or hoped to get. To punish on the basis of actual harm rather on the basis of foreseen or desired harm is to measure the extent of criminality by fortuity. It is the general premise of the Model Code that fortuity should be replaced as a measure of grading by an examination of the individual characteristics of the offender and by an evaluation of the culpability actually manifested by his conduct.

It is difficult to assess the extent to which recently drafted codes and proposals have accepted this judgment. One might suppose that prior law would create some momentum on this issue and that strict liability might be retained in the absence of explicit rejection. A number of recent enactments and proposals, however, require the Model Penal Code result on the face of the statutory language and should, for all that appears, be so interpreted. Others have specifically preserved strict liability on this issue. One can only wait for further refinement of recent legislation in the case law to determine what patterns will emerge.

(d) *Other Grading Criteria.* In accepting a classification of theft by amount stolen, the Model Code does not purport to represent that amount is the only or even the most important measure of the anti-social tendencies of the particular thief's character. Amount stolen happens to be one of the factors in ordinary theft that lends itself to legislative generalization. Other more important variables must be taken into account in the sentencing and post-sentencing individualization of punishment that a flexible system such as that provided by the Model Code will permit. Additionally, there are several other legislative generalizations that can and should be made.

Theft of firearms is made felonious because of the special danger of lawless use of stolen weapons. Theft of automobiles and other vehicles is classified as a felony without regard to the amount involved both because vehicles characteristically represent large amounts of mobile property offering special temptation to theft and because stolen vehicles often play a part in the commission of other crimes. Under Paragraph (a) of Subsection (2), the professional receiver or "fence" for stolen property is also classified as a felon in the view that one who provides a regular market for thieves represents a threat to property on a scale not measured by the values involved in a particular transaction. Paragraph (b) provides that certain categories of theft shall be punishable as misdemeanors rather than petty misdemeanors, even though the amounts involved are less than $50. These are thefts "from the person or by threat, or in breach of fiduciary obligation." These involve either special potentialities for physical violence or alarm associated with the taking, or in the case of fiduciaries, special likelihood that speculations may continue over substantial periods under circumstances that make them difficult to discover and prove. . . .

In addition, there are a host of other special categories of theft which have been given grading significance in some revised state codes and proposals. They include credit card thefts; theft of trade or scientific secrets; theft of a testamentary instrument; theft of livestock; theft of a fire extinguisher; theft by a public servant in the course of his duties; theft while armed with a deadly weapon; theft of public funds; theft of a court or other official record; looting; theft of narcotics; theft of a key or other instrument used to provide access; theft of a license plate or certificate of title; theft of check blanks; theft of explosives; theft of implements, paper, or anything else associated with the preparation of money, bonds, stamps, or other documents, instruments, or obligations of the state; and theft of mail other than a newspaper, magazine, circular, or advertising matter.

COMMENT TO § 223.1(3)

4. *Claim of Right.* Subsection (3) of Section 223.1 deals with those situations where a theft prosecution is inappropriate because the actor obtains the property of another under a claim of right. Three situations are dealt with. Paragraph (a) deals with cases where the actor is unaware that the property or service belonged to another person. Paragraph (b) covers cases where, though he knew of the ownership of another person, the actor believed that he nevertheless had a right to acquire or dispose of the property or service by acting as he did. Finally, Paragraph (c) deals with cases where property exposed for sale is taken into the actor's possession under the reasonable belief that the owner would have consented if he were present or with the intention of prompt payment when the occasion arises.

(a) *Unaware of Ownership by Another.* Subsection (3)(a) gives the actor an affirmative defense in situations where he is unaware that he is infringing the property interests of others, as where he supposes that he is appropriating abandoned property or that the property belongs to him. In these cases, therefore, the defendant's honest belief that the property is his or that it does not belong to another will be a defense to theft as defined in Article 223.

Strict application of the elements of the offense of theft as set forth in Sections 223.2 to 223.8 will lead to the same conclusion in most cases as is afforded by the claim-of-right defense in Subsection (3)(a). In Section 223.2(1), for example, it is required that the actor unlawfully take or exercise unlawful control over the property of another "with purpose to deprive him thereof." "Deprive" in turn means to withhold "property of another" or to dispose of such property under specified conditions. Since one must have a "purpose" to deprive and since deprive means to perform certain acts with the property "of another," it follows that the actor must know that the property belongs to another. Similarly, Sections 223.3 and 223.4 require that the actor "purposely" obtain property of another by deception and "purposely" obtain property of another by threat. Thus, in both of these cases, the actor is also required, in this case by operation of Subsections (2)(a)(ii) and (4) of Section 2.02, to know that the property belongs to another. Analysis of Sections 223.5 to 223.8 yields the same result.

The claim-of-right defense provided in Section 223.1(3)(a) can thus be regarded as redundant with respect to these offenses since a proper analysis of their elements requires knowledge of the proprietary interest of the other party and hence would recognize an honest, though unreasonable, mistake as a defense. The special claim-of-right defense on this ground has nevertheless been included for three reasons.

First, it seems important to make it clear beyond doubt that an honest belief that the property does not belong to another should be a defense to theft. Theft is an offense that is designed to deal with those who are prepared to appropriate the property of another to their own use. One who is unaware of another's interest does not pose the threat against which the offense is designed to guard nor the disposition to defy the property system that may warrant the concern of the penal law. This is true even in cases where deception or threat is used to obtain what the actor believes to the return of his own property. It may be in such cases that some other offense is committed, as, for example, where the defendant's threat is serious enough to violate the assault provisions of Section 211.1. But where no independent crime has been committed, it surely should not be the case that the actor is subject to a charge of theft for resorting to deceit to obtain what he believes to be the return of his own property.

Second, Section 223.1(3)(a) serves to bring to the attention of those who would use these provisions as a model that recklessness or negligence on this issue should not be permitted as the basis for theft liability. It also assures that the defense will be permitted by removing any possible ambiguity in interpretation of the elements of the theft offense. Difficulty may be thought to arise by virtue of the fact that the defense provided by Section 223.1(3)(a) is designated affirmative, while the mistake defense provided by Section 2.04 is not. As a practical matter, however, the defendant will have the burden of injecting a mistake or an honest belief that the property did not belong to another into the case. Thus, nothing would seem to turn in this instance on designation of the claim-of-right defense as affirmative, since the prosecution in both instances will be required to disprove the defense beyond a reasonable doubt.

Finally, there is one provision in the definition of theft as to which a claim of right on the ground under discussion would not be a defense in the absence of special provision. Section 223.2(2) provides in pertinent part that one is guilty of theft of immovable property if he "unlawfully transfers immovable property of another" and does so "with purpose to benefit himself or another." Technically, this provision applies to a case where the actor makes an unlawful transfer of property which he believes to be rightfully his. If he were wrong in that belief, the relevance of his mistake would be judged in this instance by a recklessness standard, if consideration were limited to the definition of the offense. The effect of Section 223.1(3)(a), however, is to raise the level of culpability applicable to the "of another" element of the offense to actual awareness or knowledge, *i.e.*, the defendant's honest belief that the property was his own would preclude liability even if the belief were wrong and had been formed recklessly or negligently. In this case, therefore, the special provision of Section 223.1(3)(a) establishes a defense that otherwise would not be available.

(b) *Honest Claim of Right.* Subsection (3)(b) deals with situations where the defendant may know that the property belongs to another but where he believes that he is nevertheless entitled to behave as he does. There is no explicit requirement, as under some statutes, that the taking be "open," though a surreptitious taking would in some cases be evidence that there was no honest claim of right.

There is debate in the cases over several situations to which the defense provided in Subsection (3)(b) will apply. One occurs where the actor believes himself privileged to appropriate the property of another in satisfaction of a debt, without any special claim to the particular property appropriated.

This belief has sometimes been held to be valid defense, even where the appropriation was by force. However, a corporate treasurer has been convicted of larceny from the corporation despite his cotention that the corporation was indebted to him as a result of a previous transaction in which he was accused of defalcations and wrongfully compelled to make good the shortage. The jury was charged that the defense failed if there was no debt in fact, and the Supreme Court of Massacusetts affirmed the conviction with a declaration that "the defendant was guilty of larceny on the evidence, even though the motive which induced him to steal from his employer was the payment of a debt which he claimed to be due him, and even though he believed his conduct was justified." [95]

Even more doubt as to the defense of claim of rights exists in a second situation, namely that of an agent or a fiduciary who profits from dealing with his principal but who believes himself entitled to the profit because, ignorantly or mistakenly, he supposed that he was under no legal obligation to refrain from such dealing or to turn over such profits to his principal. The defense was recognized in one case, where an agent was given $1,450 to buy some land, bought it for $1,150, and kept the difference.[96] On the other hand, the Supreme Court of Indiana affirmed the conviction of a fiduciary who bought bonds for $430 and resold them the same day to the estate for $2,000, the trial

---

[95] Commonwealth v. Peakes, 231 Mass. 449, 121 N.E. 420 (1919).

[96] People v. Lapique, 120 Cal. 25, 52 P. 40 (1898); *cf.* Lewis v. People, 99 Colo. 102, 60 P.2d 1089 (1936).

court having refused to instruct that the defendant might be acquitted if he had a *bona fide* belief that he was entitled to make a profit in dealing with the estate.[97] Similarly, a county official was convicted in Tennessee of embezzling certain fees for which he refused to account, despite his alleged belief on advice of counsel that the statute which ended his right to the fees and put him on a salary was unconstitutional.[98]

Subsection (3)(b) would permit a defense of claim of right in all of these situations, as well as others. The general principle is that the actor should have a defense where, although he is not in a position to claim that the property belongs to him, he honestly believes that he is entitled to acquire it and that his privilege extends to the use of force or other unlawful method of acquisition. A further example might be where an employee threatens his employer in some way covered by Section 223.4 on theft by extortion, but only for the purpose of compelling the employer to pay wages which the employee believes to be due. If the employee acted with the prescribed belief in his right to acquire the property "as he did," he would not be guilty of theft although he might be punishable under other sections of the Code for assault or coercion.

Unlike the case of Subsection (3)(a), Subsection (3)(b) provides a defense that can in no instance be derived from the definition of the theft offenses set forth in this article. It is thus a supplementary defense to any defense of mistake that might exist and is premised on the view that a genuine belief in one's legal right should in all cases be a defense to theft. Persons who take only property to which they believe themselves entitled constitute no significant threat to the property system and manifest no character trait worse than ignorance. Moreover, this position is not inconsistent with prior law. The decisions rejecting the defense represent, in the main, instances of extremely incredible claims. A trial court need not give an instruction with regard to a defense for which no credible testimony is adduced, and a jury need not believe the defendant in cases where there is such an instruction and where the defendant offers testimony that it regards as untruthful. Juries can be trusted to reject incredible claims. If there should be criminal liability for recklessness or negligence in cases where property is wrongfully obtained under a claim of right, or if there should be strict liability in such cases, this should be accomplished elsewhere than in a statute defining "theft." No such offense is included in the Model Code.

(c) *Property Exposed for Sale.* Subsection (3)(c) articulates a kind of privilege of self-service for *bona fide* customers. Most of the situations to which the provision would be applicable would fall outside theft in any event, on the ground that the owner's real or supposed consent brought the behavior within the scope of Paragraph (b). This might be the case, for example, where a customer helps himself to a newspaper from a stand without leaving his coin because he has no cash smaller than a $10 bill, or a regular patron of a shop who, finding no one in the store free to wait on him, walks off with the desired article meaning to return the next day to pay. But Paragraph (c) goes beyond these cases, precluding prosecution for theft where consent of the owner can actually be negated, as where the news vendor has on previous similar occasions made it clear to the actor that no papers are to be taken without payment. An actor who disregards such an injunction ought nevertheless not be regarded as a thief. His purpose is not in any sense fraudulent since he intends

[97] Yoder v. State, 208 Ind. 50, 194 N.E. 645 (1935).
[98] Hunter v. State, 158 Tenn. 63, 12 S.W.2d 361 (1928).

to pay promptly and, by hypothesis, the vendor is willing to part with the goods in exchange for payment. . . .

In limiting Paragraph (c) to the taking of property exposed for sale, any broad proposition that intention to pay is always a defense to theft has been rejected. It would clearly be unwise to permit the defense of intent to pay when a man obtains goods by a false credit statement, or a fiduciary "borrows" money or securities from the estate, or a depositor persuades a bank cashier to honor overdrafts after the bank president has denied him credit. . . .

COMMENT TO § 223.1(4)

5. *Theft from Spouse.* Existing law offers a diversity of solutions to the problem of criminal liability for stealing from a spouse. The common-law rule against liability survives in some states. A larger number of states have abolished or narrowed the common-law immunity by judicial decision, on the ground that the Married Women's Property Acts and the changed position of women in modern society call for treating her as an individual independent of her husband in property concerns. Under Canadian legislation, theft from a spouse may be prosecuted only if the parties are not living together and were not living together at the time of the alleged offense, except that theft committed while the parties were living together may be prosecuted if the actor was "about to leave or desert." In England, recent legislation has abolished interspousal theft immunity, although any prosecution must be specifically approved by the Director of Public Prosecutions. The penal codes of the civil law countries go so far as to exclude punishment for theft not only in the case of spouses, but also as between parents and children, less immediate ancestors and descendants, and other relatives living in a common household.

Various theories of legislation have been advanced in this area. The common-law immunity is defended on the ground that prosecution undermines the unity of the family. On the other side, it has been argued that the theft itself and the desire of one spouse to prosecute the other indicate that the family unit has already been disrupted. Moreover the family-unity theory has never been regarded as sufficient reason to bar prosecution of a spouse for non-property offenses such as assault and battery, and civil litigation between spouses with respect to property is authorized everywhere.

A second theory is that prosecution for theft from a spouse should be restricted because of the danger of miscarriage of justice. Interspousal bitterness makes the complainant's testimony especially unreliable. The actual ownership of much household property is often a matter of uncertainty, depending on informal gifts, and it will be difficult in many cases to ascertain whether the owner had or had not given his consent to, or broadly tolerated, certain kinds of misappropriation.

A third view would exclude family theft from the criminal law because misappropriation in this context is so generally tolerated that the actor cannot be regarded as deviating significantly from social norms. Household belongings, particularly, are often regarded as a common pool of wealth. Husbands and wives rifle each other's wallets. They each may pawn valuables which are technically owned by the other. A person who confines his depredations to such incidents does not threaten the property security of the community, like an ordinary thief. There is some feeling also that the possibility of depredations by a spouse is part of the risk one assumes in matrimony.

Finally, there is a belief that the criminal courts are unsuited to handle the family quarrels of which theft complaints are a symptom; that these controversies require the intervention of social agencies more commonly associated with courts handling domestic relations cases; and that in a large proportion of cases the complainant eventually abandons his original interest in jailing the accused, so that prosecution becomes impossible in any event.

Subsection (4) rejects the rule of immunity for theft from a spouse except for misappropriation of household and personal effects occurring while the parties are living together. The exception covers the situations where ownership may be matter of uncertainty or where customary disregard of strict ownership rights makes it inappropriate and dangerous to permit theft prosecutions. On the other hand, it seems necessary to preserve the possibility of prosecution in cases such as the following: (i) *H* misrepresents certain worthless securities which he owns, and thus induces *W* to accept them in exchange for valuable land which she has inherited from her father; (ii) *H* is trustee for *W* under the will of *W*'s father and embezzles $10,000 of bonds from the estate; (iii) *W* removes $10,000 of *H*'s negotiable bonds from his office safe and gives the proceeds to her needy brother or lover.

A majority of the recently revised codes and proposals do not incorporate special provisions on interspousal theft. Those that do contain a special provision are evenly divided between continuing a broader form of the immunity and following the substance of Subsection (4).

COMMENT TO § 223.2

6. *Purpose to Deprive.* Subsection (1) requires for theft of movable property that the actor have a purpose to "deprive" another of an interest in the property. The term "deprive" is defined in Section 223.0(1) to include permanent deprivations as well as certain instances in which the actor does not intend to deprive permanently or unconditionally.

Although the common-law definition of larceny was often formulated in terms of an intent to deprive permanently, convictions were sustained upon evidence that fell considerably short of proving a purpose totally and finally to deprive another of his property. Thus, it was held that a jury might find an intent permanently to deprive on the basis of evidence that the offender took the property for temporary use without intending to return it and abandoned it under circumstances that amounted to a "reckless exposure to loss." Where the intent to return was contingent on payment of a reward or on repurchase by the owner, the jury was permitted to find an intent to deprive permanently on the theory that the objective was to deprive permanently if the owner refused to pay the reward or other demand. The fact that restoration to the owner is contingent, as when the taker pledges the property, has also been held to support conviction for larceny. There is disagreement in the cases on whether a workman paid on a piecework basis could be convicted of theft where he took finished articles belonging to his employer and presented them as the product of his own effort for the purpose of increasing his wages.

Under the definition of "deprive" in Section 223.0(1), a conviction for theft would be possible in each of these situations. Also covered is the case where the actor intends to return the property without exposing it to risk of loss in the meantime but also intends to withhold it "for so extended a period as to appropriate a major portion of its economic value." For example, a person would be guilty of theft under subsection (1) if he surreptitiously "borrows" his neighbor's lawn mower for the summer, intending to return it in the fall when it would no longer be needed or useful. It would likewise be theft to take tires, a battery, radioactive substances, or other similar goods with a limited useful life, even though the actor intended to return the item taken after a prolonged use that substantially dissipated its value to the owner. On the other hand, unauthorized borrowing or use of personal property is excluded from the offense where the period is not so extended as to appropriate a major portion of its economic value or in cases where the use or disposition of the property does not make it unlikely that the owner will recover its beneficial use. Unauthorized use of automobiles and other vehicles is treated separately in Section 223.9.

Subsection (1)(b) of Section 223.0 is of course primarily designed to take account of the embezzlement case where at the time of taking the actor intends to return or pay back the money, though he plans to spend it in the meantime. The bank teller who loses the proceeds of his embezzlement at the racetrack will thus have disposed "of the property so as to make it unlikely that the owner will recover it." No new ground is broken in including such conduct within the coverage of provisions on theft.[33]

One final point about the definition of "deprive" should be noted. Section 220.3 punishes as criminal mischief conduct designed to destroy or damage the tangible property of another. It would plainly be unwarranted also to prosecute for theft in a case where, for example, the actor picked up a valuable vase preparatory to breaking it. Such cases would be excluded from theft by the requirement in the definition of "deprive" that the actor "withhold" property or "appropriate" a major portion of its economic value. Simple destruction or damage to property does not involve an "appropriation" of the property to the use or benefit of the actor. Similarly, the provision in Subsection (1)(b) of Section 223.0 dealing with disposing of the property in a manner that will make it unlikely that the owner will recover it is likewise intended to exclude destructive conduct. The provisions against theft contemplate cases where the actor uses the property for his own purposes. Close cases may arise, as where the defendant takes property, uses it for his own purposes for a while, and then destroys it when discovery is imminent, or where the defendant takes property in order to sell to a junkyard, knowing that the purchaser will destroy it in order to recycle it to another use. Such cases appropriately can be punished as theft, and the definition of "deprive" will not prevent a proper prosecution. . . .

COMMENT TO § 223.3

1. *General Scope.* Section 223.3 covers that portion of the consolidated offense of theft that derives from the traditional offense of obtaining property by false pretenses. There is some force to the view that a separate section is unnecessary if the overriding purpose is to consolidate and simplify the law of theft. Language of the sort included in Section 223.2 may be adequate as it stands to reach the conduct encompassed by a false-pretenses statute or could easily be amended to reach such conduct. There are, however, a number of special problems that have arisen in the administration of false-pretenses statutes. The problems concern chiefly specification of the kinds of deception that should be

---

[33] At common law, intent to return the very property taken (*e. g.*, a wagon) after a short period of time negated the required intent, while intent to restore equivalent property (*e. g.*, different dollar bills) was no defense to embezzlement, even where the money was actually restored before the conversion was discovered. *See* W. LaFave & A. Scott, Criminal Law 653-54 (1972).

sufficient to support conviction. It is desirable that these questions be resolved by legislation and suitable that this be done in a separate section.

The offense is defined to include one who "purposely obtains property of another by deception." The term "obtain" is defined in Section 223.0(5), as is discussed below. The terms "property" and "property of another" are defined in Subsections (6) and (7) of Section 223.0 and are discussed in the commentary to Section 223.2. The concept of "deception" is elaborated upon in Paragraphs (1) through (4) and in the last sentence of Section 223.3. This concept is also discussed below.

The section adopts a comprehensive definition of criminal fraud. The term "deception" has been substituted for "false pretense or representation." The substituted term includes misrepresentations of value, law, opinion, intention, or other state of mind, as well as certain cases where the actor knowingly takes advantage of another's misinformation, though he may not be responsible for it. There is no requirement that the deception be material or, except in the one instance noted below, that it be of such a character as would have deceived a reasonable man. It suffices for conviction that the deception was effective, whether alone or with other influences, in securing the property for the actor. Of course, a conviction is not necessarily precluded if the deception is ineffective. If the actor engages in conduct designed to deceive another for the purpose of obtaining his property but either does not obtain the property or does not obtain it as a result of the deception (as where the intended victim knows the truth), there would be liability under Section 5.01 of the Model Code for attempt.

Theft by deception under Section 223.3 requires proof of purpose. The actor must have the purpose to obtain the property of another, and he must have a purpose to deceive. If the actor believes in the accuracy of the impression he seeks to convey, he will not be guilty of a violation of Section 223.3 even if his belief is unreasonable. On the other hand, Paragraph (1) makes it clear that the actor's own state of mind may be the subject of the deception. It is not necessary for the prosecution to prove that the defendant affirmatively disbelieved the representations he made. If he creates the impression that he believes something to be true when in fact he has no belief on the subject, he has purposely deceived as to the state of his mind.

2. *Obtains.* Section 223.0(5) defines "obtain" to mean, in relation to property, "to bring about a transfer or purported transfer of a legal interest in the property, whether to the obtainer or another." Theft by deception is thus a crime designed to regulate the methods by which the transfer of a legal interest in property is achieved. It is not an offense designed to safeguard possession, nor does it protect against the use of deception to gain temporary possession or control of property or to continue a possession or control that was lawfully acquired.

It should be noted, however, that the fact that deception is used to gain possession or control does not foreclose prosecution under the consolidated theft offense in cases where a subsequent conversion occurs. Section 223.2 would cover a person who gained temporary control over property by misrepresenting the purpose for which he wanted it and who then "exercises unlawful control" over the property "with purpose to deprive." For example, a person who "borrows" a lawn mower and then sells it will not be guilty of violating Section 223.3, because his deception, though perhaps a misrepresentation of intention, did not cause the owner of the lawn mower to transfer a legal interest to the actor. However, the actor, although a lawful possessor of the lawn mower, is privileged to do only that which is consistent with the permission given; if he sells the lawn mower and pockets the proceeds, he violates Section 223.2(1). Moreover, since the consolidated theft offense is to be charged as a single offense under Section 223.1(1), this technical distinction between the coverage of Sections 223.2 and 223.3 should not result in acquittals caused by prosecutor error in selecting the original charge.

Importantly, however, transfers of temporary or possessory interests in property will not be criminal, even though accomplished by deception, unless they threaten the interests protected by Section 223.2. The actor must unlawfully take or exercise unlawful control with purpose to deprive or he must obtain a legal interest in the property by deception. Conduct short of this will not be theft. It will be noticed, moreover, that Section 223.3 does not distinguish between movable and immovable property. The focus of Section 223.3 on transfer of a legal interest makes such a distinction unnecessary in this context. Sections 223.2 and 223.3 thus work together to protect both movable and immovable property from unlawful appropriation. . . .

3. *Deception.* Paragraphs (1) through (4) and the last sentence of Section 223.3 define the term "deception" as it is used in this offense. It has been noted above that the term is intended broadly to include the many kinds of behavior that can amount to the obtaining of property by deception. Some of the specific implications of the Model Code use of the term are dealt with below.

(a) *Creating or Reinforcing a False Impression.* The traditional definition of a false pretense was the making of a false representation of fact. Language covering one who "creates or reinforces a false impression" has been substituted for the common-law concept. So far as the term "creates" is concerned, no substantive change is contemplated. The early cases construing the germinal English false-pretenses statute recognized that deceptive non-verbal behavior was within the statute. These holdings are carried forward by the Model Code formulation. Schemes designed to create a false impression in the mind of the actor should thus be included even though there has been no false representation in the sense of affirmative statements that are in fact untrue.

Paragraph (1) also reaches the reinforcement of a false impression that the victim may have entertained prior to any intervention by the actor. While it may not be said that the actor "created" the impression in such cases, the actor will be guilty of a violation of Section 223.3 if he confirms the false impression by his affirmative conduct or statements and thereby induces the victim to part with the property. Mere failure to correct a known misimpression that is influencing the owner of property would not amount to "reinforcing," except in the situations specifically covered in Paragraphs (3) and (4). Any affirmative contribution to the misimpression, however, may suffice.

Since this may prove to be a point of some subtlety in particular cases, it merits elaboration. Assume a sale of costume jewelry, which, unknown to the seller, contains a real and valuable diamond. Clearly, there should be no criminal liability if the buyer discovers after his purchase that the jewelry greatly exceeds in value the price he paid. Equally clearly, criminal liability should be possible if the buyer knows of the diamond and affirmatively represents to the seller that he is an expert, has examined the stones, and can confirm that they are only glass. Here, though the buyer may not have "created" the false impression, he surely has "reinforced" it by his deceptive statements. The difficult cases will arise where the buyer's conduct falls short of the clear and affirmative misrepresentation illustrated above but nevertheless might be viewed as an affirmative contribution to the misapprehension by the seller, if only by silence in the face of probing questions. Cases of this sort will inevitably arise. It does not seem suitable, however, to seek to resolve them in advance by a more specific rule of law. The statute either must exclude completely the reinforcement of a pre-existing false impression, a solution that allows the clever to evade the law, or it must rely on prosecutors, judges, and juries properly to apply the general principle that affirmative reinforcement of false impressions should in the main be included within the reach of theft by deception.

It should also be noted that it is the falsity of the *impression* purposely created or reinforced that is determinative, rather than the falsity of any particular representations made by the actor. Thus, deception may be accomplished by statements that are literally true or that consist of a clever collection of half-truths, *i. e.,* statements that may be literally true but that are nevertheless misleading because of the omission of necessary qualifications. . . .

(d) *No Pecuniary Significance.* The last sentence of Section 223.3 excludes certain types of misrepresentation from the scope of the section. The first excluded category is falsification as to matters having no pecuniary significance, *e. g.,* where a salesman misrepresents his political, religious, or social affiliations. Such misrepresentations may succeed in securing the buyer's patronage and in that sense it could be said that whatever is paid for the purchase is money obtained by deception. But the injury done to the buyer is not a property deprivation of the sort that should be condemned and punished as theft, since the deceived person secures exactly what he bargained for in the way of property. It seems clear, therefore, that such misstatements should be the subject of a specific exclusion from the law of theft.

This is not a case, such as misstatement of opinion or value or affirmative reinforcement of a false impression, where a statutory exclusion for deserving cases will also exclude from coverage cases where there should be liability. The irrelevance of such misrepresentation to the underlying purpose of the provisions on theft, *i.e.,* to protect against misappropriation of property interests, clearly points to a blanket exclusion. Approximately half of the recently enacted and proposed codes contain such an exclusion. Maine, on the other hand, explicitly provides that lack of pecuniary significance is no defense to a charge of theft by deception.

(e) *Puffing.* The second category of misrepresentation excluded by the last sentence of Section 223.3 precludes conviction of theft on the basis of "puffing by statements unlikely to deceive ordinary persons in the group addressed." Puffing is sometimes viewed as exaggerated commendation of a seller's wares "in terms which neither side means seriously" in a setting where both parties to the bargaining process are aware that reliance upon the literal statements is not expected. If this were the extent of the problem, a special exemption might not be needed, since the alleged deceiver could defend on the ground that he had not purposely sought to create a false impression. Indeed, since the phrasing of the exemption is in terms of statements unlikely to deceive ordinary persons "in the group addressed," in some puffing situations the defense will go forward on this basis.

The problem becomes more complicated, however, when considered in the context of mass advertising, and it is to this situation that the statutory exclusion is primarily addressed. Advertising frequently includes statements and suggestions that most will recognize as not intended to be taken literally or seriously, but that could be regarded as purposely intended to create a false impression in the minds of a certain proportion of gullible persons. The exemption in Section 223.3 is accordingly restricted to communications addressed to groups of persons, such as public advertising, in terms which will not deceive the "ordinary person" in the group. In that situation, where the message cannot be formulated according to the intellectual or critical capacity of the individual reader or hearer, it would be unfortunate to require communication in terms suitable only to the most dense member of the audience or to condemn as theft what most people would regard as, at worst, improper trade practices to be controlled by civil remedies. On the other hand, criminal penalties may well be appropriate in some situations of mass communication. There is no intent to immunize, for example, schemes that represent that the mailing of money will result in the return of property never intended to be sent or misrepresentations of fact designed to induce a purchase of worthless products.

About half of the recently drafted codes and proposals contain a provision exempting "puffing." A few define the practice in terms only slightly more elaborate than the Model Code, *e.g.*, "puffing means an exaggerated commendation of wares or worth in communications addressed to the public or to a class or group." The remainder substantially track the language of the Model Code.

(f) *Fraudulent Nondisclosure.* Paragraphs (2), (3), and (4) incorporate into the concept of punishable fraud certain cases where the actor does not purposely create or reinforce a false impression but where he either interferes with the victim's acquisition of relevant information or fails to correct the victim's misimpression in circumstances giving rise to a duty of affirmative disclosure.

Taking advantage of a known mistake that is influencing the other party to a bargain is not criminal under existing law in the absence of special circumstances imposing a duty to correct the mistake. The miner who discovers that his mine is nearly exhausted of ore may sell it to a stranger although he is fully aware that the stranger is buying under the mistaken belief that the property is still valuable as a mine. The prospector who discovers oil under the land of a stranger may buy the land without informing the stranger of his discovery although he knows that the stranger was satisfied by previous tests indicating there was no oil on the property.

Section 223.3 does not attempt to make this behavior criminal, primarily because the borderline between desirable and disapproved behavior in this area is so ill-defined that criminal sanctions are likely to impinge on conduct well within the bounds of approved commercial activity. For example, suppose a "book scout" finds what appears to be a rare edition in a dusty attic, and pays the unwitting owner 25 cents, hoping to resell to a rich bibliophile for $100. There is no community consensus on whether he should be obliged to disclose his opinion to the original owner that the volume was worth $10 or to the bibliophile that it was worth no more than $25. The book scout's argument, that when he is not retained as appraiser or counselor he should not be required to volunteer valuable professional opinion, would be received favorably in many quarters. Before resolving this as a matter of the criminal law, inquiry would have to be made into the extent to which book-scouting as a trade can survive only if this kind of transaction is tolerated, how important it is to preserve the trade, and so forth. This kind of elaborate balancing is beyond the appropriate purview of a penal statute.

However, in the situations covered by Paragraphs (2), (3), and (4) of Section 223.3, liability may be imposed without jeopardizing normal business practices and without entering the field of controversial moral obligations. Interference with the victim's sources of information, as by bribing his advisers or concealing data that would otherwise have been available, clearly constitutes a case for penal deterrence as provided in Paragraph (2). Paragraph (3) imposes an affirmative duty to correct false impressions of the victim only where the actor has previously contributed (however innocently) to the creation of the false impression or has such a relationship with the victim that the latter would be entitled to count on the actor to inform him fully and honestly. Paragraph (4), requiring disclosure of known liens and adverse claims against property that the actor is selling or mortgaging, falls well within common conceptions of moral obligation, although the courts have had difficulty in bringing such non-disclosure within false pretenses legislation, especially where the undisclosed adverse claim is of doubtful validity. Such cases should, however, be included within the coverage of provisions on theft by deception. . . .

COMMENT TO § 223.4

1. *General Scope.* This section deals with situations where threat rather than force, deception, or stealth is the method employed to deprive the victim of his property. Related offenses in present law are designated as extortion, blackmail, demanding by menaces, and, in some cases, robbery. As in the case of theft by deception, it is arguable that a separate section dealing with theft by extortion is not necessary and that the conduct covered in this section is either already covered or could easily be covered by amendment to Section 223.2. Again, however, there are a number of special problems that merit separate treatment.

The offense of theft by extortion is committed if the actor "purposely obtains property of another" by any one of a series of threats that are specified in Paragraphs (1) through (7). "Obtain" is defined in Section 223.0(5) and is discussed in the commentary of Section 223.3. "Property" and "property of another" are defined in Subsections (6) and (7) of Section 223.0 and are discussed in the commentary to Section 223.2. It is therefore necessary here to discuss only the nature of the threats that may qualify as a violation of this section.

The list of threats that may sustain a charge of extortion is comprehensive but not unlimited. In general it conforms to prevailing law at the time the Model Code was drafted, although broader provisions can be found. Threats to commit crime or accuse of crime are included, as well as threats to expose secrets that will injure another in specified ways. Also specifically included are threats to take or withhold official action, threats to engage in concerted action such as a strike when the benefit of the group that engages in the concerted action is not at stake, and threats to testify or withhold testimony with respect to legal claims or defenses. Finally, a residual provision is added, covering in general terms a threat to "inflict any other harm which would not benefit the actor."

Behavior prohibited by this section is closely analogous to that proscribed as criminal coercion under Section 212.5. There is considerable overlap between the threatened conduct covered by the two sections; the major difference lies in the purpose and effect of the coercive and extortionate threats. Criminal coercion punishes threats made "with purpose unlawfully to restrict another's freedom of action to his detriment," while extortion is included within the consolidated offense of theft because it is restricted to one who "obtains property of another by" threats.

Most recent codes and proposals also contain separate theft-by-extortion sections limited to obtaining property by threatening to inflict harm. A few, however, adopt a comprehensive provision covering both "coercion" and "extortion." As the commentary to the Minnesota code states:

[T]he crime of extortion as conceived in American statute law seems to be broader than . . . [Section 223.4] and is not confined to the receipt of money or property. In principle the offense seems to be equally great whenever the victim is forced by means of a threat to do anything against his will. Likewise, the crime is equally reprehensible when the victim suffers loss without gain to the defendant.

This approach was not adopted in the Model Code both because it was thought desirable to confine more narrowly the threats that may suffice for coercion and because the grading of the two offenses should respond to different concerns.

There are two other issues of a general nature that should be addressed. It is necessary in an extortion statute to consider "claim-of-right" situations, either where the actor is seeking to obtain specific property to which he believes himself entitled or where the actor is applying pressure because he believes himself entitled to compensation or some other benefit from another. Examples would be the case of a union engaged in lawful picketing for the purpose of seeking higher wages for its members or an accident victim attempting to pressure his supposed tortfeasor into an out-of-court settlement. Such cases are dealt with by the claim-of-right defense provided in Section 223.1(3), by exclusions of certain types of threats from the offense of extortion, and by the special defense stated in the last sentence of the section. The complexities of this issue are dealt with in Comment 2 below.

The second general point relates to culpability. Like the other specifications of forms of theft, theft by extortion is a crime of purpose. Some of the recently drafted codes and proposals have left this point to implication. There are at least three explicit variations. Several require that the actor "knowingly" acquire property by threats and others that he "purposely" or "intentionally" do so. There are also a number of codes that require the actor to obtain the property of another by threats "with intent to deprive him thereof" or with some other specific purpose.

2. *Nature of Included Threats.* There are several general points that should be mentioned as a prelude to discussion of the specific threats that are described in Paragraphs (1) through (7). Consideration of the specifics of these paragraphs will then be undertaken. Discussion of the last sentence of the section will be considered in connection with the particular paragraphs as relevant.

(a) *Implicit Threats.* It should be clear that the threat need not be express. The language of Section 223.4 is intended to cover implicit as well as explicit extortionate threats. It is sufficient, for example, that the actor ask for money in exchange for "protection" from harms where the actor intends to convey the impression that he will in some fashion instigate the harm from which he proposes to "protect" the victim. The threat may also be implicit from the situation, as where a policeman who has announced his intention to effect an arrest asks for money and releases the suspect from custody on receiving it. The section also covers oral as well as written threats, as did prevailing law.

While most recent codes and proposals follow the Model Code use of such general terms as "threaten," about a third add words that indicate more specifically the intent to include verbal and implied threats. The most common variation is a provision covering threats or menaces "however communicated." Other codes explicitly include threats whether oral or written or whether communicated "directly or indirectly."

(b) *Threats to Others.* Although many jurisdictions require that the threat be to harm the person from whom property is demanded or members of his family, Section 223.4 covers threats to injure anyone. If the threat is in fact the effective means of compelling another to give up property, the character of the relationship between the victim and the person whom he chooses to protect is immaterial. Whether a threat to injure a third person unrelated to the victim was actually effective for that purpose, or, in a prosecution for attempt, whether it was intended to be effective, can be decided by the jury or other trier of fact in the particular case. There is no justification for providing as a matter of law that threat of injury to a third party can never intimidate or that the provisions on extortion can be evaded by finding a victim who will respond to such threats. No defendant should escape liability for an effective intimidation on the ground that persons other than the chosen victim would not have been intimidated. Though the idea is expressed in different language, this judgment is supported by every recent code and proposal that has been examined.

(c) *Threats of Confinement or Restraint.* As originally proposed, the provision on theft by extortion covered threats to "subject any person to physical confinement or restraint." The list of threats included in the original provision was consolidated in the Proposed Official Draft to the form in which Section 223.4 now appears, though no change in content was intended. Most threats to subject any person to physical confinement or restraint are included in Paragraph (1), as, for example, a threat to kidnap in violation of Section 212.1 or otherwise to restrain in violation of Article 212. Paragraph (7) reaches additional cases. For example, a policeman who threatens an arrest in exchange for money would fall within language of Paragraph (7), even though the arrest was not only lawful but required by law. The benefit to the policeman from making the arrest, if any, is not the kind of benefit that would preclude application of Paragraph (7) to his conduct.

Over a dozen recent codes and proposals contain specific provisions covering threats to subject anyone to physical confinement or restraint. A few others explicitly cover threats to kidnap.

(d) *Unlawful Harm.* There is no requirement in Section 223.4 that the threatened harm be "unlawful." The actor may be privileged or even obligated to inflict the harm threatened; yet, if he employs the threat to coerce a transfer of property for his own benefit, he clearly belongs among those who should be subject to punishment for theft. The case of the policeman who has a duty to arrest illustrates the point. His threat to arrest unless the proposed subject of the arrest pays him money should be treated as extortionate even though the failure to arrest would be dereliction of duty. Statutes that require the threatened harm to be unlawful have given rise to difficulties and conflicting interpretations. The limitation was given effect in *People v. Schmitz* [22] in which the defendant, the mayor of San Francisco, was convicted of extortion on evidence that he obtained money from a restauranteur by threatening to appear before the licensing authority in opposition to the restauranteur's application for a license. The conviction was reversed on the ground that the proposed opposition was not unlawful. The New York courts, on the other hand, substantially nullified the statutory requirement of unlawfulness of the threatened behavior in dealing with the statute in force prior to the 1967 revision. In *People v. Sheridan* [23] the defendant was an elevator operator who

---

[22] 7 Cal.App. 330, 94 P. 407 (1st App.Dist.1908).

[23] 186 App.Div. 211, 174 N.Y.S. 327 (1919). *Cf.* People v. Hughes, 137 N.Y. 29, 32 N.E. 1105 (1893) (union official convicted where he obtained money under threat of continuing union boycott); People v. Barondess, 133 N.Y. 649, 31 N.E. 240 (1892).

obtained money from the prosecuting witness as the price of not reporting a defect in the latter's business elevator. In affirming an extortion conviction, the Appellate Division stated that it was no defense that the elevator was in fact defective and that it was the defendant's duty to report it: "The unlawfulness lies in the motive." [24] Since the statute had no application to a defendant whose motive was not extortion, to permit this motive to make a threatened injury "unlawful" is obviously to deprive the requirement of unlawfulness of any independent significance. Some statutes have addressed this issue by requiring that the threatened injury be "malicious," a term that invites conviction in cases where the courts are willing to find an evil motive. Almost all of the recently drafted codes and proposals follow the Model Code in not requiring that the threatened action be unlawful.

(e) *Bodily Injury or Criminal Offense.* Paragraph (1) covers threats of criminal attack on person or property but goes beyond most prior formulations in reaching a threat to commit any criminal offense. The language makes it clear, for example, that the section applies to a threat to detain a person under circumstances that would amount to kidnapping or false imprisonment and to a threat to operate a house of prostitution, perhaps as competition to another illicit operator who pays money to preserve his monopoly. As noted above, the threat is included even though the victim of the threatened offense is someone other than the person of whom money or other property is demanded. . . .

Most recent enactments and proposals follow the Model Code by including threat of any crime and by not including threat of any unlawful conduct. Most contain more elaborate specification, as, for example, express proscription of a threat to "cause damage to property." Such specification is unnecessary, however, if all crimes are included.

It should perhaps be added that general claim-of-right provision of Section 223.1(3) apply to this paragraph, as well as to other formulations of theft under this article. Some recent enactments and proposals have excluded claim-of-right situations from threats to do personal injury or to commit a crime, on the ground that such conduct is never to be tolerated. The view of the Model Code, however, is that statutes dealing with improper acquisitive behavior should be inapplicable to cases where the actor's method of obtaining property is objectionable but his objective is not. Thus, for example, a person who believes himself entitled to money or other property from another, such as unpaid wages, should not be guilty of extortion if he uses threat of bodily injury or other crime to collect the money believed to be due and if he honestly believes that he has a right to acquire the property by the method employed. Instead, such conduct should be dealt with under the provisions of Article 211 and 212. Thus, an actor who commits the offense of assault, reckless endangerment, or criminal coercion is not immunized because he sought to employ such techniques to enforce an honest claim to property, even though he may have a claim-of-right defense to extortion. The Model Code solution on this point has been accepted by a substantial minority of recent codes and proposals.

(f) *Accuse of Crime.* Legislation dealing with an extortionate threat to accuse of crime was common at the time the Model Code was drafted. Typically, it did not matter whether the accusation was true or false. Paragraph (2) covers obtaining property of another by a threat to accuse another of crime and follows prior law in making truth or falsity irrelevant. The Model Code

---

[24] 186 App.Div. at 213, 174 N.Y.S. at 329.

also adheres to the notion developed above that the accusation should be sufficient even though the person who would be accused of crime is not the same person from whom money or other property is demanded. The vast majority of recent codes and proposals contain specific provisions on threats to accuse another of crime. Many are broadly worded so as to include instilling fear that the extortionist will "cause criminal charges to be instigated" against another in ways other than by making a direct accusation.

The last sentence of Section 223.4 was added to assure that certain legitimate threats to accuse another of crime will not be regarded as extortionate. The sentence provides that it is an affirmative defense that "the property obtained by threat of accusation [of crime] ... was honestly claimed as restitution or indemnification for harm done in the circumstances to which such accusation ... relates, or as compensation for property or lawful services." This was added ... in order to assure that one who had a civil complaint for damages against another could not be convicted of extortion for threatening during negotiations to file a criminal charge. Specific provision of this sort may be unnecessary, given the general claim-of-right provision of Section 223.1(3), but the explicit provision firmly establishes the intention not to intrude into what many regard as legitimate negotiating tactics. On the other hand, one who claims more than he believes is due could not claim the benefits of either defense. The claim-of-right provision in Section 223.1(3) is triggered by an honest belief that the actor was entitled to act as he did; the last sentence of Section 223.4 is triggered by an honest claim of restitution or indemnification. Neither would be applicable to an intentionally excessive demand.

The New York code contains a similar specific claim-of-right defense, with the additional proviso that "the defendant reasonably believed the threatened charge to be true." This proviso is unfortunate, importing as it does a negligence standard as the basis for the serious offense of extortion. Most of the recently enacted or proposed codes do not contain a special provision comparable to the last sentence of Section 223.4. There are some that do, however, as well as others that relegate the matter to a general claim-of-right provision similar to Section 223.1(3).

(g) *Expose Secrets.* Paragraph (3) covers extortion by threat to "expose any secret tending to subject any person to hatred, contempt, or ridicule, or to impair his credit or business repute." As originally drafted, the extortion provision of the Model Code contained three separate paragraphs relating to such conduct. These paragraphs dealt with threats to "expose any person to hatred, contempt or ridicule," threats to "harm the credit or business repute of any person," and threats to "reveal any secret." The consolidation of these provisions into the language in Paragraph (3) changes their coverage in two respects, although, as is noted below, the conduct excluded from Paragraph (3) by this change is picked up again in Paragraph (7).

First, it would be possible to "expose any person to hatred, contempt or ridicule" without at the same time exposing any secret, just as it would be possible to "harm the credit or business repute of any person" in ways other than by revealing secrets. An example would be the threat to emphasize a prior criminal record of another for the purpose of extorting money, in a context where the prior criminal record was generally known and thus could not be said to be a "secret." While such conduct might not be thought to violate Paragraph (3) because it did not involve the revealing of a "secret," it would violate Paragraph (7) as a threat to "inflict any other harm which would not benefit the actor." The "benefit" to the actor to which this language refers, as is elaborated below in the commentary on Paragraph (7), does not include the illegitimate acquisition of property by threats to harm another person.

The second way in which the consolidation might be thought to limit the coverage of Section 223.4 relates to the exposure of secrets that do not have the effects described in Paragraph (3). This can be illustrated by the following cases. First, A discloses to B in confidence that A plans to build a factory at X, requiring a large-scale land-acquisition program. B then threatens to reveal the information publicly, thus causing land prices to rise, unless A pays him not to do so. Second, C, who works in D's factory, threatens to reveal D's secret unpatented processes to D's competition unless D pays him money not to do so. Neither of these cases would be covered by Paragraph (3) as now worded, since the threatened damage would not impair the credit or business repute of the victim and would not hold the victim up to hatred, contempt, or ridicule. Again, however, both cases would fall within the general coverage of Paragraph (7), and the net effect, therefore, is not a contraction of overall coverage.

The applicability of the general claim-of-right defense and the provisions of the last sentence of Section 223.4 should also be noted with respect to this paragraph. Threat of exposure may be thought to be a legitimate negotiating technique in situations where the claimant has an honest expectation of restitution, indemnification, or compensation; at the least it is a technique the morality of which should not be resolved by the criminal law of theft.

Finally, it should be added that the exposure of secrets or defamatory information was often listed among the extortionate threats that could be penalized in legislation existing at the time the Model Code was drafted and is commonly included in the newer statutes and proposals that have been drafted since the publication of the Model Code. Paragraph (3) employs terms broader than those used in prior law in referring to threats to expose a person to hatred, contempt, or ridicule. Many earlier statutes were limited to particular imputations, such as "deformity" or "disgrace." This broad view has been accepted generally in the modern statutes following the Model Code. In fact, most modern statutes utilize language even broader than that of the Model Code. Several focus on the threatened result of exposing "any person to hatred, contempt or ridicule" but eliminate the Model Code requirement that the means be through exposure of any secret. Many other codes explicitly proscribe threats to "expose a secret or publicize an asserted fact, whether true or false, tending to subject some person to hatred, contempt or ridicule." These variations have the advantage of providing explicit coverage of behavior that will fall within the general prohibition of Paragraph (7) but that perhaps should be covered specifically in order to avoid possible misconstruction. There is, in any event, no dispute as to the desirability of reaching such conduct as extortion.

These statutes also reflect a general acceptance of the point that the threat need not be to expose publicly. It is enough that the victim is coerced by the prospect of hostile reaction to exposure, whatever it may be and to whomever it might be made, so that he parts with property in order to prevent it.

(h) *Official Action.* Paragraph (4) speaks to situations where the threat is to take or withhold official action or to cause an official to take or withhold action. The typical case covered by this provision is extortion under color of office, as where an elevator inspector or tax collector threatens to report violations of law unless he is paid. A threat to bring about adverse official action may also be made by one who is not himself an official, as where a political leader threatens to use his power over officeholders to the disadvantage of a person who refuses to pay him. Although in a sense the threat of an ordinary layman to file a criminal complaint or a civil based upon injuries done him might be said to fall within Paragraphs (2) or (4), there is no danger that Paragraph (4) would prevent a *bona fide* claimant from making such threats in connection with an effort to secure restitution or indemnification, since the last sentence of Section 223.4 specifically provides an affirmative defense in such situations.

It should also be noted that a threat to bring about adverse official action if money or other property is not paid lies close to the offense of bribery. Indeed, the same transaction may well constitute both crimes. The difference between the two offenses is that extortion requires an element of intimidation that need not be present in the case of bribery. Some recent proposals have sought to prevent problems of mischarging by explicitly precluding the defense to extortion that the victim was a willing participant and the element of intimidation thus was not present. No similar provision is included in the Model Code, although it is meant to be clear that the crimes are not mutually exclusive. The relationship between the two offenses is examined in detail in Comment 10 to Section 240.1, to which reference should be made.

Most of the new codes and proposals include language similar to Paragraph (4). A few, however, reach only threats by public officials or employees and thus exclude threats by person who have political influence and other means of causing official action to be taken. . . .

(i) *Concerted Action.* Paragraph (5) reaches the threat of collective unofficial sanctions where, for example, an official of a trade association or union is lining his own pocket by employing the coercive power that he is supposed to wield on behalf of his organization. It would also apply where a representative of a consumer group threatened to picket or boycott a store or business unless payments were made to induce him to withhold such action. This conduct obviously needs to be distinguished from situations where a demand is made on behalf of the organization and in order to achieve benefits to which the organization itself may be entitled. Paragraph (5) thus includes the threat only "if the property is not demanded or received for the benefit of the group in whose interest the actor purports to act." Where the demand is on behalf of the organization, the paragraph does not apply even though the demand may go beyond any honest claim of right. Such cases are excluded from extortionate threats because it would be unwise to subject these bargaining processes to the risk of criminal sanctions, where guilt might well turn on nice questions of what is a "lawful objective" of a strike or other similar concerted activity.

Most recent codes and proposals incorporate a provision similar to Paragraph (5). Many do not, however, and some of these also lack a counterpart to residual provision in Paragraph (7). The result is to omit any coverage of this activity.

(j) *Testify or Withhold Testimony.* Paragraph (6) goes beyond most prevailing legislation at the time it was drafted in proscribing extortionate threats to give or to withhold testimony in civil or criminal matters. This provision has been followed, however, in most recent codes and proposals. . . .

(k) *Any Other Harm.* Any particularization of criminal threats is bound to be incomplete. Paragraph (7) thus provides that a threat to "inflict any other harm which would not benefit the actor" is also sufficient to constitute theft by extortion. About half of the recent enactments and proposals have recognized the need for such a residual category. Some states have followed the Model Code language, while others have adopted a provision based on the New York formulation. . . . There are also some statutes that contain the specific threats listed by the Model Code but omit a residual clause. The result is a narrowing of coverage that seems clearly undesirable. Finally, there are a number of states that include additional specific categories of threats, some of which would be subsumed under Paragraph (1) and others under Paragraph (7) of the Model Code. . . .

It may be helpful if some illustrations are given to indicate the kinds of cases that come within Paragraph (7). One would be the case of the foreman in a manufacturing plant who requires the workers to pay him a percentage of their wages on pain of dismissal or other employment discrimination. Another would be the friend of the purchasing agent of a large corporation who obtains money from an important supplier by threatening to influence the purchasing agent to divert his business elsewhere, or the variation where the purchasing agent himself insists on personal payments by means of the same threat. The section would even apply to a law professor who obtains property from a student by threatening to give him a failing grade or to influence a prospective employer to hire someone else.

The employer in the first illustration (at least with respect to wages) or the corporation itself in the second would not be within the scope of Paragraph (7) if it made the same threats, because the employer has a recognized interest in minimizing wages paid and the buyer a recognized interest in reducing the cost of supplies. Their freedom to press for these advantages may, of course, be restricted by other laws requiring a minimum wage, adherence to contractually stipulated wage scales, or forbearing from price discrimination, but such conduct should not be included within the laws of theft.

The phrase "which would not benefit the actor" is thus meant to preclude a theft prosecution where the purpose of the threat is to secure economic benefit — the obtaining of property — for which the actor may have some claim. The claim need not be legitimate in the sense that the actor believes that he has a claim of right to the property that would trigger the provisions of Section 223.1(3). An actor whose behavior is reached only by Paragraph (7) would escape criminal conviction if he shows a legitimate interest even though his demand be excessive or unreasonable. The line is thus drawn between one who in an economic bargaining context attempts to maximize his own advantage and one who attempts to use his position, status, or knowledge, or any other unique characteristic of a situation, to his own personal advantage. It is impossible to catalogue in advance all of the situations in which this might occur and hence desirable that a general principle should be stated to inform the prosecutors and the courts of the nature of the line that must be drawn.

COMMENT TO § 223.5

1. *Background and Purpose.* Theft penalties are not imposed on persons who merely learn of the whereabouts of lost property but do not assume some control over it. If it is desirable to provide criminal sanctions for the failure to communicate helpful information to the owners of lost property, this should be done by separate legislation not carrying the moral imputation of theft or the potentially severe sanctions traditionally associated with it. On the other hand, those who find property and assume more than casual control over it are, under certain circumstances, appropriate subjects of prosecution for theft.

Section 223.5 includes as theft the failure to take reasonable measures to restore lost, mislaid, or misdelivered property to its owner with the intent to deprive the owner of the property. Traditional theft law was applied to such conduct only with great difficulty. Common-law larceny was in theory confined to trespassory interference with possession of the owner, a concept difficult to apply in the case of a finder who appropriated a lost article. The courts nevertheless extended larceny to finders by using the fiction that the owner retained "constructive" possession of lost property — or at least of "mislaid" property that was intentionally deposited by an owner in the place where it was found by the actor. Section 223.5 eliminates the largely irrelevant issue of whether the owner remains in "possession" of lost or mislaid property. It seems obvious that the guilt of a taker of "found" property should not turn on whether the owner intentionally put the property where it was found. The gist of the offense is not a putative wrong in the actor's method of acquisition of the property but a purposeful appropriation without taking reasonable steps to restore the article to the owner. Section 223.5 accordingly applies whether the property is property described as "lost" or "mislaid."

The provision with respect to property "delivered under a mistake as to the nature or amount of the property or the identity of the recipient" deals with situations which are even more difficult to fit into traditional larceny than are the lost-property cases. For example, one who accepts a $10 bill knowing that the other person thinks he is handing over a $1 bill acquires it without trespass or false pretense. Moreover, he may not be in any of the employee or fiduciary relations that were enumerated in the typical older embezzlement statutes. Consequently, special legislation or judicial sleight-of-hand was required to reach persons taking advantage of such mistakes. Similarly, if the owner or his agent voluntarily hands the property over to the accused while laboring under a misapprehension as to the identity of the recipient, it requires strenuous manipulation of concepts to disregard the apparent transfer of title as well as possession and to hold that the accused is guilty of larceny because he committed a trespass against the transferor's possession. A prosecution for false pretenses may also be frustrated because the actor may not have created or reinforced the misimpression. Yet the recipient, knowing that the transfer to him is inadvertent, is in a moral and physical situation with respect to the property much like that of the finder of lost property. Moreover, he knows who is rightfully entitled to the property and can easily take steps to restore the property. Accordingly, Section 223.5 imposes theft sanctions against one in this situation who fails to take reasonable measures to restore. Most recent codes and proposals also specifically cover theft of misdelivered property. Some, however, are restricted to theft of lost or mislaid property.

It is necessary to limit the reach of Section 223.5, on the other hand, in order to avoid impinging on certain types of tolerated sharp trading. For example, it is not proposed to punish the purchase of another's property at a bargain price on a mere showing that the buyer was aware that the seller was misinformed regarding the value of what he sold. The language of Section 223.5 is accordingly limited to situations where the mistake is as to "the nature or amount of the property or the identity of the recipient."

It could be argued that the conduct covered by Section 223.5 is already adequately reached by the language in Section 223.2(1) relating to one who "exercises unlawful control over" property of another "with purpose to deprive him thereof." The advantage of explicit coverage, on the other hand, is that the conceptual difficulties with applying traditional larceny or embezzlement law to these situations can unmistakably be discarded. As noted, traditional theft law generally had reached such conduct only by manipulation of antecedent concepts. There is every reason to continue the trend of inclusion without at the same time posing the analytical subtleties that traditional law required.

Finally, it should be noted that the terms "property," "property of another," and "deprive" are defined in Section 223.0. Each of these terms is discussed in the commentary to Section 223.2.

2. *Culpability.* The prosecution must prove under this section that the defendant knew the property was lost, mislaid, or delivered under a mistake as to the nature or amount of the property or the identity of the recipient. Among the recent codes and proposals, it appears that only Oregon omits the requirement of knowledge and in effect imposes liability for negligence by defining the offense to include one "who comes into control of property that he knows or has good reason to know to have been lost, mislaid" or misdelivered. In addition to the requirement of knowledge under the Model Code, the actor must have a purpose to deprive the owner of the property and must know that he has failed to take reasonable measures to restore the property to a person entitled to have it. Thus, appropriation of property that the taker believes to be abandoned would not be theft. Nor would it be theft to assume or retain control of lost property with purpose to restore to the owner, even though it might be said that the finder had not acted with reasonable dispatch to restore the property. Negligence is not a proper basis of liability for theft. Several recent proposed and enacted codes require an intent to deprive the owner permanently of the possession, use, or benefit of the property. Georgia and Minnesota omit an explicit requirement of intent to deprive and instead focus on the fact that the actor appropriates property to his own use without first taking reasonable measures to restore the property to its owner.

The common-law view of larceny as an infringement of the possession of another required a determination of the actor's state of mind at the moment of finding. An honest state of mind at that point would preclude the felony conviction. Moreover, the subsequent formation of a purpose to deprive would not be criminal since the actor would already be in possession. The search for an initial fraudulent intent appears to be largely fictional, and in any event poses the wrong question. The realistic objective in this area is not to prevent initial appropriation but to compel subsequent acts to restore to the owner. The section therefore permits conviction even where the original taking was honest in the sense that the actor then intended to restore; if he subsequently changes his mind and determines to keep the property, he will then be guilty of theft. Similarly, the section bars conviction where the finder acts with reasonable promptness to restore the property, even though he may have entertained a purpose to deprive at the time he acquired the property or at some other time during his possession. Section 223.5 thus focuses on the operative event of a purpose to deprive accompanied by the failure to take reasonable measures to restore. . . .

COMMENT TO § 223.6

1. *Background and Purpose.* Section 223.6 incorporates into the law of theft the traditionally distinct crime of receiving stolen property. This innovation has been adopted by a majority of the recent codes and proposals.

The need for a separate offense of receiving stolen property is apparent when considered against the other possible theories of prosecution traditionally available. The historic restriction of larceny to a crime of "trespass" against another's possession excludes the receiver, who does not himself commit a trespassory taking but acquires the property by voluntary delivery from the original thief.

Embezzlement and false pretenses also were defined in terms of a relationship between the possessor or owner of property and the person who makes the initial appropriation. Furthermore, ordinary conceptions of accomplice liability would not make the receiver liable for the original taking, unless he aided or abetted the commission of that crime. Nor, unless he tried to frustrate law enforcement by harboring the thief or assisting his escape, would the receiver be guilty as an accessory after the fact to the original theft. Even if he were, moreover, he would normally be subject to lesser sanctions than those available for the thief. It is easy to understand, therefore, why traditional doctrine required that receiving stolen property be punished as a distinct and separate offense.

Yet both analytical and practical grounds suggest that receiving should be assimilated to theft. Analytically, the receiver does precisely what is forbidden by Section 223.2(1) — namely, he exercises unlawful control over property of another with a purpose to deprive. From a practical standpoint, it is important to punish receivers in order to discourage theft. The existence and functioning of the "fence," *i.e.,* a dealer who provides a market for stolen property, is an assurance to thieves, and especially to professional thieves, of the ability to realize gain from their unlawful activity. It is also frequently difficult to differentiate those who take from those who hold stolen property for disposition, and it is therefore not uncommon for prosecutors to charge suspected thieves with both taking and receiving.

Consolidation of receiving with other forms of theft affords the same advantages as are involved in other aspects of the unification of the theft concept. Consolidation reduces the opportunity for technical defenses based upon legal distinctions between the closely related activities of stealing and receiving. One who is found in possession of recently stolen goods may be either the thief or the receiver. If the prosecution can prove the requisite state of mind to deprive the true owner of the property, it makes little difference whether the jury infers that the defendant took directly from the owner or acquired the goods from another person who committed the act of taking. Consolidation also has a consequence favorable to the defense by precluding conviction of both offenses for the same transaction. Under prior law, multiple liability occasionally occurred, as where the defendant was held guilty as a principal in the original theft for helping to plan that crime and also of the "separate" offense of receiving for taking his share of the proceeds. . . .

4. *Culpability.* Section 223.6 requires a culpability of "purpose" with respect to the element defined by the phrase "receives, retains, or disposes of movable property of another." It also provides that this action must be taken "knowing that it [the property] has been stolen, or believing that it has probably been stolen, unless the property is received, retained, or disposed with purpose to restore it to the owner." Subsection (2) then details instances in which this requisite knowledge or belief is presumed to exist. This language disposes of a number of issues related to culpability that warrant separate treatment.

(a) *Knowledge or Belief Without Purpose to Restore.* Theft convictions generally require a purpose to deprive another of his property. In terms, Section 223.6 does not require such a purpose for criminal receiving, but the net effect of its provisions is the same. First, the actor either must know that the property has been stolen or must believe that it probably has been stolen. Second, the actor's receipt, retention, or disposition of the property is criminal, unless his conduct is undertaken "with purpose to restore it [the property] to the owner." Since a purpose to restore defeats conviction, and since the prosecution must establish beyond a reasonable doubt that the actor did not have such a purpose, the culpability required under Section 223.6 can properly be assimilated to a purpose to deprive the victim of his property. As a practical matter, the absence of a purpose to restore will be proved by showing that it was part of the receiver's plan to avoid detection and to realize for himself the benefits of the property. Though stated differently in order to accommodate the elements of the receiving offense, the culpability required by Section 223.6 is thus consistent with the culpability otherwise provided for theft in Article 223.

American receiving statutes in effect at the time the Model Penal Code was formulated typically adopted the language of the original English statute, which required that the actor know of the stolen character of the property at the time he received it. Taken literally, this requirement of knowledge could mean that the receiver must know the details of each of the elements of conduct and culpability that make up the offense of the original thief. Such a requirement would of course impose an impossible burden on the prosecution, for it is unlikely that the receiver would know or be interested in the precise particulars of the original theft [12] and even more unlikely that the prosecutor could uncover evidence of such awareness. For this reason, "it is everywhere held that positive knowledge is not required." [13]

The Model Code statement of the offense in terms of the receiver's belief that the goods have probably been stolen completely avoids this problem. The receiver need not "know" of the details of the theft, nor need he be certain that a theft has in fact occurred. It is sufficient, as it should be, that the receiver holds himself out to receive, retain, or dispose of property that "probably" has been stolen and that he is aware of that probability. Formulation of the culpability standard in these terms is both an accurate description of the person who should be treated as a criminal receiver and a provable criterion of liability.

Recent codes and proposals are sharply divided among three basic approaches to the question of required culpability for criminal receiving. About a third continue the requirement that the receiver "know" that the property in question is stolen property. A slight plurality agree with the Model Code judgment that knowledge or belief "that it has probably been stolen" is the appropriate standard. The remainder adopt the position taken by some older statutes and penalize receiving with "reasonable grounds for believing the property stolen," thereby imposing liability for negligence. The proposed federal criminal code as enacted by the Senate imposes liability for recklessness with regard to the fact of receiving property "that has been stolen."

COMMENT TO § 223.7

1. *Background.* Common-law larceny and traditional false-pretense statutes have generally been limited to the taking of property. Though arguably viewed as a species of "property," labor or professional services has not been included within the traditional scope of that term in ordinary theft statutes. Theft of services thus was not ordinarily a criminal offense in the absence of special legislation. . . .

---

[12] *See* United States v. Werner, 160 F.2d 438 (2d Cir. 1947), per L. Hand, J.: "The receivers of stolen goods almost never 'know' that they have been stolen, in the sense that they could testify to it in a court room. . . . Nor are we to suppose that the thieves will ordinarily admit their theft to the receivers: that would much impair their bargaining power," quoted in W. LaFave & A. Scott, Criminal Law 685 n.32 (1972).

[13] *Id.* at 685.

2. *The Offense.* Section 223.7 defines "services" to include labor; professional service; transportation; telephone or other public service, such as gas or electricity; accommodations in hotels, restaurants, or other similar establishments; admission to exhibitions, such as athletic contests, musical performances, and the like; and the use of vehicles or other movable property. The term "services" is defined to include these specified services but is not limited to them. Anything that can be classified as a service that the actor "knows is available only for compensation" falls within the reach of the section. While this broad definitional approach has been followed by most recent enactments and proposals, a few provisions are limited to specified kinds of services.

One consequence of the assimilation of theft of services to theft in general is that the offense will be graded according to the amount involved. In most situations, *e. g.,* defrauding hotels and restaurants, using slugs in telephones and vending machines, or evading transportation and admissions charges, the small sums involved will result in classification of the offense as a petty misdemeanor carrying a maximum term of imprisonment for 30 days. Higher maxima were common in the general theft-of-services statutes in force before the Model Penal Code was drafted, but no reason appears for punishing defrauding of services more severely than theft of tangible property of equivalent value. Most new codes and proposals follow the Model Code approach and grade theft of services according to the amount involved. Several, however, grade theft of services as a misdemeanor regardless of the value of the services obtained or diverted. Since the amount involved in most thefts of services is small, this scheme results in higher penalties than those authorized by the Model Code in many cases. In large-scale theft of services, of course, the punishment is less severe under these statutes.

Section 223.7 goes beyond most prior legislation in two significant respects. Subsection (1) deals with securing services by "threat" as well as by deception, and Subsection (2) covers the equivalent of embezzlement in relation to services. The approach to theft of services is intended to be as broad as the comprehensive definition of theft of property in Article 223. The elaboration of deception and threat in Sections 223.3 and 223.4, as well as the comprehensive scope of the embezzlement and larceny counterparts in Section 223.2, thus is fully applicable to the theft of services. One respect in which this formulation expands the law existing at the time the Model Penal Code was drafted relates to embezzlement of services, where services paid for by one person are diverted without his consent to the benefit of some other person not entitled thereto. Recently promulgated codes and proposals are in basic agreement with the inclusiveness of Section 223.7 in regard to its coverage of obtaining services by threat. A majority of recent codes and proposals also include provisions covering diversion of services.

The presumption of fraud established by the last sentence of Subsection (1) was not uncommon in prior statutes dealing with hotels and inns. Section 223.3(1) specifically includes deception as to intention or other state of mind, and that provision would be read as a part of Section 223.7. Deception as to intention to pay is a natural inference from the conduct that is stipulated to give rise to the presumption. The effect of the presumption is elaborated in Section 1.12(5) of the Model Code. . . .

COMMENT TO § 223.8

1. *Background and Scope.* Section 223.8 is designed to bring within the law of theft certain situations that traditionally have occasioned difficulty. The problem arises whenever the actor's behavior arguably constitutes merely a breach of contract rather than a misappropriation of property of another. Section 223.8 recognizes that in some situations one who promises to make certain payments or other disposition of property should be punished for dealing with the property as his own. At the same time, the section does not purport generally to substitute criminal prosecution for civil remedies under the law of contract. The challenge, therefore, is to distinguish default that would be assimilated to theft from non-performance that should be left to the traditional remedies for breach of contract. . . .

2. *Elements of the Offense.* The conduct proscribed under Section 223.8 consists of essentially two elements: (i) the obtaining of property upon an agreement or subject to a known legal obligation to make a specified payment or other disposition, whether from the property obtained or its proceeds or from one's own property to be reserved in an equivalent amount; and (ii) dealing with the property as one's own and failing to make the required payment or disposition. A culpability of "purpose" applies to each of these elements. There is also specific language making the section applicable notwithstanding that it may be impossible to identify particular property as belonging to the victim at the time of the failure to make the required payment or disposition. The section concludes with a series of presumptions applicable to government officials and fiduciary employees. Each of these elements warrants further elaboration.

(a) *Circumstances of Acquisition.* As noted above, Section 223.8 requires that the actor "obtain" the property, and Section 223.0(5) defines "obtain" in the narrow sense of bringing about a transfer of a legal interest in the property. . . .

(b) *Agreement or Legal Obligation.* Section 228.8 applies to one who takes the property upon agreement or legal obligation "to make specified payment or other disposition, whether from such property or its proceeds or from his own property to be reserved in equivalent amount." It is explicitly required that any legal obligation to this effect be known. The inclusion of the word "purposely" before "obtains" imposes the same requirement with respect to the terms of an agreement by virtue of the provisions of Section 2.02(4).

As is noted in Comment 1, the extent to which ordinary contract law is invaded by the section will in large part be determined by the explicitness of the agreement and the extent to which a specific, fiduciary-like reservation is required. It is plain that these words should be narrowly construed so as to confine the operation of the section to cases that are distinguishable from violations of Section 223.2 only in the sense that there may be difficulties as to method of acquisition or control over the property. . . .

(c) *Disposition of the Property.* Section 223.8 provides for theft penalties if the actor "deals with the property obtained as his own and fails to make the required payment or disposition." It is also specifically provided that this result obtains even though it may be impossible to identify specific property as belonging to the victim at the time of the failure to pay or make appropriate disposition. By operation of Section 2.02(4), the purpose requirement of the provision extends to each of these elements.

The words "deals with the property as his own" are designed to import the element commonly referred to by other statutes as conversion. It is enough if the actor commingles the funds with his own and otherwise treats the property as though it were not subject to the specific obligation that has been undertaken. Mere carelessness, moreover, does not suffice. The actor must know that he is not living up to his agreement and must purposely deal with the property as his own and fail to make the required payment or disposition. An appropriate way to limit the extent to which this language might yield unwarranted extensions of the law of theft would be to read it to be the substantial equivalent of the "purpose to deprive" that is required by Section 223.2(1). A strict reading of the required culpability together with a strict requirement of segregation of funds should effectively minimize the number of contract situations to which the provision can be applied. . . .

(d) *Presumptions.* The last sentence of Section 223.8 states two presumptions applicable to an officer or employee of the government or a financial institution. Such persons are presumed to know any legal obligation that is relevant to liability under this section. They are also presumed to have dealt with the property as their own if there is a failure to pay or account upon lawful demand or if an audit reveals a shortage or falsification of accounts.

As set forth in Section 1.12, the effect of a presumption under the Model Code is to shift the burden of production of evidence but not the burden of persuasion. It seems appropriate to cast the burden of explanation on the employee or public officer on these occasions, perhaps even in prosecutions for ordinary embezzlement. . . .

3. *Additional Provisions.* The Institute took no position with regard to certain statutes penalizing additional categories of default, *e.g.,* failure to pay wages or failure of a commission merchant to pay the consignor. To the extent that these are conceived as regulations of the manner in which business shall be carried on, they belong in regulatory codes and should not entail the severe sanctions that accompany a conviction for theft. The Institute also took no position on the desirability of sanctions for public officers and other officials who engage in conduct violative of regulations designed to safeguard funds in their custody. Again, however, theft penalties are inappropriate, and the sanctions should be regulatory in nature.

COMMENT TO § 223.9

1. *Background and Scope.* Nearly all states have legislation penalizing unauthorized taking, use, or operation of motor vehicles. These laws are designed to reach temporary dispossession. The typical situation dealt with is the "joyride," *i.e.,* the taking of another's automobile without his permission, not for the purpose of keeping it but merely to drive it briefly. The offense is typically committed by young people, and the car is generally recovered undamaged. Such behavior would not amount to larceny, which, as traditionally defined, requires proof that the actor intended to deprive the owner permanently. Under the Model Penal Code, theft may be committed not only where the actor contemplates permanent dispossession of the owner but also where the actor contemplates deprivation for an extended period of time or a disposition of the property under circumstances that make recovery by the owner unlikely. Nevertheless, there is still need for a non-felony sanction against the disturbing and dangerous practice of driving off a motor vehicle belonging to another. Such joyriding jeopardizes the vehicle itself, a considerable amount of temptingly mobile property, and, since the circumstances are conducive to irresponsible behavior in the operation of the vehicle, jeopardizes the lives of the riders and others.

The question arises whether to extend the principle of the section so as to penalize temporary deprivation of movable property other than motor vehicles. A few state statutes impose misdemeanor penalties for the unauthorized use of any movable property. Under such a law, a girl would be a criminal if she wore her roommate's dress to a party without the roommate's consent. This extension of criminal liability is rejected because it goes beyond prevailing moral notions and cannot be justified as necessitated by the dangerousness of the behavior. A better case can be made for extending Section 223.9 to non-motor vehicles, *e.g.,* sailing craft, bicycles, air gliders, and horses or other animals that can be ridden or driven. Section 223.9 was not extended to such behavior for several reasons: lack of evidence of any substantial social problem from the temporary misappropriation of these categories of property, unwillingness to make crimes out of petty infringements of property rights, availability of other penal sanctions where the owner suffers a loss, and availability of theft penalties where the deprivation, though temporary, is of substantial duration or highly likely to prevent safe recovery by the owner.

The overwhelming majority of recent codes and proposals contain provisions similar to Section 223.9. While a plurality are limited to motor-propelled vehicles, others use language covering aircraft and boats or "any vehicle." A few specifically include animals that can be ridden or driven.

2. *Operates.* Legislation in effect when the Model Code was drafted typically designated the prohibited conduct as taking, using, or operating without the consent of the owner. The single term "operates" was selected for Section 223.9. "Taking" would ordinarily have application only to activities preliminary to operation. Such preliminary conduct could be punished as an attempt under Section 5.01 of the Model Code. On the other hand, there would be no substantive objection against making a comparable section expressly applicable to taking as well as operating. If the legislature chooses to bring animals within the scope of such a prohibition, the terms "take" or "use" would seem appropriate.

To penalize a non-operational "use" of a vehicle without the owner's consent, however, would extend the section beyond its rationale. A man who climbs into a parked truck in order to conceal himself from the weather or to sleep is not using the vehicle in any way that involves the dangers of "joyriding." A closer question is presented by the case of the non-operating passenger in a vehicle that is being operated without the owner's consent. There should be reluctance to authorize the conviction of a young person whose sole connection with the transaction is to accept a ride in a car taken and operated by another. The deterrent purposes of the law would seem to be served, on the other hand, by prosecution of the operator and those who can be held responsible as accomplices in the operation of the vehicle. A possible intermediate position would be to provide a presumption that all persons in a vehicle being operated without the owner's permission are accomplices in such operation. There seems to be no strong case, however, for extending liability beyond the accomplice provisions that otherwise will be fully applicable....

COMMENT TO § 224.5

1. *Background and Scope.* At the time this section was drafted, some 48 states had legislation supplementing the ordinary laws of theft and false pretenses in the context of bad checks.[1] There seem to have been four main reasons for this

---

[1] *See* F. Beutel, Experimental Jurisprudence ch. X to ch. XIII (1957), summarizing the statutes of all states in a table at 282-85 and proposing a Model Bad-Check Statute at 419. The study is

development: first, elimination of the necessity of proving that property was obtained by means of the check, as would be required under a theft or false-pretenses statute; second, circumvention of the limitation in false-pretenses law that a false promise is not a punishable misrepresentation; [2] third, creation of a presumption under certain circumstances of fraudulent purpose or knowledge that the check would not be paid; and fourth, establishment of more severe grading, particularly for what would otherwise be petty theft, for certain types of bad-check offenses.

The theft provisions of the Model Penal Code eliminate the second reason entirely and attenuate the first. Fraudulent promises are expressly brought within the offense of theft by deception as defined in Section 223.3(1). Moreover, the term "property" is broadly defined in Section 223.0(6) so that many situations not conventionally regarded as the "obtaining of property" are brought within the scope of the theft offenses. For example, the deposit of a worthless check resulting in a credit to the depositor's account would be an obtaining of property,[3] as would extinction of a pre-existing debt in exchange for a bad check.

It nevertheless still seems desirable to cover the issuance of bad checks in a separate provision. The case for a presumption of fraudulent purpose or knowledge would apply even to the most common transaction where goods or services were obtained by the use of a worthless check. Similarly, the case for upgrading bad-check offenses beyond the penalties available for petty theft is unaffected by other provisions of the code. Moreover, it seems appropriate to reach the issuance of bad checks in situations where property is not obtained thereby, as in the case of a gift. One who issues a bad check under such circumstances knows that, although he is not cheating the recipient, the check is likely to be negotiated for cash, credit, or property and thus will have an adverse impact on ordinary commerce.

Section 224.5 therefore has three major objectives. The most important is to establish for bad-check situations presumptions that can be used in prosecutions for the misdemeanor offense defined here or for the felony offense of theft by deception in cases where large amounts of money or property are involved. Additionally, Section 224.5 focuses upon the issuance or passing of a bad check with the requisite knowledge and thus eliminates any requirement that property be obtained. Finally, the offense is graded as a misdemeanor even where the amount involved is very small. Statutes accomplishing these objectives have been consistently included in recently revised codes and proposals. In contrast to the Model Penal Code, however, some new codes limit bad-check statutes to situations where property is directly obtained.

2. *Culpability and Presumptions.* Section 224.5 aligns itself with those pre-existing bad-check laws that defined the criminal state of mind as knowledge that the check will not be paid rather than as an intent to defraud. Knowledge that the check will not be paid seems adequate for the misdemeanor offense defined here. Prosecution for theft by deception, accompanied both by higher culpability levels and more severe sanctions remains available where significant

---

reviewed in Cavers, Science, Research and the Law: Beutel's "Experimental Jurisprudence," 10 J.Leg.Ed. 162 (1957). *See* also R. Perkins, Criminal Law 315-18 (2d ed. 1969); Note, 14 Miami L.Rev. 486 (1960).

[2] A check could be regarded as merely a promise that the drawer's bank will pay.

[3] For contrary case law, see Immel v. State, 228 Md. 566, 180 A.2d 703 (1962) (no property is obtained when actor has not yet drawn upon a fraudulently obtained bank credit).

property rights are involved. The lower culpability level is a common feature of recently drafted bad check laws. Several new codes, however, continue to require an intent to defraud or its equivalent.

The second sentence of Section 224.5 establishes in two situations a presumption that the actor knows the check will not be paid, namely where the issuer of the check had no account with the drawee at the time the check was issued and where payment was refused for lack of funds and the issuer refused to make prompt payment. The latter instance is qualified by a requirement of presentation within 30 days after issuance and by the provision of a 10-day period during which the issuer has the opportunity to satisfy the obligation. The presumptions do not apply in cases of a post-dated check or order.

As noted above, the presumption of knowledge is probably the most important practical reason for retaining special bad-check provisions. Consider the position of the hotel keeper or merchant who finds that a check is drawn on a ficititious or inadequate account. In the fictitious-account situation, it is highly improbable that the transaction was innocent. In the case of checks on real but inadequate accounts, the chance of innocent miscalculation by the drawer is much greater but is ordinarily negatived by a refusal to make the check good. The amounts involved may be small, and the drawer may be a transient against whom swift action must be taken. It seems entirely appropriate to create a basis for swift action and for prosecution without requiring proof of fraudulent objective, putting the burden on the issuer to come forward with some evidence of innocent mistake.

Recently drafted bad-check provisions have in general accepted presumptions structured in this manner. A few states have also accepted the important corollary that the presumptions should be applicable to theft prosecutions where significant sums of money are involved. New York and New Hampshire have eliminated from the presumption the provision of a 10-day period during which the issuer has the opportunity to satisfy the obligation. Instead they have made payment within 10 days an affirmative defense. Kansas, which requires the higher culpability level of intent to defraud, achieves a similar purpose to that of the Model Penal Code by allowing the presumptions to be *prima facie* evidence of intent to defraud.

3. *Grading.* Section 224.5 classifies the offense as a misdemeanor. At the time it was drafted, most existing statutes graded the offense as a felony, at least where the amounts involved exceeded a specified minimum. It seems unlikely that felony sanctions will afford any particular advantage in dealing with bad-check situations, especially in light of the availability of felony conviction under Section 223.3 in cases where the offender obtains property in excess of $500 by means of one or a series of bad checks. In cases where the amount involved is less than $50, the offense is graded as a misdemeanor rather than as a petty misdemeanor, as would theft of such amounts by deception. Maintaining the integrity of this type of document warrants special treatment of this form of deception even though the amounts involved may be very small. Most recent legislation on this subject has accepted misdemeanor grading for the separate bad-check offense. Some states still classify the offense as a felony if the face value of the check exceeds a certain amount. Kansas has authorized a higher penalty for habitually passing worthless checks.

COMMENT TO § 224.6

1. *Purpose.* This section is based on legislation enacted in a number of states to deal with fraudulent use of a relatively new credit device. It fills a potential gap in the law relating to obtaining property by false pretenses. Sections 223.3 and 223.7 of the Model Code cover the theft of property or services by deception. It is questionable whether they reach the credit card situation because the user of a stolen or cancelled credit card arguably does not obtain property or services by means of any deception practiced on the person providing the property or services. The actor's implicit representation that the issuer of the card will reimburse the merchant is true: the seller will collect from the issuer of the credit card because issuers assume the risk of misuse of cards in order to encourage sellers to honor the cards readily. Thus, it is the non-deceived issuer who is the victim of the practice.

Most new criminal codes and proposals have included a separate offense addressing the subject of credit-card fraud. Additionally they have added new sections which cover the theft or forgery of a credit card itself. Several states, however, have not dealt separately with stealing a credit card or theft with a credit card but have included the offenses covered by Section 224.6 under general theft statutes.

2. *Elements of the Offense.* Section 224.6 provides that it is an offense to use a credit card for the purpose of obtaining property or services with knowledge that the card is stolen, forged, revoked, cancelled, or for any other reason unauthorized. Some new codes have followed the Model Penal Code in not requiring any criminal state of mind beyond knowledge that use of the card is unauthorized. However, most new codes, as well as many older statutes, require an "intent to defraud."

The definitions of such terms as "property," "services," and "obtains" in Section 223.0 are made applicable to this section by Section 224.0. The term "credit card" is defined in the third sentence of Section 224.6 itself. That definition provides that a "credit card" is a "writing or other evidence of an undertaking to pay for property or services delivered or rendered to or upon the order of a designated person or bearer." This would seem to apply only to the use of an actual card that evidences an obligation on the part of the issuer. It would not appear to cover the situation where a person uses a fictitious number on a mail-order form or gives a fictitious telephone credit card number to an operator. Many new codes have explicitly covered these situations in legislation against credit card fraud.

Section 224.6 distinguishes between the use of stolen, forged, revoked, or cancelled cards, on the one hand, and use of cards outside the authorization of the issuer, on the other. The second sentence of the section gives the actor an affirmative defense in the latter case upon proof by a preponderance of the evidence that he had the purpose and ability to meet all obligations to the issuer arising out of his use of the card. The situations chiefly contemplated were those of the holder of an expired credit card and those where the user exceeded credit limits established by the issuer. Cards are readily renewable and credit limits easily exceeded. It seems undesirable to penalize good-faith use of a card by one to whom it has been issued merely because he has delayed or omitted some minor step required to perfect or maintain his right to continue to use the credit of the issuer or because he has failed adequately to keep track of all charges previously incurred.

Only two states have followed the Model Penal Code in providing an affirmative defense for good-faith use. Those states that include "intent to defraud" as an element of the offense presumably rely on this *mens rea* requirement to cover these situations.

3. *Grading.* The grading of the credit card offense as a felony of the third degree where the amount involved is over $500 and otherwise as a misdemeanor parallels the grading for theft and bad-check passing. As in the case of bad checks, the offense is not reduced to the level of a petty misdemeanor even when the amount involved is quite small. The rationale, in the case of both credit cards and checks, is that these methods of defrauding lend themselves to repeated violations by transients so as to undermine reliance on useful credit mechanisms. . . .

COMMENT TO § 240.1

1. *Scope.* Section 240.1 classifies bribery as a felony of the third degree. The offense reaches both the person who offers, gives, or agrees to give a bribe in an official or political matter and the public servant or other covered individual who solicits, accepts, or agrees to accept a bribe. As is explained below, the three subsections of the offense are designed to deal in some particularity with a series of difficult problems that were not commonly faced in bribery legislation prior to the drafting of the Model Penal Code.

The offense covers the bribery of many persons other than full-time employees of government. It includes bribery of advisors and consultants to government, bribery of voters and political party officials, and bribery of any one who exercises official discretion in a judicial or administrative proceeding. Jurors, for example, are specifically included. The offense does not, however, cover witnesses. Section 241.6 deals with witness bribery along with other illegitimate efforts to influence the conduct of a witness. The Model Code also deals separately with bribery unrelated to a governmental function or proceeding. Specifically, Section 224.8 covers bribery of persons who hold themselves out to the public as disinterested appraisers of commodities or services, and Section 224.9 adds a prohibition against rigging a publicly exhibited contest. . . .

Although the elements of the bribery offense are discussed below in detail, it may be appropriate here to summarize the impact of Section 240.1 on logrolling activity. Paragraph (1) limits to a "pecuniary benefit" the kind of offer that cannot be made to a public official in exchange for his vote or other exercise of official discretion. Section 240.0(6) defines "pecuniary benefit" to mean something the primary significance of which is economic gain. Thus, an exchange of legislative votes or other political favors of primarily non-economic significance is excluded from the definition of the offense.

Paragraph (2), on the other hand, prohibits the offering of "any benefit" as consideration for the exercise of official discretion in the context of a judicial or an administrative proceeding. The term "benefit" is defined quite broadly in Section 240.0(1). The term "administrative proceeding" is defined to include any proceeding "the outcome of which is required to be based on a record or documentation prescribed by law, or in which law or regulation is particularized in application to individuals." Thus, the trading of votes in judicial or administrative hearings is prohibited as bribery.

Paragraph (3) extends the prohibitions against logrolling by prohibiting the offer of any benefit for the violation of a known duty by a public servant or a party official. The effect of this provision is to prohibit the trading of votes or other logrolling that leads a public servant to violate the specific duties of his office as opposed to a general obligation of fidelity to the public interest or other implicit moral obligation. Thus, specific obligations imposed on a public servant by statute, administrative regulation, or executive order cannot knowingly be violated in exchange for any "benefit."

Finally, the term "benefit" as defined in Section 240.0(1) excludes "an advantage promised generally to a group or class of voters as a consequence of public measures which a candidate engages to support or oppose." This provision, derived from Paragraph (a) of the original draft, excludes from all three paragraphs of the bribery offense campaign promises and other similar undertakings that candidates traditionally promise and occasionally perform. . . .

4. *Conduct and Culpability.* The operative language with respect to each of the paragraphs of the offense of bribery is that one is guilty "if he offers, confers or agrees to confer upon another" any benefit or pecuniary benefit, as the case may be, "as consideration for" prescribed conduct by the bribe recipient. The bribe recipient is also covered if he "solicits, accepts or agrees to accept from another" the prescribed benefit "as consideration for" his official action. The language of the statute contains no explicit statement of the required culpability. Under Section 2.02(3), this silence might be thought to indicate that "recklessness" is the operative culpability with respect to each of the elements of the offense. As the following discussion explains, however, the question is more complex than a mechanical application of Section 2.02(3) would suggest.

(a) *Offers or Solicits as Consideration for.* The offense of bribery is defined in a manner that includes a completed agreement between the person who offers the bribe and the person who receives it. It also permits prosecution of inchoate conduct intended to achieve that objective. The terms "offers" and "solicits" clearly refer to such inchoate behavior and are designed to include what might be regarded as an attempt to give or to receive a bribe.

The term "solicits" is intended to be interpreted consistently with the meaning of the concept in Section 5.02. That section states that a person is guilty of solicitation to commit a crime if, "with the purpose of promoting or facilitating its commission," he "commands, encourages or requests" another person to engage in conduct that would constitute the offense. Section 5.02(2) specifically provides that a failure of communication is no defense if the actor's conduct was designed to effect communication. Section 5.02(3) establishes a renunciation defense, suitably circumscribed to assure that the abandonment is voluntary and complete and that it is manifested by conduct that prevented commission of the solicited offense.

In the context of bribery, one who "solicits" a benefit "as consideration for" his official conduct is thus one who, with the purpose to promote or facilitate his receipt of a benefit in exchange for his official action, commands, encourages, or requests another person to supply the benefit. Both the foreclosure of the defense of failure of communication and the availability of the renunciation defense would be fully applicable to bribery within the limitations set forth in Section 5.02.

The solicitation aspect of the offense is thus, in effect, a crime of purpose; the actor must have as his conscious objective the receipt of a benefit as consideration for official conduct on his part. The term "offers" as it applies to the bribe giver similarly implies purposeful conduct. The person who offers a bribe is engaged in inchoate conduct that has as its objective the achievement of an agreement that a benefit will be exchanged for official action. Indeed, the offeror of a bribe would be guilty of solicitation of a criminal offense under Section 5.02 by virtue of "encouraging" or "requesting" that the bribe recipient engage in criminal conduct. It thus is sound to treat the inchoate behavior of both parties in the same manner and to apply to both of them the benefits and limitations of the solicitation offense as defined in Section 5.02. Again, therefore, the offering aspect of the offense is a crime of purpose; the actor must have as his conscious objective the conferring of a benefit as consideration for official conduct on the part of the recipient of the offer. Logically, both failure of communication of the offer and its voluntary and complete renunciation should also have the same impact that Section 5.02 provides for solicitation.

This does not mean, it should be noted, that the bribery offense includes all inchoate behavior and thus excludes the possibility of a charge of attempted bribery. Section 5.01 authorizes an attempt prosecution for anyone who engages in a substantial step designed to culminate in the commission of the offense. There may well be conduct short of an actual effort to communicate with the other party that will be sufficient to constitute such a substantial step. For example, withdrawal of funds and taking them to a surreptitious meeting may well suffice, together with other evidence of intent, to constitute attempted bribery even though no formal effort to communicate an actual offer was made. Similarly, a charge of solicitation could be maintained under Section 5.02, as in the case of an effort by one person to induce another to bribe a public official.

It is also important to emphasize that bribery, like solicitation and attempt, is not an offense that focuses solely upon culpability. The requirement that the actor "solicit" or "offer" a bribe demands proof of objective conduct which, by analogy to the law of attempt, has corroborative force with respect to the required purpose of influencing official behavior. It is therefore not enough that the actor intends that official behavior be influenced. He must engage in steps to procure that end, and that conduct must properly be described as amounting to an actual solicitation or offer of a bribe. The same point must be kept in mind, moreover, with respect to the remainder of the elements of the offense as they are discussed below.

(b) *Agrees to Confer or Agrees to Accept as Consideration for.* The bribery offense also extends to one who "agrees to confer" or who "agrees to accept" a benefit as consideration for official action. These terms are subject to an analysis similar to that made above in connection with "offer" and "solicit." "Agree to confer," as well as "agree to accept," is language of conspiracy, language which implies an understanding of the terms of the agreement and the objective of the agreement. Thus, one who agrees to confer a benefit upon another as consideration for official action by the other party, both as a matter of the common sense of these terms and by analogy to the law of conspiracy, is one who knows that he is committing himself to confer a benefit and who desires that the benefit be in exchange for official action. The same is true of one who agrees to accept a benefit as consideration for his official action. Logically, as well as a matter of policy, other doctrines developed in the Model Code as corollaries of the law of conspiracy should also be applied here. Thus, the term "agrees" should be construed as expressing a unilateral concept, much as the words "agrees with such other person . . . that they or one . . . of them will engage in conduct which constitutes such crime" are construed in Section 5.03. The result is that "agrees" does not necessarily mean a bilateral arrangement signifying an actual meeting of the minds. It is sufficient if the actor believes that he has agreed to confer or agreed to accept a benefit for the proscribed purpose, regardless of whether the other party actually accepts the bargain in any contract sense. Similarly, the doctrine of renunciation as developed in Section 5.03(6) should be applicable to one who agrees to confer or agrees to accept a bribe.

(c) *Confers or Accepts as Consideration for.* It has been established that the terms "offers," "agrees to confer," "solicits," and "agrees to accept" imply a purpose that the arrangement be the exchange of a benefit as consideration for the performance of an official function. The remaining question is whether the words "confers" and "accepts" should be similarly interpreted. It may lead to undesirable results if they are not.

Given the established applicability of the bribery offense to inchoate behavior, it would be possible to construe "confers" and "accepts" as signifying a completed bilateral arrangement — in effect an illegal contract to exchange a benefit as consideration for the performance of an official function. To do so, however, would impose a burden of proof on the prosecution that seems wholly unwarranted. The evils of bribery are fully manifested by the actor who *believes* that he is conferring a benefit in exchange for official action, no matter how the recipient views the transaction. The person who actually pays money or confers a benefit in order to influence official action should be subjected to the penalties of bribery whether or not the official goes along with the scheme. Similarly, the public official who accepts a benefit for this purpose presents the same criminological case regardless of whether the person who confers the benefit meant to enter into such an arrangement. It is wholly appropriate, therefore, to view the action of conferring a benefit or accepting a benefit entirely from the point of view of the actor. If he meant to confer a benefit as consideration for official action or to accept a benefit for that purpose, the offense of bribery is complete.

A contrary interpretation of the bribery offense would not necessarily change this result, since a reading of bribery to require an actual agreement between the parties would mean that a charge of attempted bribery could be filed in cases where no actual agreement existed. It seems unnecessarily complex, however, to require the prosecutor to use different theories depending on whether he thinks he can establish a mutual understanding or only a purpose by the defendant to reach an understanding, particularly where both theories would lead to the same grading of the offense. The principle of *ejusdem generis* therefore suggests that each of the operative terms — "offers," "confers," "agrees to confer," "solicits," "accepts," and "agrees to accept" — should be read to apply to inchoate and unilateral behavior. Each defendant should be judged by what he thought he was doing and what he meant to do, not by how his actions were received by the other party....

5. *Defined Terms.* In addition to the words that have been discussed above, Section 240.1 uses a number of terms that have been defined in Section 240.0. Each of these is considered below.

(a) *Benefit.* Section 240.0(1) defines the term "benefit" comprehensively to mean "gain or advantage, or anything regarded by the beneficiary as gain or advantage, including benefit to any other person or entity in whose welfare he is interested." The purpose of defining the term so broadly is to reach every kind of offer to influence official or political action by extraneous incentives. For example, an offer to admit the child of a judge to a particular school, college, or private club in exchange for favorable action on a case would constitute a "benefit" within this definition, as would solicitation of sexual relations by a law enforcement officer as consideration for his overlooking illegal behavior. These acts would be covered by Paragraphs (2) and (3) of Section 240.1, respectively.

As explained in the commentary on logrolling, the definition of "benefit" excludes "an advantage promised generally to a group or class of voters as a consequence of public measures which a candidate engages to support or oppose." This is designed to exclude campaign promises and other general commitments that a candidate typically makes in order to get votes. The limitation of the exclusion to a group or class of voters includes in the definition of "benefit" promises to an individual, such as the promise by a candidate for the bench that he will vote a certain way in a particular class of cases in exchange for support in the election. The opportunity for subversion of the judicial process by such promises is dissipated if they are made to a group or a class of persons; it is much greater if they are made to a single individual or to several individuals in a manner hidden from the public view. The words "group or class" should thus be construed to include a large enough number of people so as to make the promise essentially a matter of public record on an issue of public rather than private concern. . . .

(b) *Pecuniary Benefit.* Section 240.0(6) defines "pecuniary benefit" as "benefit in the form of money, property, commercial interests or anything else the primary significance of which is economic gain." Because the word "benefit" is included in the definition of "pecuniary benefit," the clause in Section 240.0(1) relating to benefits to any other person or entity in whose welfare the actor is interested is also applicable to pecuniary benefits. Thus, Paragraph (1) of the bribery offense would punish an offer of money to the wife or relative of a public official on the same terms as it would reach an offer directly to that official. The concept of economic gain used in the definition of "pecuniary benefit" is also meant to be construed broadly. It is intended, for example, to include cases where a public servant is offered a job in private industry as an inducement to take official action favorable to his prospective employer or where a corporate employee who sits in the state legislature is offered a promotion or a raise in return for his vote on a pending bill. . . .

The Model Code contains no special provision relating to campaign contributions. The result is that a person may be convicted of bribery for offering a campaign contribution, and a candidate may be guilty of bribery for receiving such a contribution, if the other requirements of the offense are met. Most importantly, the prosecution must show that the offer was made or accepted "as consideration for" the recipient's exercise of official discretion or violation of known duty. Such proof will be relatively easy where the "campaign contribution" is made available for the candidate's personal use and much more demanding where the money is used to defray legitimate campaign expense. In many factual contexts, the issue is likely to be subtle and difficult, but there seems to be no better way to put the question than to ask whether the payment was offered or received "as consideration for" official action to be taken by the candidate after election. Additionally, the prosecution will be required to show that the contemplated official action concerned a matter of private advantage rather than a benefit accruing to a group or class of voters as a consequence of action on a public issue. If these proof requirements are met, conviction under the Model Code may result even though the payment took the form of a campaign contribution duly reported as required by law. . . .

(c) *Public Servant.* Section 240.0(7) defines "public servant" to mean "any officer or employee of government, including legislators and judges." Nearly all modern codes and proposals include legislators and judges within the term "public servant" as it is used in the general bribery offense, although some older statutes maintain separate bribery provisions relating to various categories of officials. . . .

Not only top government officials are covered by the Model Code definition, but any government employee, however lowly, is covered as well. Almost all modern codes and proposals agree that the term should be so understood. New York, for example, includes "any public officer or employee of the state or of any political subdivision thereof" and "any person exercising the functions of any such public officer or employee." All of the other recent codes and proposals are just as broad. . . .

The definition of "public servant" in Section 240.0(7) also includes "any person participating as juror, advisor, consultant or otherwise, in performing a governmental function." The purpose is to include persons who are temporarily in the government service as well as those who hold a more permanent status. This too is common practice in new codes and proposals, although it is not as universally accepted as other portions of the Model Code definition of "public servant.". . .

Finally, it should be noted that witnesses are excluded from the definition of "public servant" in Section 240.0(7) because the subject of witness bribery is dealt with in Section 241.6 along with other forms of tampering with witnesses. Some of the recent codes and proposals have included witnesses in general bribery provisions, though most have treated the matter separately.

(d) *Party Official.* Section 240.0(5) defines "party official" to mean "a person who holds an elective or appointive post in a political party in the United States by virtue of which he directs or conducts, or participates in directing or conducting party affairs at any level of responsibility." Most states traditionally have not dealt with the bribery of party officials, but a number of the recently enacted codes have followed the suggestion of the Model Penal Code and included such persons within the general bribery provision. Several recent proposals follow suit.

Here, in contrast to public servants, the focus of the Model Code is upon persons with some managerial responsibility rather than all persons who are in some way connected with a political party. Most of the modern codes with provisions covering the bribery of political party officials, however, do not limit the offense in this manner. At least seven state codes define "party official" to include all officials and employees of a political party. . . .

(e) *Administrative Proceeding.* Section 240.0(8) defines "administrative proceeding" to include "any proceeding, other than a judicial proceeding, the outcome of which is required to be based on a record or documentation prescribed by law, or in which law or regulation is particularized in application to individuals." The term is used in Paragraph (2) of the bribery offense to include those proceedings that are analogous to the judicial process. Thus, quasi-judicial proceedings will be included, as well as some proceedings directed toward the formulation of regulations if the law contemplates that the outcome shall be based on evidence and findings. The definition will also cover a significant range of actions that might be called "executive" or "administrative," as where the official action applies a general rule to an individual. Examples would be the granting or revoking of a license, awarding veteran's disability compensation, or awarding or withholding welfare or social security. . . .

6. *Scope of the Offense: Paragraph (1).* Paragraph (1) reaches the offer or acceptance of a "pecuniary benefit" as consideration for "the recipient's decision, opinion, recommendation, vote or other exercise of discretion." It applies to

bribes offered to or accepted by a "public servant, party official or voter." Private citizens are thus included in situations where they satisfy the definition of "public servant" or "party official," as those terms are defined, or where the bribery relates to their conduct as voters.

The official action that is the subject of Paragraph (1) focuses upon decision-making, *i.e.,* upon the exercise of discretion by the designated persons. It is designed to include minor ministerial acts as well as major decisions of policy. It follows prevailing law in making it immaterial whether the decision for which the bribe is offered would have been made in the same manner without the bribe or whether the result of the decision is viewed as correct or incorrect. Situations where no exercise of discretion is involved are covered in Paragraph (3) dealing with the violation of a "duty.". . .

7. *Scope of the Offense: Paragraph (2).* As noted above, Paragraph (2) was added in order to apply "benefit" rather than "pecuniary benefit" to discretionary action in judicial or administrative proceedings. The integrity of proceedings of this character and the impropriety of any extraneous attempt to influence their course or outcome seem plain. Recent codes and proposals that follow the Model Penal Code approach to logrolling are unanimous in the broad preclusion of benefits that are sought to be conferred in this context.

8. *Scope of the Offense: Paragraph (3).* Paragraph (3) extends the coverage of bribery to non-discretionary situations in which payment is offered or accepted as consideration for violation of a "known legal duty" by the recipient. It is clear from the wording of the provision that the requirement of knowledge applies both to the bribe giver and the bribe recipient, although the fact that one of the parties does not know of the duty will not defeat conviction of the other. The phrase "legal duty" is not defined in the Model Code, but it is intended to be interpreted broadly to apply to any specific and clearly delineated obligation of a public servant or party official. Possible sources of such a duty include the state constitution, statutes, administrative regulations, executive orders, and developed traditions concerning performance of official functions. The breadth of this concept is limited by the requirement that the duty exist at law and by the requirement that the actor know of the duty and that the contemplated action would constitute a violation of it.

The fact that only a violation of duty is encompassed within this paragraph makes it clear that the bribery offense does not apply where the law contemplates payment of fees to a public servant or where tips or other compensation received by a public servant are not inconsistent with his duties. Such conduct may be covered under Paragraphs (1) and (2) if payment is made or accepted as consideration for an exercise of discretion, but otherwise it does not constitute bribery. Potentially illicit gifts to a public servant are dealt with as such under Section 240.5 *infra.* Since Section 240.5 is relatively narrow in scope, a gap in the coverage of the Code will exist for some cases of tips or compensation paid to a public servant for providing a service that he has a duty to perform without compensation. This gap is quite deliberate. Payment to a public servant to induce performance of a non-discretionary act that he has a duty to perform without compensation is undoubtedly undesirable. Administrative and legislative sanctions addressed to such misconduct may well be appropriate. The practice is widespread, however, and in many quarters it is tolerated quite openly. This suggests that community standards of behavior have not yet crystalized sufficiently to warrant imposition of criminal penalties for such behavior, especially at the felony level. Caution is particularly appropriate in dealing with the ordinary citizen who offers the customary tip for non-discretionary action with no thought of corrupting government processes or obtaining unfair private advantage. Accordingly, the primary means of controlling such conduct should be disciplinary action within the civil service. Additionally, it may be appropriate to enact special legislation outside the penal code for imposition of minor and essentially non-criminal sanctions. . . .

9. *Recipient Unqualified to Act.* The last sentence of Section 240.1 provides that it is no defense to a prosecution for bribery that a person whom the actor sought to influence was not qualified to act as desired "whether because he had not yet assumed office, or lacked jurisdiction, or for any other reason." This provision follows prevailing law and is justified on the same ground that argues for dispensing with the so-called "impossibility" defense with respect to attempts. The disposition to influence official conduct in the manner proscribed by this section is an adequate basis for intervention of the criminal law whatever the formal capacities of the person to whom the bribe is offered. Moreover, the fact that the offense is defined in its inchoate form makes it appropriate to apply theories of inchoate liability that the Model Code has used with respect to the crimes of attempt, conspiracy, and solicitation.

The language of the preclusion may seem to be worded so that literally it would apply only where the defendant was the person who sought to influence the official conduct of another. It is intended, however, to apply with equal force where the defendant is a public official who solicits or accepts a bribe. . . .

10. *Economic Coercion as a Defense.* There are a number of cases that have discussed the possibility that extortion or other forms of economic coercion should be accepted as a defense to bribery. Broad statements can be found to the effect that bribery and extortion "are mutually exclusive." Such pronouncements can be taken for the proposition that a defendant who is charged with one of these offenses can successfully defend by proving the other. There is an obvious problem with such an implication and with any practice that leads to an acquittal of the defendant for one crime solely because he proves that he committed another. The situation presented by these cases can best be analyzed by separate treatment of the liability of the purported bribe giver and the purported bribe receiver.

(a) *The Bribe Giver.* The case to be considered involves the situation where the defendant has made payments of money to a public official in exchange for favorable action and where he stands charged with bribery. With respect to that offense, both the bribe giver and the bribe receiver are properly viewed as guilty of a criminal offense. The difficulty arises from the fact that the law of extortion punishes only the person who receives money from another; the victim of the extortion is not subject to criminal sanctions but is viewed as one whose property has, in effect, been stolen. The question is whether the guilt of the bribe giver is mitigated by the fact that he may be regarded as the victim of extortion.

If such a defense is recognized, it can be expected that those who are charged with offering a bribe will routinely seek to characterize themselves as unfortunate victims of extortion rather than as influence seekers who voluntarily paid money to another in order to secure favorable official action. Moreover, it will often take a subtle examination of the facts in order to determine which characterization is more nearly accurate. To put it another way, it will not be too difficult for skilled defense counsel to turn the trial of an alleged bribe giver into a debate on the motives of the bribe recipient and on whether he initiated the plan by threatening to take adverse action against the victim-defendant. As the New York Court of Appeals has observed:

"the essence of bribery is the *voluntary* giving of something of value to influence the performance of *official duty*," whereas the essence of extortion is "duress." Although the theoretical distinction between the two crimes is clear, the line of demarcation may not, in practical application, always be clear, particularly where, as here, the allegedly extorsive demand for payment was couched in the form of polite suggestions, and it is claimed that the payments were solicited from a receptive and willing donor.[135]

The theory of giving a defense to the bribe giver in this situation appears to be "that if a government officer threatens serious economic loss unless paid for giving a citizen his due, the latter is entitled to have the jury consider this, not as a complete defense like duress but as bearing on the specific intent required for the commission of bribery." [136] In those jurisdictions that describe the *mens rea* associated with bribery as a "corrupt intent," it would be possible to conclude that responding to economic or other coercion by a public official is not "corrupt" and therefore not bribery. However, if the "specific intent" required for bribery is simply an intent to influence official conduct, it would be hard to conclude that the motivation for the payment — whether it be to secure an unwarranted advantage or to prevent the official from taking a threatened adverse action — negates the intent in any analytical sense. The defendant has nevertheless paid the money "with the intent to influence" the official conduct. The question whether extortion by the public official negates the intent that is required for bribery thus may turn on close analysis of the elements of the offense as set out by the specific statute involved.

As elaborated above, the Model Code defines the offense with respect to the bribe giver to include one who "offers, confers or agrees to confer upon another . . . any pecuniary benefit as consideration for" the exercise of official discretion.[137] This requires that the actor intend that the benefit be paid in exchange for official action. In the situation under discussion, this intent would exist even if the defendant were responding to extortionate threats by the public official. Threats of that character would provide evidence of the actor's motive in making the payment and, if anything, reinforce the conclusion that the purpose of the arrangement was to purchase official action. It is plain as an analytical matter, therefore, that the offense of bribery as defined in the Model Code would not permit the so-called extortion defense.

Moreover, denial of the extortion defense for the bribe giver seems clearly correct as a matter of policy. The private citizen who responds to an official's

---

[135] People v. Dioguardi, 8 N.Y.2d 260, 273, 203 N.Y.S.2d 870, 881, 168 N.E.2d 683, 692 (1960) (emphasis in original).

[136] United States v. Barash, 365 F.2d 395, 401-02 (2d Cir. 1966), *appeal after remand,* 412 F.2d 26, *cert. denied,* 396 U.S. 832 (1969). The defendant was a certified public accountant and an attorney who was alleged to have made bribe payments to internal revenue agents in connection with their office audits of the defendant's clients. The statute involved in the prosecution was 18 U.S.C. § 201(b)(1), which defines the offense as "whoever . . . corruptly gives, offers or promises anything of value to any public official . . . with intent . . . to influence any official act . . . ." If the internal revenue agents had indeed initiated the payments by threats of adverse action, the court was thus prepared to hold that this would not be a "corrupt" payment "with intent to influence" an official act. The court observed that "a jury could conclude that a payment solely to eliminate a roadblock to what a citizen is entitled is not to 'influence' any official act." 365 F.2d at 402 n.7.

[137] The quotation is from Paragraph (1). Paragraphs (2) and (3) differ in important respects from Paragraph (1), but the differences do not affect the analysis of this question.

threat of adverse action by paying money to secure more favorable treatment evidences thereby a willingness to subvert the legitimate processes of government. It is not acceptable to pay kickbacks or under-the-table compensation to a public servant, even if such payment is required in order to obtain official action that is rightfully due. Such conduct constitutes a degree of cooperation in the undermining of governmental integrity that is inconsistent with complete exoneration from criminal liability. The correct decision, of course, is to refuse the illicit overture and to report it to the appropriate authorities. Only by refusing to immunize the payor from criminal liability can the penal law encourage resort to this option.

This conclusion is reinforced by certain practical considerations. To permit litigation of the extortion defense where both the fact of payment and its intended impact are clear is likely to impair conviction of many bribe givers who merit punishment under any reasonable conception of public policy. Whether the transaction partakes more of bribery or of extortion will often be a cloudy question, and there is no compelling reason to try to differentiate between the two characterizations. In either event, payment made as consideration for official action is a reprehensible invasion of government integrity. It therefore seems justified to avoid this potential for confusion by removing the issue from trial and appellate litigation.

To be sure, there may be cases where extortionate threats by a government official make the action of the bribe giver seem less blameworthy than it might be otherwise. Under a sentencing structure as flexible as that contained in the Model Code, however, these factors can adequately be taken into account at the sentencing stage. Sentencing provides the opportunity to consider where the primary fault lies and whether the defendant should be considered a fully equal partner in the scheme, even to the point of reducing the grade of the conviction of the bribe giver to the misdemeanor level if such action seems appropriate. It is not at all unusual for the defendant's motives for acting as he did to be relevant primarily at the sentencing stage. This seems to be a good occasion for the application of that principle. Accordingly, it is the position of Section 240.1 that the defense of extortion or economic coercion is unavailable to one who is charged with offering, conferring, or agreeing to confer a bribe and that the matter should be regarded as relevant, if at all, at the time of sentencing. . . .

(b) *The Bribe Receiver.* The case of the purported bribe receiver is much easier than that of the bribe giver. To allow one accused of receiving a bribe to defend on the ground that he exacted the payment by coercion is plainly silly. The impairment of governmental integrity is at least as great where extortion is involved, and the reprehensibility of the actor's conduct is, if anything, even greater.

The technical analysis of the Model Code provision with respect to this situation closely follows the analysis given with respect to the bribe giver. One who "solicits, accepts or agrees to accept from another . . . any pecuniary benefit as consideration for" discretionary action can be convicted of bribery,[144] no matter by what method the payments were induced. The use of threats or coercion does not negate any of the elements of the offense as they have been elaborated in the preceding commentary.

---

[144] *See* note 137 *supra.*

There is, however, a grading point that deserves mention. Section 223.4(4) authorizes prosecution for theft by extortion where property of another is obtained by means of a threat to take or withhold action as a public official. Where money is paid as consideration for forbearance from the threatened harm, the Model Code would allow prosecution under either bribery or extortion. Both offenses may be punished as felonies of the third degree, and it is, therefore, generally irrelevant which theory is used.[145] In one situation, however, a practical difference exists. Where extortion involves less than $500, it may be classified under Section 223.1(2) as a misdemeanor. Conviction of bribery on the same facts would render the defendant liable to third-degree felony penalties. This might be viewed as a grading anomaly that should preclude unfettered prosecutorial discretion as to the choice of theory. Perhaps it could be argued that extortion should thus be a defense to bribery, at least to the extent of reducing the grade of the latter offense to the level of sanctions authorized under the extortion provision.

There are two answers to this contention. First, the decision to grade all bribery as a third-degree felony is based on the premise that subversion of governmental processes is a serious evil to be met by serious sanctions. This rationale would apply to payments induced by threats as well as payments voluntarily made and accepted. Hence, the bribe receiver who extorts the payment justifiably may be punished for a felony without regard to the grading of extortion. Second, as is revealed in the discussion of the grading of bribery below, there are some relatively minor instances of bribery where reduction of the offense to the misdemeanor level may be considered appropriate without regard to any relationship between bribery and extortion. If there are cases of bribery-extortion that warrant misdemeanor treatment, the judge will be free to adopt this course under Section 6.12 and thus to achieve a parity between the grading of the two offenses. Since the Model Code sentencing structure is so flexible, in other words, the grading differential can be accommodated on a case-by-case basis.

The position of the Model Code excluding the defense of extortion or economic coercion by the bribe receiver has been universally accepted, it would appear, in the recently drafted codes and proposals. Most, as the Model Code, are not explicit on the point, though it seems clear that they should be interpreted to foreclose the defense. . . .

11. *Grading.* Bribery statutes in effect when the Model Code was drafted generally provided for felony sanctions, although the bribery of voters quite commonly was treated as a misdemeanor. In principle, it would seem desirable to provide a grading of the offense that ranged in seriousness from petty offers to traffic policemen to corruption of high government officials in matters involving the general welfare of the state or large sums of money. Prosecution might also be facilitated by classifying minor derelictions as misdemeanors.

---

[145] Section 1.07(1) *supra* would permit a prosecution for either bribery or extortion or for both at the same time. Section 1.07(1)(d) would only permit a conviction for one of the offenses, however, since extortion would in effect be a specific instance of the general bribery offense.

In cases where extortion is charged but not bribery, the prosecutor must of course show that the money or other property was obtained by threat. It thus will be a defense to extortion that the money was voluntarily paid without any threats by the public official and in this sense bribery will continue to remain a defense to extortion. Moreover, in cases where both bribery and extortion are charged, the offenses may be graded differently if small amounts of money are involved. Thus, it may avoid confusion and unnecessary litigation if bribery is the theory of prosecution in all cases where such a charge seems possible.

It is difficult, however, to draft such a provision. The felony could be limited to bribes involving official proceedings or high officials designated by rank or minimum salary and to pecuniary bribes exceeding a specific sum. An alternative might be to limit the felony to cases involving "substantial impairment of official integrity." The difficulty of drafting a satisfactory set of legislative grading criteria ultimately persuaded the Council to abandon the attempt and to leave to the court the option to reduce felony convictions to the misdemeanor level in accordance with the general authority of Section 6.12. The criteria of Section 6.12, authorizing reduction in grade where, "having regard to the nature and circumstances of the crime and to the history and character of the defendant," it would be "unduly harsh" to impose a felony sentence or conviction, invoke the basic concerns that a more detailed grading scheme would involve. . . .

COMMENT TO § 240.2

1. *Rationale.* Section 240.2 covers threat of harm to achieve improper influence in official and political matters. This offense is a complement to the crime of bribery. As defined in Section 240.1, bribery covers offer of benefit to a public servant, party official, or voter for the purpose of influencing the recipient's official action or vote. Section 240.2 proscribes use of threat against the same classes of persons with the same illicit objective. This congruence of rationale between the two offenses is reflected in drafting similarities. Thus, Paragraphs (a), (b), and (c) of Section 240.2(1) closely parallel Paragraphs (1), (2), and (3) of Section 240.1. Paragraph (d) of Section 240.2(1) contains an additional provision without analogue in the bribery offense. It deals with the related subject of *ex parte* communications made to judicial and administrative officers with the purpose of influencing improperly the outcome of official proceedings.

At the time the Model Code was drafted, penal legislation against use of threat to influence official action was much less common than was legislation against bribery. There were, however, numerous special statutes protecting jurors, others involved in the judicial process, legislators, and law-enforcement officers. The prevalence of laws against improper influencing of jurors, masters, referees, and the like evidences a widespread judgment that pressures other than offer of benefit may obstruct the administration of justice. Statutes in effect when the Model Code was drafted varied significantly in their approach to this danger. The broadest formulations reached "any attempt to influence" a verdict. More commonly, the statutes required that the attempt to influence be "corrupt" or "improper." Sometimes, there was added a requirement that the influence be by communication outside the regular course of proceedings. Some prior legislation also included administrative proceedings, congressional investigations, and corrupt influencing of legislators and voters.

2. *Threat of Harm.* The chief difficulty in drafting a statute of this sort lies in drawing the line between permissible and impermissible threats. Many kinds of harm may be threatened or inflicted without contravening accepted standards of behavior and without impairing the integrity of government. A threat to withdraw political support, for example, is not only a legitimate means of influencing political decisions but is in most instances constitutionally protected. More commonly, use of threat may be either appropriate or blameworthy depending on the motives of the actor and the sympathies of the observer. Thus, for example, a public official's threat to discharge a subordinate over a difference in policy may be legitimate supervision or reprehensible interference with the independence of another public servant. And a threat to arrest or prosecute may

be a proper means to induce another to abide by the law or a method of improper intimidation. These distinctions are too subtle for resolution by the blunt instrument of criminal prosecution. However one may characterize the facts of a particular case, it would be intolerable to subject all such decisions to review under the penal law.

One approach to this problem would be to restrict the prohibited threats to those made with a "corrupt" intent. This formulation would pass the issue to the courts without definitive legislative guidance. The courts would be expected to differentiate the legitimate from the illegitimate and would do so on the basis of whatever factors commanded the attention of judges. No doubt the courts would discharge this duty in a generally sensible fashion, but there are serious problems, both theoretical and practical, with unstructured delegation to judges of the responsibility for resolving fundamental policy decisions on a case-by-case basis. These difficulties have been canvassed in connection with the bribery offense. For the reasons there explained, use of the elastic concept of "corrupt" intent has been abandoned as a statutory device for defining the scope of bribery and of this offense as well.

The alternative approach reflected in Section 240.2 parallels the solution eventually adopted for the crime of bribery. Threat of any harm is proscribed if made with purpose to influence the exercise of discretion in a judicial or administrative proceeding or to secure official action violative of a known legal duty. Thus, an attempt to reach a judge in a pending case or to influence a public official to violate a specific obligation of his office will be protected against threats to foreclose a mortgage, to bring a criminal prosecution, to publicize a private scandal, to withhold business patronage, etc. In each instance, the threat must be made with a purpose to influence the conduct of the official in the ways detailed in Paragraphs (b) and (c) of the offense. These provisions parallel Paragraphs (2) and (3) of the bribery statute, and reference should be made to the commentary to Section 240.1 for an elaboration of their content.[11]

A slightly different approach is adopted for a threat made to influence the exercise of discretion by a public servant, party official, or voter. This conduct is covered in Section 240.2(1)(a), which closely parallels Paragraph (1) of the bribery offense. The bribery provision is limited to offer of "pecuniary benefit," *i.e.*, gain or advantage of primarily economic significance, in order to exclude from bribery certain types of political compromises not involving the payment of money. Similarly, the scope of Section 240.2(1)(a) is limited to threat of "unlawful harm" in order to exclude from coverage accepted behavior, such as threat of political opposition, with respect to the exercise of discretion by a public servant, party official, or voter. The term "unlawful" includes threat of physical attack, threat of property damage forbidden by penal statute or by the law of torts, and threat to discharge a public servant in violation of applicable civil service statutes or regulations. Even if the threatened harm would ordinarily be only a civil wrong, its use to coerce official or political action merits criminal sanctions. Thus, the referent of the term "unlawful" is the body of pre-existing law, both penal

---

[11] There are two points of difference that should be noted. The first is the substitution of threatened harm for the conferring of a benefit, a change that reflects the different substantive coverage of the two sections. The second relates to culpability and the explicit statement of purpose to influence in the paragraphs of Section 240.2. In view of the purpose requirement implicit in Section 240.1 and developed in detail in the commentary to that section, this difference in wording will have little impact. The requirement that the actor "know" the legal duty involved in Section 240.1(3) is also explicitly carried forward in Section 240.2(1)(c).

and civil, that deals with the type of harm threatened. The fact that the content of this body of law is specific and ascertainable is what commends use of "unlawful" rather than "corrupt" to designate the types of threat that are forbidden.

Finally, it should be noted that the term "harm" is broadly defined in Section 240.0(3) to include any "loss, disadvantage or injury, or anything so regarded by the person affected, including loss, disadvantage or injury to any other person or entity in whose welfare he is interested." Harm to third persons is thus explicitly included, and the term is defined, as is "benefit" with respect to bribery, in a manner that reflects the actual evaluation of the official involved rather than a disinterested and objective determination of "harm." This subjectivity seems warranted on the ground that even an idiosyncratic perception of "harm" may be exploited by the threatener to work a real impairment of the integrity of government. . . .

3. *Ex Parte Contacts.* Subsection (1)(d) is designed to reach improper influence by means short of bribery or threat. It includes "private" communications addressed to public servants who will exercise discretion in judicial or administrative proceedings. It prohibits any communication designed to influence the outcome on the basis of considerations other than those authorized by law.

Subsection (1)(d) does not reach attempts to influence legislators or ordinary executive officials in their exercise of discretion or performance of duties. The reason for the exclusion is that there is no tradition or commonly accepted morality governing the kinds of communications that may appropriately be addressed to such officials. All sorts of pleas for special favors are made to legislative and executive officials, both by organized lobbyists and by ordinary citizens. The probability of serious subversion of good government is not so clear in such cases as when the pressure is accompanied by an offer of benefit or threat of harm or when the pressure is applied in a proceeding of the sort that must be based upon a formal record of testimony.

This is not to say that improper influences beyond the scope of Subsection (1)(d) present no problems or that the integrity of government cannot seriously be threatened by such behavior. Special legislation dealing with lobbying and codes of proper official behavior are certainly appropriate measures to be considered in this area. They should be enforced primarily by civil disciplinary measures, however, and are in any event beyond the scope of the Model Code.

Subsection (1)(d) is confined to "private" communications in order to prevent it from being applied to the press and to other forms of public comment. Communication in briefs or other documents made part of the public record are also excluded from coverage. Even with these qualifications, some members of the Institute expressed the fear that the provision would jeopardize flexible informal regulatory practices under which parties have felt free "in good faith" to communicate relevant information privately to officials of administrative agencies. These members would have preferred limitation of the provision to "corrupt" influence. Use of the term "corrupt," however, would have all of the disadvantages here that led to its rejection in connection with bribery and influencing by threat. Private approaches to administrative officers are nearly always made on the basis of avowed good purposes, such as to avoid delay or to make sure that the true public interest (as conceived by the proponent) will be served. Coverage only of "corrupt" attempts to influence would either rob the provision of any significance or leave the courts with the wholly unstructured task of defining through criminal prosecutions the limits of appropriate *ex parte* contact. The offense as drafted, on the other hand, is reasonably informative.

Moreover, application of this provision to communications that are merely inappropriate rather than reprehensible is precluded by the requirement of specific purpose. The actor must have a purpose to influence the outcome of a proceeding "on the basis of considerations other than those authorized by law." Nothwithstanding the usual irrelevance of awareness of illegality, this language is intended to require not only that the actor intend to influence the outcome on the basis of certain factors but also that he know that those considerations are not authorized by law. Anyone who acts without such knowledge need not be apprehensive of conviction under this section. . . .

4. *Unqualified Official.* The last sentence of Subsection (1) precludes defenses based on the fact that the person whom the actor sought to influence was not qualified to act in the desired way, "whether because he had not yet assumed office, or lacked jurisdiction, or for any other reason." A similar provision is contained in the last sentence of Section 240.1. Reference to the commentary on that section should be made for an elaboration of its purpose. The same reasons that support exclusion of the defense with respect to bribery seem equally applicable here.

5. *Grading.* Subsection (2) grades the offenses defined in this section at the misdemeanor level except in cases where a crime is threatened or where a threat is made with the purpose of influencing a judicial or an administrative proceeding. The latter situations are graded as third-degree felonies. All offenses under Subsection (1)(b) thus will be felonies of the third degree, and all offenses under Subsections (1)(a) and (1)(c) will be felonies of the third degree if a threat of crime is involved. The remaining offenses will be misdemeanors. . . .

COMMENT TO § 240.3

1. *Rationale.* Section 240.3 obviates a difficulty of proof sometimes encountered in bribery prosecutions. Where both the fact of payment to a public servant and an exercise of official discretion favorable to the payor are established, common sense suggests that bribery has occurred. Yet in some cases, prosecution for that offense may fail for lack of evidence that the defendant offered or solicited or agreed to confer or accept the payment in advance of the official action. Where the prior understanding is reached with sufficient secrecy or subtlety, the actors may escape conviction for bribery even though they have acted to undermine the integrity of government in exactly the manner condemned by that offense. Section 240.3 reflects the judgment that complete exoneration from liability is inappropriate, even though conviction for bribery is not obtainable. This conclusion is grounded in part on the view that compensation for past official action often represents a prior understanding which the prosecution has failed to prove. More importantly, however, Section 240.3 is grounded on the judgment that criminal sanctions are warranted where no prior approach or undertaking was made. Even where the compensation is genuinely retrospective in character, it implies a promise of similar compensation for future action. This implication may be less virulent than the direct offer of payment for future action, but it poses a not dissimilar threat to governmental integrity. And apart from this sort of illicit suggestion, one who compensates a public servant for past favorable action puts pressure on others to make similar payments in order to forestall the risk of possible adverse action by a disappointed official. For these reasons, Section 240.3 imposes misdemeanor penalties on compensation for past official behavior without regard to proof of any offer, solicitation, or agreement before the fact. . . .

2. *Elements of the Offense.* Section 240.3 is patterned after the definition of bribery in Section 240.1. Reference to the commentary to that section therefore will be of asssitance to an understanding of this offense. Specifically, the first sentence of Section 240.3 applies to a public servant who solicits, accepts, or agrees to accept a pecuniary benefit as compensation for an exercise of official discretion favorable to another or for an action violative of his duty. As in the bribery offense, the words "solicits, accepts or agrees to accept" are words of purpose. Thus, they convey a requirement that the actor have a particular conscious objective — in this case, solicitation or acceptance of payment "as compensation for" official action. The conduct of the actor may be unilateral and inchoate, *i.e.,* liability does not depend upon a consummated agreement to which both parties fully accede.

The range of official conduct to which this prohibition applies is also determined by reference to the bribery offense. Section 240.3 protects against the subtle evils of retrospective compensation the same kinds of official action for which prospective payment is proscribed in Section 240.1. Specifically, the provision covers any violation of duty and any exercise of discretion "favorable to another." It is not necessary that the beneficiary of such action be the payor. Thus, Section 240.3 reaches the public servant who accepts compensation from one individual for an exercise of discretion favorable to another. The official action, however, must either involve discretion or constitute a violation of duty. The section does not punish acceptance of compensation for *performance* of duty. This exclusion is warranted on the ground that there can be no illegitimate private advantage where the public servant only does that which duty requires him to do. As was noted above, regulation of compensation for performance of duty may be accomplished by supplementary legislation of a generally non-penal character.

The commentary to Section 240.1 also explains the meaning of the term "pecuniary benefit." This limitation to a benefit of primarily economic significance is necessary in the context of discretionary actions in order to exclude from bribery and related offenses legislative vote-trading and other forms of acceptable political compromise. It is arguable, however, that Section 240.3 should reach solicitation or acceptance of any "benefit" in those circumstances where a similar breadth of coverage is achieved by Section 240.1. Those circumstances include an exercise of official discretion in a judicial or administrative proceeding and any action violative of a known legal duty. Again, the context of these categories of coverage is explored in the commentary to Section 240.1.

The second sentence of Section 240.3 adds coverage of one who "offers, confers or agrees to confer compensation acceptance of which is prohibited by this Section." The "offers, confers or agrees to confer" language is drawn from the bribery statute and should be construed here, as there, to convey a requirement of purpose that reaches inchoate and unilateral conduct. The prohibition applies to the same range of official conduct, and is limited by the same requirement of pecuniary benefit, as is liability of the public servant who solicits or accepts the compensation. . . .

3. *Grading.* The offenses covered by this section are graded at the misdemeanor level. Assuming that the official action really has not been influenced by advance promise of gain, the consequences of payment seem less serious than the harm done by outright bribery. In the absence of contrary proof, moreover, this assumption plainly should govern the level of liability to which the actor should be held. Accordingly, the misdemeanor penalty seems adequate. . . .

COMMENT TO § 240.4

1. *Scope and Rationale.* Section 240.4 applies to retaliation for past official action. This offense is a complement to Section 240.3 and is justified by many of the same reasons that support criminal provisions for compensation for past official favor. In this context, the need for a special provision is lessened by the fact that many of the more serious forms of retaliation are independently criminal. It remains true, however, that retaliation can be accomplished by unlawful acts that are not crimes but that should be proscribed as such when they are used in response to action lawfully taken by a public servant. Retaliatory conduct is not only especially reprehensible when engaged in for such a motive, but it also implies a threat of further retaliation for future adverse action and thus poses a danger to the integrity of government. Section 240.4 is designed to protect against these evils. . . .

The conduct proscribed by this offense is inflicting harm "by any unlawful act." As is explained in the commentary to Section 240.2, the term "unlawful" includes any criminal or civil wrong for which the law provides a remedy. The alternative of defining the offense to include any harm in retaliation for official action would be too broad. Under the Section 240.0(3) definition of "harm," the concept would include public criticism, withdrawal of friendship or political support, or any other kind of loss or disadvantage. Many of these harms must be tolerated, no matter what the purpose of the actor, and indeed some of these instances of harm constitute protected activities under the first amendment. It should be noted, however, that instances of unlawful "harm" are not limited to harm to the public official. The definition of "harm" in Section 240.0(3) explicitly extends to any "loss, disadvantage or injury to any other person or entity in whose welfare . . . [the public servant] is interested."

Section 240.4 does not specify the required culpability. The words "in retaliation for," however, imply purpose. This offense, therefore, should be read in like manner to Section 240.3 to require that the actor have a particular purpose — in this case to cause the harm in order to retaliate for lawful conduct by a public servant. The words "anything lawfully done . . . in the capacity of public servant" are intended to provide a generic description of the range of conduct for which retaliation is proscribed. It is not meant to require specifically that the actor know of the lawfulness of the public servant's conduct, as would follow from the provisions in Section 2.02. Similarly, the "unlawful act" engaged in by the perpetrator of the offense need not be known by him to be unlawful. It is sufficient if he knows of the nature of the conduct and if it is in fact conduct that the criminal or the civil law recognizes as unlawful.

Misdemeanor penalties seem adequate for this offense, both because the impact on the integrity of government seems less serious than in cases of bribery and threats to influence future conduct and because the most serious forms of retaliation will be independently criminal and can be prosecuted without resort to this section. Section 240.4 thus applies to less aggravated forms of harm and can be analogized to Section 240.3 in terms of the appropriate penalty classification. . . .

COMMENT TO § 240.5

Section 240.5 covers gifts to public servants. This provision resembles some prior legislation dealing with gifts by importers to customs officers, by banks to banking officials, by carriers and utilities to regulatory authorities, by businessmen to food and drug inspectors, etc. Unlike these antecedents, Section 240.5 states general prohibitions applicable to broad categories of persons and conduct. The difficulty of framing satisfactory generalizations of this sort is not inconsiderable, and it may be thought preferable to deal more specifically with narrower categories of public servants in ways more carefully reflective of their particular responsibilities. In some instances, at least, it might be better to handle the problem of gifts to public servants through disciplinary or other non-penal sanctions against the offending official rather than through resort to criminal prosecution. Two countervailing considerations, however, support inclusion of this provision in the Model Code. First, gifts of the sort here covered quite generally create the appearance of a threat to government impartiality, even if that evil in fact is not realized. Second, some instances of bribery may go unpunished for failure of adequate evidence that the benefit was offered or accepted "as consideration for" official action. In such a case, Section 240.5 functions as a lesser included offense to bribery and provides misdemeanor sanctions where it is impossible to establish the requirements of felony liability.

Subsections (1) through (4) of this provision deal with different classes of public servants. Each of these prohibitions reaches an individual who solicits, accepts, or agrees to accept a pecuniary benefit from a person known to be the subject of, or interested in, pending action. Subsection (5) excludes from coverage lawful fees, gifts arising from some independent relationship, and trivial benefits, such as tips, that involve no substantial risk of undermining official impartiality. Subsection (6) follows the pattern of the offenses in Article 240 by including the person who makes the gift within the criminal prohibition in terms comparable to the person who receives the gift. The offense is a misdemeanor. This grade is consistent with Sections 240.3 and 240.4 *supra,* which also deal with forms of government corruption less serious than outright bribery or threats to accomplish the same purposes. . . .

COMMENT TO § 240.6

1. *Rationale.* Section 240.6 covers a kind of transaction that closely resembles bribery. Specifically, the section prohibits compensation of a public official for advice or assistance to a private interest in a matter likely to come before him for discretionary action. In the usual case, such compensation will exceed the legitimate worth of any services rendered. In other words, the value of those services is likely to derive in large measure from the public servant's subsequent opportunity to validate his advice or assistance by favorable official action. Compensation for such action is nothing more or less than bribery, but in order to convict the actor of bribery, the prosecution must prove that the payment was offered or accepted "as consideration for" an exercise of official discretion. That issue is clouded by the existence of a plausible alternative reason for compensating the public servant. The risk, therefore, is that the simple ruse of hiring a public official as a private consultant will defeat prosecution for bribery, even in those cases in which conviction should be possible. That danger, of course, is not acute where the purported *quid pro quo* for compensation is patently fictive or trivial; but where the services rendered are not susceptible to precise valuation or where the benefit lies in the fact of employment rather than in the rate of compensation, there is real prospect that private compensation may be an effective smokescreen for bribery.

Section 240.6 is designed to forestall that prospect. It defines a separate offense that is not dependent on proof that payment was offered or accepted "as consideration for" official action. Instead, the section constructs a prophylaxis against bribery by prohibiting compensation to a public servant for advice or other assistance to private interests on a matter with respect to which he "has or is likely to have an official discretion to exercise." As is appropriate in light of the lesser proof requirements, Section 240.6 is graded less severely than bribery. Even for misdemeanor sanctions, however, it is important to note that this provision is not justified solely as a means of reaching cases of unproved bribery. Assuming, as one must, that the payment was in actuality not made or accepted with the intent to influence official action, such conduct is objectionable on other grounds. At the very least it creates a dangerous conflict of interest. The public servant who accepts payment for advice or assistance to a private party, even without an implicit understanding or subtle promise of influence, cannot be expected to retain utter objectivity when he confronts that same matter in his official capacity. The mere fact of serving two masters constitutes a threat to both the appearance and reality of impartial government. Similarly, the private party who offers or makes compensation that he knows to be unlawful, as Subsection (2) requires, cannot be regarded as blameless simply because the prosecution fails to establish the specific purpose that distinguishes bribery.

It is recognized, of course, that Section 240.6 does not reach all forms of the evil against which it is directed. For example, it applies to services but does not cover arrangements by which a public servant might supply goods or land in connection with some public project pending before him. Nor does this section reach the situation where a public official shares indirectly in compensation paid to his private partners or to other business concerns in which he may be interested. In short, Section 240.6 makes no attempt to deal generally with problems of conflict of interest. Coverage of this field in model penal legislation appears impracticable in view of the variety of business and governmental circumstances that must be taken into account and the preferability of a regulatory approach backed by disciplinary or other non-penal sanctions. It nevertheless seems appropriate to include in the Model Code the most obvious case where a public servant serves two masters under circumstances highly suggestive of bribery and not in any event defensible on other grounds.

2. *Receiving Compensation.* Subsection (1) of Section 240.6 covers the public servant who solicits, accepts, or agrees to accept compensation for advice or other assistance concerning a matter likely to come before him for official action. The words, "solicits, accepts or agrees to accept" are taken from the definition of bribery in Section 240.1, and reference should be made to that commentary for an elucidation of their meaning. Here, as in the bribery offense, these words imply a requirement of purpose — in this case, a purpose to accept payment as compensation for advice or other assistance to private interests on a matter of the sort designated. The word "compensation" is intended as a synonym for "pecuniary benefit," a phrase defined in Section 240.0(6) to include any gain or advantage "the primary significance of which is economic gain."

The kinds of services for which compensation is proscribed are described at some length. Subsection (1) covers compensation "for advice or other assistance in preparing or promoting a bill, contract, claim, or other transaction or proposal" that is likely to come before the public servant for discretionary action. Earlier drafts of this provision would have applied to payment for any "services in relation to any matter" as to which the official will exercise discretion. In the course of debate, members of the Institute objected to this formulation as too broad. Although the excess coverage was not always identified with precision, it is clear that the criticism was justified in at least one respect. The earlier formulation would have reached compensation for services of a mundane or mechanical sort that do not involve any exercise of judgment or expertise by the public servant. As finally adopted, Section 240.6(1) cures this defect by limiting its prohibition to the kinds of services that implicate the public servant's judgment, opinion, values, or expertise — specifically, "advice or other assistance in preparing or promoting a bill, contract, claim, or other transaction or proposal." It is with respect to this sort of promotional assistance that the dangers of unproved bribery and conflict of interest are acute. Section 240.6 is thus directed toward the prevention of such abuses.

The more important limitation on the scope of Subsection (1), however, is that it reaches only advice or assistance on a matter with respect to which the public servant "knows that he has or is likely to have official discretion to exercise." The provision does not apply to matters with respect to which the public servant must execute some non-discretionary duty. In such a case, compensation for assistance to private interests can corrupt the functions of government in only one manner — by inducing the public servant to violate his duty. If he does so, a prosecution for bribery almost certainly can be made out. If he does not do so, there cannot have been the kind of subtle undermining of governmental integrity at which this section is aimed. Of course, there remains the potential for conflict of interest and the appearance of bias. This prospect is well illustrated by the case of *United States v. Drumm,*[4] where a government poultry inspector was retained by large suppliers to advise them on their packing and shipping practices. Section 240.6 would not reach such an arrangement unless Drumm's inspection duties involved some discretionary judgment on his part. Whether otherwise such conduct should be made criminal is a difficult question. Perhaps the best solution would be a requirement that employees disclose such conflict-of-interest relationships for appraisal by their superiors, with dismissal or minor penalty for violating the rule. In any event, in deference to the apprehensions expressed by members of the Institute and in adherence to the general policy of conservative use of penal sanctions, Section 240.6 is restricted to advice or promotional assistance on pending legislation, claims against the government, proposals for contracts, and other matters with respect to which the public servant may exercise official discretion.

3. *Paying Compensation.* Subsection (2) of Section 240.6 covers the private payor of compensation to a public servant. Although this provision might be interpreted to apply broadly to any unlawful payment to a public servant, the context makes clear that it is intended to reach only such compensation as is proscribed by Subsection (1). The provision is somewhat unusual in that it requires knowledge of illegality. This departure from usual policy is warranted on the ground that most persons affected by this provision will be laymen who cannot be expected to know of the many rules, both penal and civil, governing various classes of public officials. The public servant, on the other hand, may be held accountable for knowledge of the various legal and ethical rules governing his employment. . . .

---

[4] 329 F.2d 109 (1st Cir. 1964).

COMMENT TO § 240.7

1. *Selling Political Endorsement.* Subsection (1) of Section 240.7 prohibits the sale of political influence or endorsement. Although the terms of this provision reach the government official who exercises a power of appointment or approval, that is not its principal application. The public servant who accepts payment for official action is guilty of bribery under Section 240.1, and there is no need to resort to this offense. Instead, this section is aimed chiefly at the third party who solicits or accepts money as consideration for his recommendation or endorsement concerning official action. . . .

2. *Other Trading in Special Influence.* Subsection (2) of Section 240.7 is designed to reach the same sort of harm committed by a different class of persons. Subsection (1), in effect, deals with the sale of influence by persons whose employment, status, or prior experience puts them in a position to have an impact on the affairs of government. Subsection (2) deals with the sale of influence by persons who by virtue of kinship, friendship, or other special relationship to a public servant are in a position to exert the same type of special influence. Specifically, it provides misdemeanor sanctions for any person who solicits, receives, or agrees to receive any pecuniary benefit "as consideration for exerting special influence upon a public servant or procuring another to do so." "Special influence" is defined to include the relationships mentioned above, specifically including any person who has the "power to influence . . . apart from the merits of the transaction." Obviously, there is some overlap in the coverage of Subsections (1) and (2). Some instances of the sale of influence may be prosecuted under either provision. It is not necessary, however, to mark a clear distinction between these subsections, for both address the same evil and carry identical sanctions. . . .

3. *Paying for Endorsement or Special Influence.* Subsection (3) complies with the policy of Article 240 to punish the payor as well as the payee of any prohibited benefits. Like the counterpart provisions in the other sections in this article, it should be interpreted to be co-extensive with the reach of Subsections (1) and (2).

APPENDIX C

CRIMINAL PROCEDURE

INTRODUCTION

A. The Study of Criminal Procedure

An understanding of criminal procedure rules and practice is important for several reasons. First of all, criminal procedure is highly structured and has developed distinct stages. It is important to know the sequence of steps commencing with investigation and culminating in postconviction review. Furthermore, rules of criminal procedure not only prescribe the sequence of events that lead to a determination of guilt or innocence, but also define the manner in which those steps must be carried out. A principal objective of criminal procedure is ascertainment of guilt or innocence. After a case has moved through preliminary stages and presentation of proof at trial, a court or jury determines whether or not a defendant is guilty of the substantive crime(s) charged.

Procedural rules do not exist in a vacuum, however. Both practical and constitutional constraints have contributed to the development of contemporary criminal procedure. For example, to bring a case to trial, police investigation is usually necessary. Hence law enforcement officers must be authorized to search for and seize evidence of guilt, interrogate suspects, and identify alleged wrongdoers. Ancillary to these specific investigative actions it may be necessary to take a suspect into custody, that is, to arrest. After a successful investigation and apprehension of a suspect, the system proceeds to adjudicate guilt or innocence. But guilt or innocence as to what? Defendants are not tried for being bad persons; trial is conducted to ascertain whether or not a defendant has committed specified violations of law. Therefore, a defendant must be charged with having committed an identified offense or offenses. This is important not only so that a judge or jury can evaluate the evidence and determine guilt or innocence, but also so that defendants will know precisely the charges that must be answered. This illustrates some of the practical considerations that are prerequisites to determining guilt or innocence.

However, as stated previously, although determination of guilt or innocence is an objective of criminal procedure, it is not the sole objective. The Bill of Rights and its counterparts in state constitutions recognize the tendency of government in the zealous pursuit of crime to encroach upon the liberty of citizens. Consequently, these constitutions limit the power of the state to fashion a process to determine guilt or innocence. Because the investigative stage is so important, the fourth amendment to the United States Constitution prohibits unreasonable searches and seizures and prescribes minimum criteria for issuance of arrest and search warrants. There are many other limitations on procedures that may be used by the state in pursuing and prosecuting alleged criminals. Our criminal procedure represents an accommodation between the need to have a logical process for determining guilt or innocence and practical measures that relate to and further that determination, and the need for a procedure that is fair and encroaches on the liberties of citizens to the least degree feasible yet permits adjudications of guilt. Since these objectives are not entirely consistent, in that effective crime control may be thwarted by considerations of fairness or human dignity, we must anticipate that criminal procedure will not always operate smoothly.

It is important to understand the principles and rules of procedure (and not merely to have a technical knowledge of procedural rules), not only to grasp how society deals with those suspected of crime, but also to perceive the consequences when procedural rules are violated. To a considerable degree, both federal and state criminal procedure has become "constitutionalized." In brief, this means that the federal and state constitutions require as well as prohibit various rules, techniques or practices in criminal procedure. Therefore, a failure of government to conform to a rule of procedure may produce not simply a technical violation of law but a violation of constitutional rights as well. However, a violation of a rule of procedure does not ordinarily insulate a suspect against prosecution; in some instances, the contravention of even a constitutional rule may have no significant consequences so far as ultimate trial is concerned. Thus, when there has been an unlawful arrest and nothing more, from a practical point of view there will be no effect on subsequent procedural stages. If evidence is secured through an unlawful arrest, depending on circumstances courts may preclude its introduction at trial. When a court refuses to allow a prosecutor to introduce evidence obtained in violation of constitutional rights, it invokes an exclusionary rule fashioned by appellate courts. Finally, a violation of a constitutional rule of procedure, in limited circumstances, may preclude subsequent prosecution of a case. For example, when a defendant has been denied the sixth amendment right to a speedy trial, the Supreme Court has prohibited subsequent trial.[1]

In responding to violations of constitutional rights, courts in most instances have tried to neutralize procedural harm by preventing the prosecution from exploiting official misconduct. Since violation of constitutional rights frequently produces evidence a prosecutor intends to use as part of the case against an accused, courts sometimes exclude evidence obtained in violation of procedural rules. Therefore, in familiarizing oneself with the rules of procedure one does not undertake a mere exercise in technicalities. One learns not only the prescribed manner in which a criminal investigation and prosecution go forward, but also the very significant consequences that may accrue when procedural rules have been breached.

B. Constitutions and Procedure: The Notions of Procedural Due Process

In the study of criminal procedure it is critical to develop an understanding of the relationship between criminal procedure and certain constitutional doctrines and rules. Relevant constitutional provisions may be classified as:

1. Traditional notions of due process
2. Explicit constitutional rules of procedure contained in amendments to the United States Constitution.
3. Bills of rights in state constitutions.

1. Traditional Notions of Due Process

The concept of due process is deeply rooted in Anglo-American law. Reference to trial in accordance with the "law of the land" was one of the conditions demanded under Magna Carta.[2] Due process is an elusive term. However, the generally accepted meaning is the right of a person to be free from *arbitrary* governmental action.[3] Procedural due process requires that government use fair means in arriving at a determination that may affect a person adversely (such as the determination of guilt). Certain procedural ingredients are thought fundamental to this notion of fairness. These include notice of charges against a person and time and place of hearing on these charges, an opportunity for a defendant to refute the charges, and a hearing on the charges before an impartial tribunal that makes a determination based on evidence adduced at the hearing. The fifth and fourteenth amendments to the United States Constitution, applicable to the federal and state governments respectively, provide that no person shall "be deprived of life, liberty, or property without due process of law."

2. *Explicit Constitutional Rules of Procedure Contained in the Amendments to the United States Constitution*

The first eight amendments to the United States Constitution embody several explicit rules of criminal procedure. Examples are the prohibition against unreasonable searches and seizures,[4] and the rights to counsel,[5] jury trial,[6] and confrontation of one's accusers.[7] These rules do not express merely general notions of fairness but supplement in specific detail the fundamental elements of fairness. Early decisions by the Supreme Court applied the first eight amendments (Bill of Rights) only to the national government, so those amendments that contained rules of criminal procedure were applied only in federal prosecutions.

The fourteenth amendment, however, operates as an express limitation on state procedures; in applying the "due process" language of the amendment to state criminal proceedings the Supreme Court was originally concerned only with "fundamental fairness." That a state proceeding varied from what was required in federal prosecutions did not invalidate it as long as the procedures conformed to standards of decency and fairness that characterize a civilized society. For example, to allow the prosecution to appeal a conviction of second-degree murder because of an improper construction of law in a lower court, with the result that a defendant was ultimately convicted of first-degree murder, was not considered fundamentally unfair, notwithstanding that such a practice was prohibited in federal prosecutions under the double jeopardy provision of the fifth amendment.[8] However, failure to supply a defendant with counsel in a capital case tried in a "lynch mob" atmosphere was ruled fundamentally unfair.[9]

In recent years the United States Supreme Court has moved away from the fundamental fairness approach and has incorporated into the fourteenth amendment most of the specific rules of criminal procedure in the Bill of Rights and applied them to state criminal proceedings. With the exception of the right to indictment by grand jury, nearly every rule of criminal procedure in the first eight amendments to the Constitution now stands as a limitation on state criminal procedure. This application of the specific provisions of the first eight amendments to state criminal proceedings has been characterized as a "revolution" in the criminal law. It commenced in 1960 and has been accomplished in less than twenty years — a relatively short period for the development of new constitutional doctrine. The changes required in inherited state criminal procedure have been substantial, yet students must be cautious not to equate changes in law with changes in the manner in which officials carry out the law.

This constitutionalization of criminal procedure has two implications. First, it enables federal courts to review convictions obtained in state courts if infringement of a defendant's federal constitutional rights has been alleged. Second, the application of constitutional rules of procedure to both federal and state proceedings has brought about a certain measure of uniformity in criminal procedure in the United States. Some aspects of procedure are untouched by the Constitution; in these areas each state may fashion its own approach. For example, to a considerable extent states may decide how much pretrial discovery to allow. Furthermore, even though a constitutional norm, e.g. the right to a jury trial, is involved, states may exercise choice on matters ancillary to the right, for example, how many jurors are required or how many peremptory challenges are available. Since virtually every rule of constitutional criminal procedure has been applied to state proceedings, much of the work of the courts now consists of filling in the gaps and delimiting the scope of the various constitutional rules. This incorporation of specific constitutional rules has not, however, completely superseded the more generalized "fairness" test under due process. Notwithstanding the absence of a specific constitutional rule of criminal procedure, a court may require adherence to certain procedures on the basis that "fairness" requires it, or prohibit certain procedures because they are fundamentally unfair.

3. Bills of Rights in State Constitutions

All states have provisions governing criminal procedure in the bill of rights segments of their constitutions. In many respects these are identical or at least similar to the rules in the federal Bill of Rights. It is essential for a student to master constitutional rules of criminal procedure in his or her state. Even though an issue relates to a federal constitutional right, it is better practice also to refer to the corresponding state right. Furthermore, in some states particular state constitutional rules may be broader than the federal rules. Under these circumstances a defendant has a right to insist upon a procedural right not mandated in the United States Constitution, or to object to a particular investigative or trial procedure prohibited under the state constitution but not similarly prohibited under the federal Bill of Rights.[10]

C. An Overview of the Criminal Justice System

In the study of criminal procedure, there is a tendency to focus on narrow problems affecting a particular stage of prosecution. This orientation is sometimes confusing, and as a result students derive a somewhat distorted perspective of the criminal justice process. The brief overview that follows sketches the full panorama of the criminal justice system and may provide a better understanding of how and where things fit.

1. Arrest

The first significant step taken by government against an individual is usually arrest, i.e. taking a suspect into custody. Furthermore, it is at the arrest stage that various legal principles and rules first come into play. An arrest may occur when a law enforcement officer observes an individual perpetrating a crime, the so-called "presence arrest," or entertains probable cause to believe that the arrested person has committed an identified felony. The same information that will legitimate an arrest may be laid before a magistrate to support an application for issuance of an arrest warrant; traditionally, arrest for lesser misdemeanors may only be made on warrant if an officer has not made a presence arrest. When a choice exists between an application for an arrest warrant and a warrantless arrest, there is no constitutional requirement that an officer resort to warrant practice.[11] However, unless there are exigent circumstances or consent, police officers cannot enter an arrestee's dwelling to arrest without an arrest warrant,[12] and if a wanted person is on a third person's premises, consent or a valid search warrant is required.[13] An arrestee's person and anything he or she may be carrying can be searched incident to a valid custodial arrest,[14] as may the passenger compartment of a vehicle in which an arrestee was riding immediately before arrest.[15]

In some cases arrest is not the first significant step. Sometimes before an arrest can be made, police must use various investigative techniques — surveillance of suspects, interviews with prospective witnesses, solicitation of information from informants, or interrogation of a suspect. Either as part of the pre-arrest investigation or coincidental with arrest, a search for evidence, again with or without a warrant, may be made. However, investigating officials are required to resort to search warrants rather than to search for and seize evidence without a warrant, unless exigent circumstances are present.[16] In federal cases and in complex state cases such as public corruption or white collar crime, a grand jury may conduct its own investigation by summoning witnesses before it and can indict defendants who are not then in custody. In such an instance, the court to which the indictment has been returned issues a bench warrant for the defendant's arrest.

Most states provide an alternative to arrest in minor offenses like traffic violations. Under this alternative procedure a violator, instead of being arrested, may receive a summons from an officer requiring the violator to appear in court on a particular day.

2. Booking

Arrested persons usually undergo a procedure termed "booking," usually at a police facility. This involves obtaining a limited amount of biographical information from the arrestee, fingerprinting, and photographing.

3. Preliminary Appearance

Although a brief period of detention is lawful for purposes of booking, arresting officers are required to produce an arrested person before a judicial officer immediately, which as interpreted means without unreasonable or unnecessary delay.[17] At that time, an officer or court clerk prepares a preliminary pleading, often called a complaint, setting forth the criminal charges that will form the basis of the later proceedings. The defendant (note that initiation of charges changes the accused's status from suspect to defendant) is informed of the charges, advised of the right to counsel, including assigned counsel if the defendant is financially unable to retain personal counsel, under the laws of some states is advised about the privilege against self-incrimination, and, in a state in which informations are used as the standard charging documents for trial, told of the statutory right to a preliminary examination. The judge before whom a preliminary appearance is made also is responsible for determining the defendant's eligibility for pretrial release and for fixing the form or forms of such release.

4. Pretrial Release

In traffic and other minor misdemeanor cases, state law may authorize the posting of a cash deposit with a police facility desk officer, which allows the arrestee to leave immediately and to appear in court when required. In felony and serious misdemeanor cases, however, a judge must decide preconviction release questions. Pretrial release traditionally has been accomplished through a process called bail, in which an arrestee provides some form of security to underwrite appearance in court when required. In its oldest form, this required real property owners of the county or district to encumber their land conditioned on the defendant's appearance in court. However, in the modern era bail is arranged in the form of a surety bond; the issuing surety company usually requires a deposit of cash or securities equal to the penalty amount of the bond from which it can obtain indemnity if a default occurs. Under the eighth amendment, the amount of bond is to be set at a figure sufficient to ensure a defendant's appearance in court, but cannot be set higher so as to punish a defendant by making it inevitable that he or she remain in pretrial detention. In some cases bail is based on predetermined schedules in which a specific amount of security is set for each offense. This is widely used for misdemeanor offenses.

In recent years, legislation has allowed the alternatives of (1) a cash or securities deposit with the court, (2) a ten percent deposit system, according to which only ten percent of the face amount of a deposit (e.g. $500 on a $5000 required deposit) is actually left with the court, and (3) a release on a defendant's own recognizance ("R.O.R."), in which no deposit or payment is required immediately. Whether required by statute or not, contemporary practice is to use the least restrictive of these alternatives appropriate to bring a defendant into court. Within these statutory or rule alternatives, the judge before whom a defendant is first brought fixes the form of pretrial release; after indictment or information, control over preconviction release conditions vests in the court with trial jurisdiction. If a defendant cannot immediately meet the form, conditions, and amount of preconviction release fixed by a court, he or she must be remanded to jail. However, if at any time the preconviction release conditions set by the court are complied with, the defendant immediately is to be released from confinement by custodial officials. Supplementary judicial action is not required.

5. Preliminary Hearing

A preliminary hearing is held in most jurisdictions soon after arrest and preliminary appearance. Practice varies from state to state. In some states a hearing is held within hours of arrest, while in others it may occur a certain number of days afterwards. The scope of the preliminary hearing varies, but may include the following:

(a) Advice of constitutional rights and appointment of counsel for indigents.
(b) Determination of probable cause to move the case to the next stage.
(c) Bail redetermination.
(d) Decisions on preliminary motions submitted on behalf of the arrestee.
(e) Perpetuation of witness testimony.

If a case is dismissed at preliminary hearing, the arrestee is discharged from custody. However, this does not necessarily terminate the matter; a discharged defendant is subject to rearrest if police subsequently acquire additional evidence sufficient to establish probable cause. Moreover, in federal practice and in states requiring grand jury indictments for felonies, if a grand jury indictment intervenes between preliminary appearance and the time at which a preliminary examination ordinarily should be held, no examination is held even though that might be a useful defense discovery device. In a state in which, at least in routine cases, an information is filed by a prosecuting or district attorney, if a judicial officer finds probable cause the case is referred to the prosecutor. That official may file charges based on anything brought forth at the preliminary examination, but cannot go beyond that. A preliminary examination can be waived by a defendant, but in that event, in an information state, the original complaint sets the maximum scope for the prosecutor's information.

6. Formal Charge — Indictment or Information

Up to this point matters have progressed based on a complaint filed either by a law enforcement officer or a private citizen. Complaints are not final charges but merely a formal justification for continuing an individual in custody or on preconviction release status and proceeding to preliminary examination. The formal charge on which trial is held in federal and a minority of state courts is an indictment returned by a grand jury. In the rest, the trial pleading is an information prepared and filed by a prosecuting attorney. A grand jury is a body of citizens that performs the accusatory function. It hears evidence and determines whether or not a formal charge should be made against a particular person. Grand jury proceedings are ex parte rather than adversary, in that the ultimate accused has no right to be present personally or through counsel or otherwise to participate.

In a majority of states grand juries are used only sparingly or not at all. Instead, when a defendant has been bound over after preliminary examination, the prosecuting or district attorney may file an information. In most of these states, an information cannot be filed against one discharged at examination; a few jurisdictions, however, allow an information to be filed without a bind-over.

The chief constitutional control over the content of an indictment or information is the fifth amendment right of an accused to know the nature and cause of the accusation lodged against him or her. The patterns for charging crimes are usually set through charging manuals or by indirection by reference to pattern jury instructions. However, in American criminal proceedings relatively little information actually is conveyed even through those pleadings sufficient to meet constitutional minimum standards. Traditionally, a device called a bill of particulars has been available to defendants to elicit additional information, but that information is likely to be meager in scope. Discovery procedures today constitute the usual means through which the defense learns the details of prosecution evidence and the theory of the prosecution case.

7. Arraignment

Just as in a civil case a defendant must respond to a plaintiff's complaint, so in a criminal prosecution a defendant must respond to formal charges. The stage of the prosecution at which this is accomplished is called the arraignment, or arraignment on the indictment or information. At arraignment, a defendant is ordinarily advised once more of certain constitutional and statutory rights. If he or she cannot afford counsel and counsel has not been previously appointed, an attorney will be provided and further proceedings stayed until counsel has had an opportunity to interview the defendant and render advice bearing on the procedural steps to follow. The formal charge (indictment or information) is read, and the defendant will be asked to plead to it. Arraignment is presided over by a judge, who explains the plea alternatives to the defendant. Ordinarily the plea choice is simple: guilty or not guilty.

The vast majority of criminal cases is disposed of by guilty pleas, either at arraignment or subsequently. Almost always, these guilty pleas are based on an agreement between prosecution and defendant (and defense counsel); a defendant agrees to plead guilty in return for charge or sentence concessions by the prosecutor. The plea, however, must be ratified or accepted by the trial court if it is to take effect. The process of agreement is called plea bargaining and is a pervasive characteristic of the American criminal justice system.

Guilty plea practice is strictly controlled by constitutional standards. A defendant must be represented by counsel or have accomplished a valid waiver of that right. When the counsel right is availed of, defense counsel must have had an adequate opportunity to advise the client beforehand about the choices he or she must make. The court must advise the defendant of the nature of the charge(s) to which a guilty plea is to be tendered, including mandatory minimum penalties and the maximum penalties provided by law, of the procedural consequences of a relinquishment of the constitutional safeguards governing trial that a guilty plea will accomplish, and of the fact no trial will be held.[18] The court must obtain from the accused acknowledgments of factual circumstances corresponding to the elements of the offense to which a guilty plea is tendered or, if a defendant will not do so personally, must see that a record is made based, for example, on earlier trials of the same defendant in the same matter, a grand jury or preliminary examination transcript, or evidence from witnesses.[19] It is also necessary to bring out on the record the nature of the agreement underlying the plea, if there has been one,[20] and an acknowledgment that the plea is voluntary.[21] A complete record must be made of the entire plea proceeding.[22]

Federal practice and the procedural law of many states recognize an alternative plea of nolo contendere, by which a defendant does not formally acknowledge guilt but submits to judgment and sentence. A practical benefit flowing from reliance on a nolo plea is that a defendant has made no admission of guilt that can be used to his or her disadvantage in related civil or criminal litigation. It is necessary to establish a factual basis for a nolo plea other than through the defendant's own admissions; otherwise, the procedures constitutionally required are identical to those necessary for a valid guilty plea.[23] A court need not accept a nolo plea, and may force a defendant to elect between a guilty and a not guilty plea.

If a defendant pleads guilty or nolo, a judgment of guilt is entered and the case proceeds to sentencing. An underlying plea agreement must be kept; if it is not, the court that accepted the guilty or nolo plea may either enforce the agreement or vacate the guilty plea.[24] The defendant then may plead not guilty or negotiate further for a different guilty or nolo plea agreement.

A defendant who pleads not guilty forces the prosecution to prove the state's case in a trial. If an accused refuses to plead at all, i.e. "stands mute," a plea of not guilty is entered by the court and the case will proceed to trial.

8. Pretrial Motions

In the federal jurisdiction [25] and most states, a defendant who wishes to raise certain legal questions affecting the pending case must do so before trial, by filing pretrial motions. The most common motions include a motion to quash or dismiss, which challenges the sufficiency of the pleading, and a motion for a bill of particulars, which asks for additional information about the charge in the indictment or information. These motions are commonly filed before arraignment. Another motion of signal importance in recent years has been the motion to suppress, used to challenge the admissibility of evidence at trial on the ground it has been obtained in violation of the defendant's constitutional rights.[26] Such a motion may extend to tangible objects seized by the police, confessions, and eyewitnesses' identification testimony. However, although motions to suppress evidence on fourth amendment grounds must be made before trial, attacks on the constitutional admissibility of confessions and identification testimony may be reserved for trial (and heard in the absence of the jury), and need not always be submitted through a consolidated pretrial motion to suppress. Nonetheless, many states find it more expedient to resolve all constitutional evidentiary problems before trial through an omnibus motion hearing. A motion to suppress usually requires an evidentiary hearing to establish whether a defendant's rights have been violated through governmental acquisition of evidence.

9. Discovery

Pretrial discovery still is not as widely used in criminal prosecutions as it is in civil cases, but its use nevertheless is expanding rapidly. In jurisdictions that recognize pretrial discovery in criminal cases, discovery motions ordinarily must be made before trial.

The principal forms of discovery are depositions[27] and access to and inspection of evidence.[28] There is no constitutional objection to reciprocal discovery, i.e. counter-discovery for the prosecution against the defense, as long as there is no disparity in the scope of discovery available to either party.[29] However, the scope of prosecution discovery is determined by state statute or rule, and not all states recognize prosecution discovery at all or in plenary form.

The prosecution is under a constitutional duty to disclose without a precedent defense motion all data that may either exculpate a defendant or mitigate the seriousness of the offense(s) charged.[30] There also is a claim to impeaching data affecting important prosecution witnesses.[31] If material not falling within either category is withheld, however, in violation of purely procedural requirements, there is no federal constitutional defect unless the defense shows that the undisclosed data were material; if the defense has made only an undifferentiated request for anything that might prove useful to it, there has been no denial of federal constitutional rights.[32]

A discovery function is achieved through provisions requiring defendants to file notices of intent to rely on the defense of alibi[33] or mental disease or defect,[34] coupled with information about the details of the defense and the witnesses to be relied on.

10. Trial

(a) Time of Trial

After pretrial motions have been disposed of, a case is docketed for trial. In many states the prosecutor controls the trial docket and determines when a case is set for trial. Modern systems of court administration, however, place control of calendaring in the hands of a court executive or administrator. The mere fact a case has been set for trial does not mean it will in fact proceed to trial. As cases approach their trial dates, many defendants who pleaded not guilty change their pleas to guilty. Furthermore, some cases are dismissed on prosecutor motion if for one reason or another, based on subsequent investigation or change of circumstances, the case no longer justifies prosecution. Such a dismissal is called a nolle prosequi, or simply a nol pros.

The sixth amendment right to a speedy trial affects commencement and completion of trial proceedings. However, no precise time period is established under the speedy trial provision; courts must balance the reasons for delayed trial against the harm actually wrought to the defense through delay.[35] More specific time restrictions on procedural stages are established today through court rule or statute, e.g. the federal Speedy Trial Act of 1974.[36]

(b) Jury Selection

If a case proceeds to trial, it follows a ritualistic pattern evolved over many centuries. Not every case is tried to a jury. In every state there is a class of minor offenses triable by a judge alone (bench trial), and jury trial can be waived.[37] The federal constitution allows trials before a jury of fewer than twelve persons,[38] and a verdict need not be unanimous.[39]

If trial is to be by jury, a jury is empaneled from a group of citizens summoned for jury duty, called the venire. Methods of selecting potential jurors vary from state to state. However, because a defendant has a right to be tried by a group of citizens representing a cross-section of the community, systematic exclusion of groups because of race, sex, etc. is prohibited.[40]

Individual jurors are selected through voir dire examination in which venirepersons are examined by court, counsel, or both to determine eligibility to sit. A prospective juror with obvious bias may be challenged for cause and excused.[41] Both prosecution and defense have a set number of peremptory challenges by which a juror may be excused without assigning any reason.

(c) Stages in a Criminal Trial

The following are the principal functional steps in a typical criminal trial:

Opening of the case by the prosecution. The prosecutor as the representative of the "People," "Commonwealth," "State" or "United States" is the moving party responsible to present the government's case against the defendant. He or she is likely to commence by introducing himself or herself to the jury, and identifying the judge, defense counsel, and the defendant, who sits at the counsel table. Next, the prosecutor explains to the jurors the nature and significance of the case, something about the order of proceedings to follow, and at least a brief summary of the prosecution theory of the case and the evidence expected to be adduced. The prosecution's opening statement is important enough in providing a basic education for jurors that under the doctrine in most states it cannot be dispensed with.

Opening statement by defense counsel. Defense counsel may, but need not, make an opening statement immediately following the prosecution's opening statement. Some attorneys rarely postpone the defense opening, for fear the prosecution's statement may make so favorable an impression on the jurors' minds that it will be harmful to the defense; an immediate defense opening may dispel that effect. Others routinely defer their opening until after the prosecution has rested its case-in-chief. A defense description of the defense case in relation to that of the prosecution can be much more ample at that time, and defense witnesses, who will be called to testify immediately after, may make a much more effective impact on a jury than if the prosecution's proof has intervened between the defense opening and presentation of the defense case. The choice will be made tactically in each case.

Prosecution case-in-chief. Because judge and jury are in effect at rest and waiting to be persuaded, the prosecution has the burden of establishing, ultimately at the level of proof beyond a reasonable doubt, every element of the crime(s) charged in the indictment or information. This is done through the testimony of witnesses. If real or demonstrative evidence, including documents, is to be submitted, foundation for it must be laid through witness testimony. After foundation has been laid, items are formally proffered as exhibits. All witness testimony is elicited through questions, first from the proponent on direct examination, and then through cross-examination by opposing counsel. Although, according to tradition, specific answers to precise questions are the vehicle for testimony, witnesses may well be allowed to make narrative statements on direct examination, clarified through specific questions by proponent's counsel. Cross-examination, however, must be tightly controlled through specific questions. If there is doubt about credibility, personal and background data may be elicited through the process known as impeachment, designed to expose falsehood.[42]

Tradition relies on expert witnesses summoned by the respective parties to establish scientific facts.

Presenting the defense case. After the prosecution has completed its case-in-chief, it rests. It is traditional at that point for the defense to move for dismissal of the case based on a prosecution failure to establish even a prima facie case of guilt. Should there be such a deficiency, the trial court will allow the prosecution to reopen its case to supplement its proof, but if its case truly were deficient and it had presented all the evidence available to it, the court would have to dismiss the case as requested. Because the defendant has been in jeopardy from the time the jury was sworn to receive the case,[43] the defendant could not thereafter be tried again.[44]

If the motion to dismiss is denied, as it almost always is, the defendant must decide whether or not to present affirmative defense evidence. There is, of course, no duty of any sort resting on the defense to present defense witnesses. In particular, the privilege against self-incrimination ensures that no defendant can be called to the witness stand by the judge, prosecutor or counsel for a codefendant, and no prosecution comment can be made about a defendant's decision not to testify in personal defense.[45] Defendants who elect to offer no defense proof simply incur the risk that jurors may find the prosecution's proof credible beyond a reasonable doubt. That is not true, however, of affirmative defenses; these the defense has the burden of pleading, going forward with evidence and persuading by the requisite burden of persuasion (usually the civil-case standard of preponderance or greater weight). That the burden of persuasion on affirmative defenses constitutionally can be assigned to the defendant seems established by *Patterson v. New York,*[46] but states of course may decline ever to do so as a matter of state law.[47]

If the defense offers affirmative proof, the prosecution is allowed to present evidence in rebuttal. This, however, must answer only the new dimensions created by the defense case; the prosecution cannot reserve part of its principal evidence in order to spring it on the defense in the form of a rebuttal case. (Such a tactic would in any event be risky, for if the defense should offer no proof, the prosecution would have no opportunity to offer additional proof.)

At the conclusion of all the evidence, the defense may move for a directed verdict of acquittal, but this should not be granted if even a single dispute of law or fact has emerged at trial.

At the conclusion of proof, and after requests for instructions have been submitted by both parties to the court, as mentioned below, counsel make closing arguments. Jurisdictions differ somewhat as to who goes last, defense or prosecution, but most allow the prosecution to speak last because it bears the ultimate burden of persuasion.[48] Both counsel are supposed to eschew prejudicial arguments, but since the prosecution has no appeal against acquittal, the case law generally evaluates defense claims of prosecutor misconduct in that regard.

(d) Judge and Jury

At trial the judge is the umpire, seeing to it that the rules governing admissibility of evidence and procedure are adhered to by counsel. In carrying out this function, the judge rules on objections by counsel. Examination and cross-examination of witnesses, however, are with rare exceptions the responsibility of counsel, for it is not compatible with a judge's position as umpire for him or her to conduct extensive questioning of witnesses.

One of the most important functions performed by the judge is to instruct the jury on the law. Since jurors are lay people and not experts in law, it is necessary to explain various legal terms so that they can relate the facts to the law. Counsel submit requests for instructions before final argument begins, and the court selects those it wishes to give. It also may give certain instructions on its own initiative, although state practice determines how extensive those must or may be. Today, in many states, instructions are based on model or pattern jury instructions promulgated by a highest appellate court with rulemaking powers or, in some jurisdictions, informally by a state bar association. An instruction of law should be given if the requesting side has elicited any evidence through direct or cross-examination necessitating an explanation of legal principles to the jury so that it knows what to do with the proof if it finds it credible. In most states, judges are prohibited from commenting on the evidence, but even in the federal jurisdiction and small minority of states in which English traditions are preserved, allowing judicial comments on evidence, appellate courts have taken a quite restrictive view as to the propriety of exercising that power.

After the instruction process has been completed, the jury is given the case for deliberation. Deliberations must be conducted in a private place, and nobody can be present other than the jurors. If a court wishes, it can sequester a jury, i.e. have its members accommodated in hotel rooms and provided meals under guard so as to forestall any contact with anyone other than the officers having them in charge. If a jury is not sequestered, its members return to their homes when court is not in session, but are admonished not to discuss the case with anyone and not to read or view anything bearing on the trial. If a jury cannot agree, it reports that fact to the court. The court may ask the jury to consider the case a while longer to see whether an agreement is possible, but this cannot be couched in a way or continued for such a length of time that jurors will feel they are being coerced into agreement; pressures of this sort on hold-out jurors are not proper.

When a jury reaches a verdict it announces it in court in the defendant's presence, and the court then enters a judgment on the verdict. A jury that cannot agree on a verdict is called a hung jury. A defendant can be tried before another jury if the first trial is inconclusive. The decision to retry rests in the discretion of the prosecutor.

11. Posttrial Motions

Under traditional criminal procedural law, after a verdict of guilty a defendant may submit either or both of two posttrial motions. One is a motion in arrest of judgment advancing jurisdictional defects going to the basic power of the court to enter a lawful judgment of conviction. That motion might renew claims of double jeopardy, attacks on the indicting grand jury based on denial of equal protection through exclusion of certain classes of citizens from eligibility to serve as jurors, or assertions of the unconstitutionality of the statute on which the prosecution was based. Jurisdictional attacks should have been made before trial as well as after, but if a court truly lacks judicial powers in a criminal case, a defendant should be able to advance that fact after conviction. A second is a motion for a new trial, which embodies all attacks on the propriety of trial court rulings on points of evidence and procedure, as well as a claim that the jury abused its factfinding discretion when it found the evidence sufficient to convict. A judge considering a motion for a new trial is often viewed to sit as a "thirteenth juror," [49] empowered to vacate a conviction because of personal doubts a defendant actually is guilty.

When a motion in arrest is granted, further proceedings may be impossible because no lawful basis for them remains. If an indicting grand jury was unconstitutionally empaneled, however, it is possible to lay the same data before a new grand jury, constitutionally empaneled, and to obtain a valid new indictment on the basis of which retrial can be held. When a court grants a motion for a new trial, it sets aside the judgment and orders a new trial. A motion for a new trial is available only to the defendant, and serves to waive any double jeopardy protection the defendant otherwise might have had in relation to the offense(s) of which he or she was convicted.

The double jeopardy concept dictates that a prosecutor is bound by a jury's verdict of not guilty; only a defense appeal resulting in a reversal based on grounds other than legal insufficiency of trial evidence [50] will permit retrial of those offenses for which the defendant was convicted, but not any greater offenses of which he or she is deemed to have been acquitted.[51] The prosecution, however, may appeal an order granting a defense motion for a new trial, for if it is successful the appellate judgment restores the trial court jury's verdict of conviction, and does not expose the defendant to a second full trial which the double jeopardy clause is intended to forestall.[52]

12. Sentencing

If posttrial motions have not been filed, or have been denied, the case moves into the sentencing stage. In most states, sentence is imposed on a defendant by the trial judge; a handful retain the early nineteenth century tradition of jury sentencing. Sentencing alternatives available to a trial court are provided in the jurisdiction's penal code; this topic is covered in Chapter 10 of the main text. Data for trial court use in assessing sentence are usually gathered in the form of a presentence report prepared by the probation service. Evidence rules do not govern judicial sentencing, although there is a constitutional requirement that sentencing data used by a court be accurate.[53] A sentencing court constitutionally may consider the fact that a defendant committed perjury while testifying in personal defense.[54] The defendant has a constitutional right under the sixth amendment to be present at imposition of sentence and to address the court at sentencing (called the right of allocution).

13. Appeal

At common law, nobody had a right to an appeal. In most American jurisdictions, however, a convicted defendant has a statutory, but not a constitutional,[55] claim to at least one level of appellate review of any legal matters properly preserved for later consideration. In the federal jurisdiction and some states, review extends to sentence as well as legal errors at trial.[56] There is no double jeopardy or other federal constitutional bar to such prosecution sentence appeals, because an appellate court's substitution of a more onerous punishment does not subject a defendant to the hazards of a repeated trial, the harm at which the double jeopardy clause is directed.[57] Adequacy of trial evidence to support conviction is considered a legal issue; otherwise, American courts neither reevaluate facts nor engage in supplemental fact determinations in criminal cases.

14. Postconviction Review

Traditionally, defendants who appealed unsuccessfully or failed to invoke appeal in a timely fashion had no further remedy, unless through habeas corpus they could establish a want of jurisdiction to convict. However, because federal courts may review the conviction of any state prisoner assertedly held in violation of the federal constitution (a statutory basis for federal habeas corpus),[58] and must hold evidentiary hearings on prisoner applications unless there has been a recent adequate state court determination of the matters presented to federal judges,[59] there has been strong pressure on states to create plenary postconviction review procedures through which all federal constitutional issues, and perhaps other legal questions as well, may be submitted for decision.[60] Federal prisoners must make use of a special plenary proceeding in lieu of habeas corpus.[61]

FOOTNOTES

1. Strunk v. United States, 412 U.S. 434 (1973).
2. HOWARD, MAGNA CARTA, TEXT & COMMENTATY 43 (1964).
3. Pound, *The Development of Constitutional Guarantees of Liberty*, 20 NOTRE DAME LAW. 389 (1945).
4. U.S. CONST. amend. IV.
5. U.S. CONST. amend. VI; Argersinger v. Hamlin, 407 U.S. 25 (1972); Gideon v. Wainwright, 372 U.S. 335 (1963). The right includes the alternative of personal defense. Faretta v. California, 422 U.S. 806 (1975).
6. U.S. CONST. amend. VI; Codispoti v. Pennsylvania, 418 U.S. 506 (1974); Duncan v. Louisiana, 391 U.S. 145 (1968).
7. U.S. CONST. amend. VI; Globe Newspaper Co. v. Superior Court, 102 S. Ct. 2613 (1982).
8. Palko v. Connecticut, 302 U.S. 319 (1937).
9. Powell v. Alabama, 287 U.S. 45 (1932).
10. Force, *State "Bills of Rights": A Case of Neglect and the Need for a Renaissance*, 3 VAL. U.L. REV. 125 (1982).
11. United States v. Watson, 423 U.S. 411 (1976).
12. Payton v. New York, 445 U.S. 573 (1980).
13. Steagald v. United States, 451 U.S. 204 (1981).
14. Gustafson v. Florida, 414 U.S. 260 (1973); United States v. Robinson, 414 U.S. 218 (1973).
15. New York v. Belton, 453 U.S. 454 (1981). Cargo areas may be searched if officers have reasonable grounds to believe contraband may be transported there. United States v. Ross, 102 S. Ct. 2157 (1982).
16. Chimel v. California, 395 U.S. 752 (1969).
17. *See, e.g.*, FED. R. CRIM. P. 5(a).
18. FED. R. CRIM. P. 11(c) incorporates federal constitutional doctrines established by the Supreme Court.
19. FED. R. CRIM. P. 11(f); North Carolina v. Alford, 400 U.S. 25 (1970).
20. FED. R. CRIM. P. 11(e)(2).
21. FED. R. CRIM. P. 11(d).
22. FED. R. CRIM. P. 11(g).
23. FED. R. CRIM. P. 11(b).
24. Santobello v. New York, 404 U.S. 257 (1971).
25. FED. R. CRIM. P. 12.
26. FED. R. CRIM. P. 41(e), (f).
27. FED. R. CRIM. P. 15.
28. FED. R. CRIM. P. 16.
29. Wardius v. Oregon, 412 U.S. 470 (1973).
30. Moore v. Illinois, 408 U.S. 786 (1972); Brady v. Maryland, 373 U.S. 83 (1963); Napue v. Illinois, 360 U.S. 264 (1959). Knowing prosecution use of false or perjured evidence is itself a due process violation. Mooney v. Holohan, 294 U.S. 103 (1935).
31. Davis v. Alaska, 415 U.S. 308 (1974).
32. United States v. Agurs, 427 U.S. 97 (1976). *See also* United States v. Valenzuela-Bernal, 102 S. Ct. 3440 (1982).
33. FED. R. CRIM. P. 12.1.
34. FED. R. CRIM. P. 12.2.
35. Barker v. Wingo, 407 U.S. 514 (1972).
36. 18 U.S.C. §§ 3161-3162 (1976).
37. Duncan v. Louisiana, 391 U.S. 145 (1968).
38. Williams v. Florida, 399 U.S. 78 (1970). However, a jury cannot be composed of fewer than six persons, even in minor cases. Ballew v. Georgia, 435 U.S. 223 (1978).
39. Apodaca v. Oregon, 406 U.S. 404 (1972) (10 out of 12 jurors); Johnson v. Louisiana, 406 U.S. 356 (1972) (9 out of 12 jurors). However, the verdict of a six-person jury must be unanimous. Burch v. Louisiana, 441 U.S. 130 (1979).
40. Duren v. Missouri, 439 U.S. 357 (1979); Alexander v. Louisiana, 405 U.S. 625 (1972). A defendant need not be in the excluded class to raise the constitutional objection. Peters v. Kiff, 407 U.S. 493 (1972).
41. On the required scope of voir dire concerning racial bias, *see* Rosales-Lopez v. United States, 451 U.S. 182 (1981); Ristaino v. Ross, 424 U.S. 589 (1976); Ham v. South Carolina, 409 U.S. 524 (1973).

42. "Scarcely a trial occurs, in which some witness does not lie." J. Frank, Courts on Trial 85 (1949).

43. Crist v. Bretz, 437 U.S. 28 (1978). At bench trial, jeopardy attaches when the first prosecution witness is sworn. *Id.*

44. Hudson v. Louisiana, 450 U.S. 40 (1981); Burks v. United States, 437 U.S. 1 (1978).

45. Griffin v. California, 380 U.S. 609 (1965). However, trial courts can instruct juries that no adverse inference is to be drawn from a defendant's failure to testify, even though the defense does not wish such an instruction to be given, Lakeside v. Oregon, 435 U.S. 333 (1978), and must give such an instruction at defense request. Carter v. Kentucky, 450 U.S. 288 (1981).

46. 432 U.S. 197 (1977).

47. *See* Engle v. Isaac, 456 U.S. 107 (1982).

48. *See, e.g.,* N.Y. Crim. Proc. Laws § 260.30(8)-(9) (McKinney 1975).

49. Tibbs v. Florida, 102 S. Ct. 2211 (1982); Hudson v. Louisiana, 450 U.S. 40 (1981).

50. Burks v. United States, 437 U.S. 1 (1978).

51. Price v. Georgia, 398 U.S. 323 (1970); Benton v. Maryland, 395 U.S. 784 (1969).

52. United States v. Wilson, 420 U.S. 332 (1975).

53. Townsend v. Burke, 334 U.S. 736 (1948).

54. United States v. Grayson, 438 U.S. 41 (1978).

55. Abney v. United States, 431 U.S. 651, 656 (1977); *In re* Gault, 387 U.S. 1, 58 (1967).

56. *See generally* American Bar Association Standards for Criminal Justice, Appellate Review of Sentences (2d ed. 1980).

57. United States v. DiFrancesco, 449 U.S. 117 (1980).

58. 28 U.S.C. § 2241(c)(3) (1976). *See* Lehman v. Lycoming County Children's Servs. Agency, 102 S. Ct. 3231 (1982), concerning the scope of federal habeas corpus relief.

59. 28 U.S.C. § 2254(d). *See* Marshall v. Lonberger, 103 S. Ct. 843 (1983); Engle v. Issac, 102 S. Ct. 1558 (1982); Sumner v. Mata, 455 U.S. 591 (1982).

60. *See generally* American Bar Association Standards for Criminal Justice, Postconviction Remedies (2d ed. 1980).

61. 28 U.S.C. § 2255 (1976); this is usually called a "2255 motion." *See generally* United States v. Frady, 456 U.S. 152 (1982).